BASTIEN

PIANO FOR ADULTS

A Beginning Course: Lessons • Theory • Technic • Sight Reading

Jane Smisor Bastien, Lisa Bastien, & Lori Bastien

Preface

Congratulations on your advancement into Book 2! We offer you our best wishes for continued success at the piano.

Sincerely,

Jane Smisor Bastien, Lisa Bastien, and Lori Bastien

Table of Icons

This icon is used as a reminder to check your answers in the answer key. The answer key may be found on page 151.

This icon is used whenever follow-up exercises are presented.

This icon is used when a historical or theoretical piece of information is given.

This icon is used to review important information which has been presented previously.

This icon is used to indicate pieces that have *Accompaniment Recordings* available through the IPS (see instructions on the inside front cover how to access). The recordings are also available separately in a 2-CD pack (KP2CD). The circled number inside the icon indicates the particular CD track on Disc One or Disk Two.

ISBN 0-8497-7305-9

CONTENTS

CHAPTER 5 - Group 2 Keys

CHAPTER 6 - Reading in A Major

CHAPTER 7 - Reading in E Major

CHAPTER 8 - New Scales and Triads

APPENDIX

Chapter 1
Reading in G Major

NEW CONCEPTS

- Accidentals ♯ ♭ ♮
- G Major Scale and Chords

REVIEW CONCEPTS

- Key Signature
- Primary Chords
- Root
- Block Chord
- Broken Chord
- Triad
- Common Time 𝄴
- Cut Time 𝄵
- Root Position
- D.C. al Fine
- V7 Chord
- Inversion

An **accidental** is a sharp (♯), flat (♭), or natural (♮) sign. When an accidental appears in the music, it applies for the duration of the measure. A barline cancels an accidental.

MEET ME IN ST. LOUIS, LOUIS

Words by Andrew B. Sterling
Music by Kerry Mills

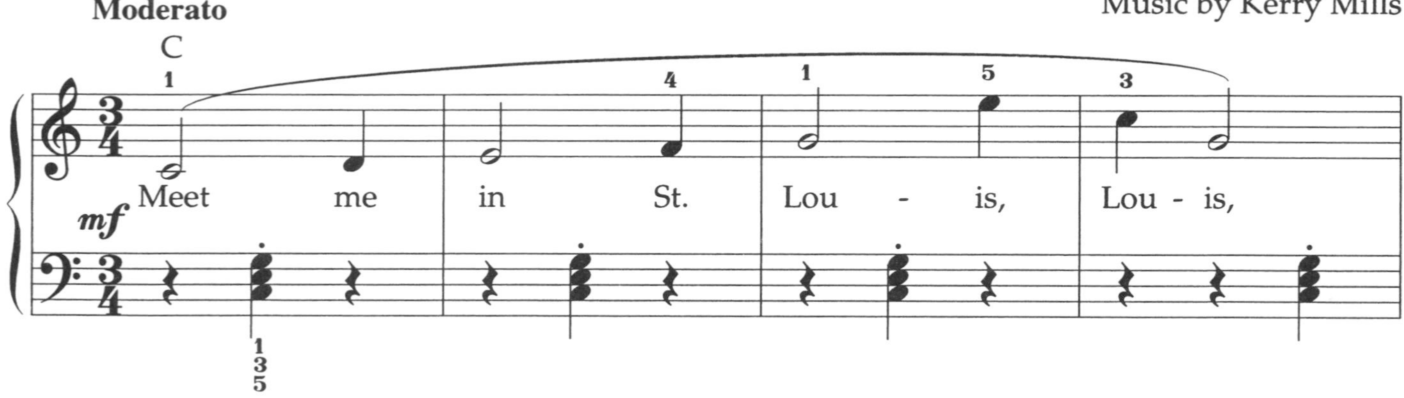

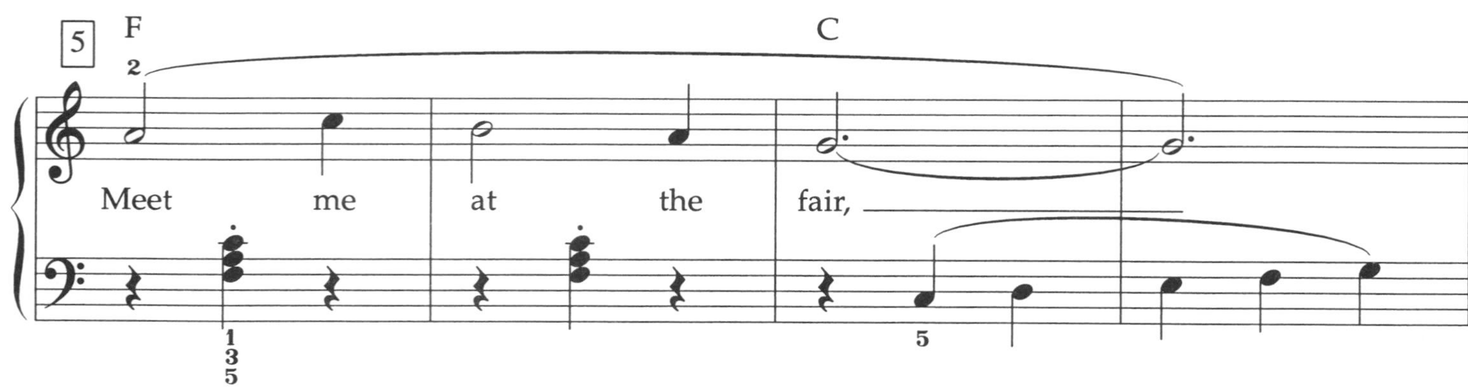

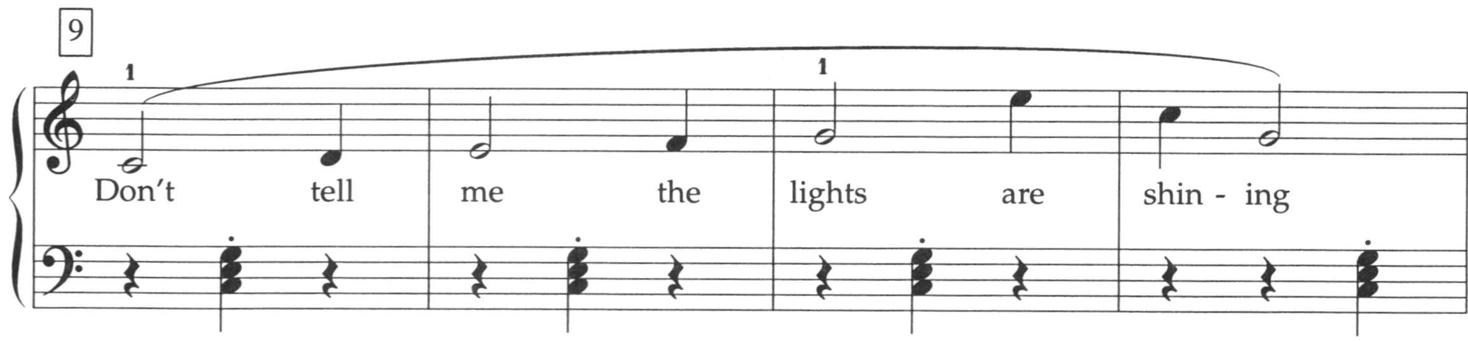

13
D7
G
An - y place but there, We will
17
E7
Am
dance the Hoo - chee Koo - chee, I will
21
D7
G
be your toot - sie woot - sie; If you will
25
C
Meet me in St. Lou - is, Lou - is,
29
F
G7
C
Meet me at the fair.

EAST RIVER BOOGIE

Moderato

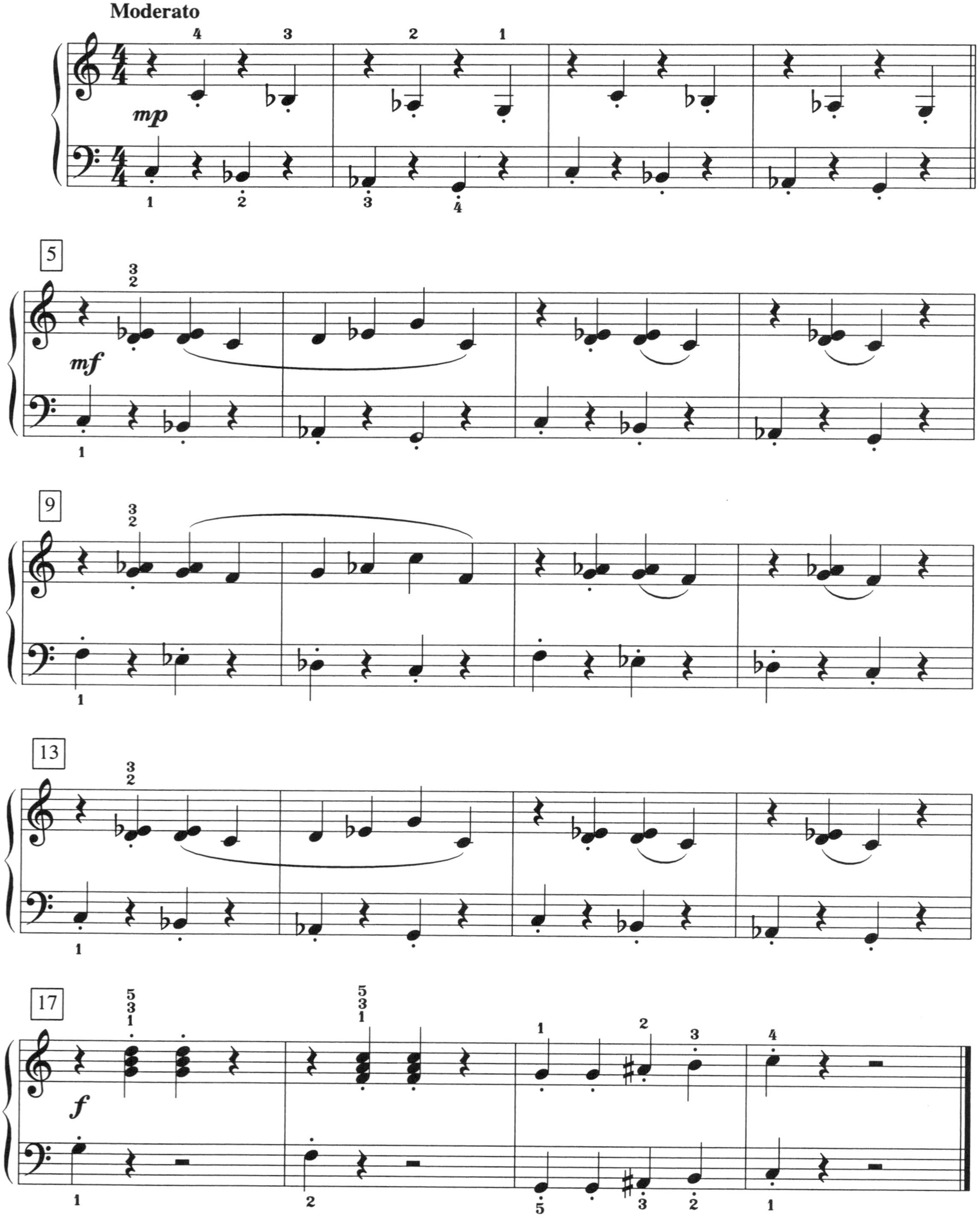

GOOD MORNING BLUES

Traditional Blues
Adaptation

Medium Blues

mf

5

★

9

Good morn-ing blues, blues how do you do? Good

13

morn - ing blues, blues how do you do? I'm

17

do-in' all right, good morn-ing how are you?

★ A thin double barline can be used to show the end of a musical section. The end of a section can occur in the middle of a measure, as it does here.

The **key signature** is the sharp(s) or flat(s) located at the beginning of each staff. It indicates which notes are sharp or flat throughout the piece.

Key Signature

Key of G
1 sharp: F♯

G Major Scale

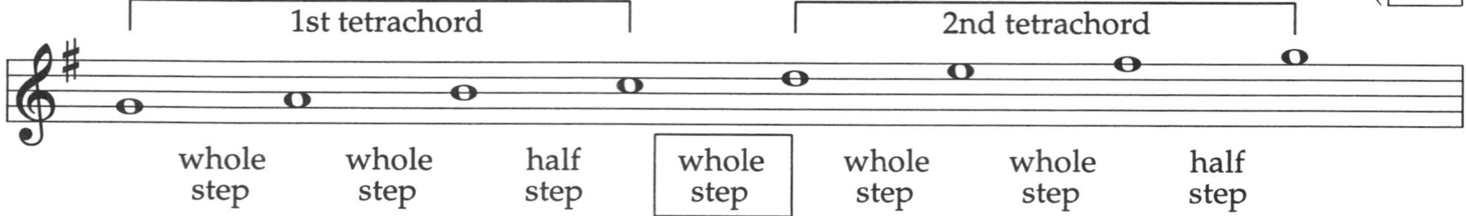

Primary Chords in the Key of G Major

I, IV, and V chords are called **primary chords**. These three chords are the most important chords in any key. In a Major key, they are all Major chords.

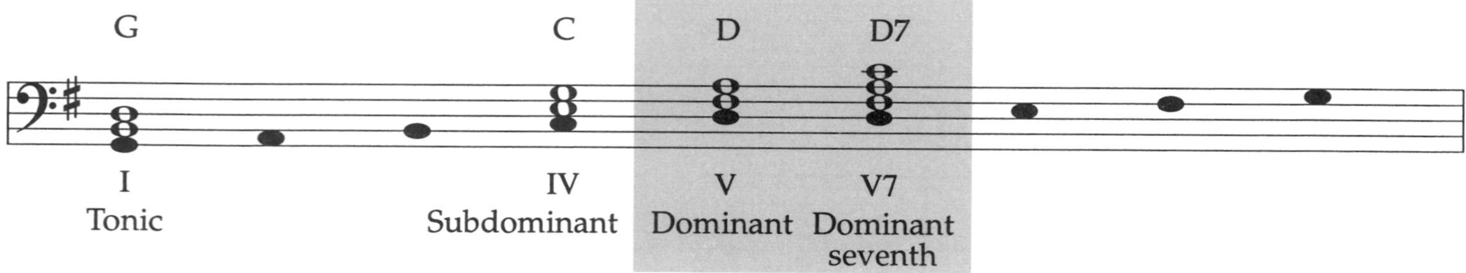

Note: In most cases in this book, the V7 chord will be used rather than the V chord.

G MAJOR SCALE AND CHORDS

Play hands separately first. Memorize the fingering.

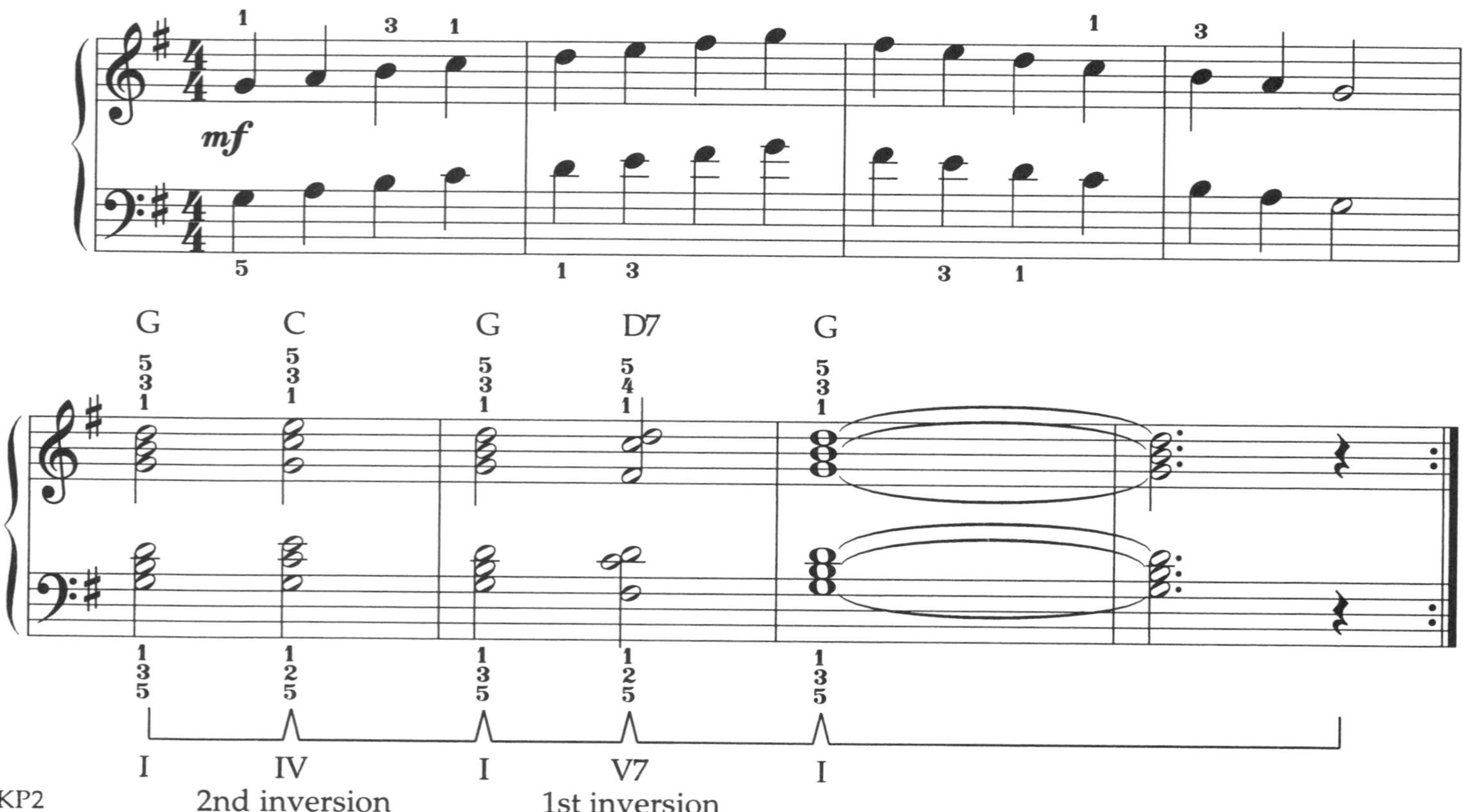

D.C. al Fine is an abbreviation for the term *Da Capo al Fine,* which means to return to the beginning and play to the *Fine* (end).

PRELUDE IN G

DISC ONE 7 ♩ = 88

Allegretto

mf

5

Fine

rit. 2nd time

9

mp

mf

13

D.C. al Fine

mp

f

rit.

Block chord
notes in a chord played simultaneously

Broken chord
notes in a chord played one at a time

A seventh chord has four notes consisting of a root, a 3rd, a 5th, and a 7th.

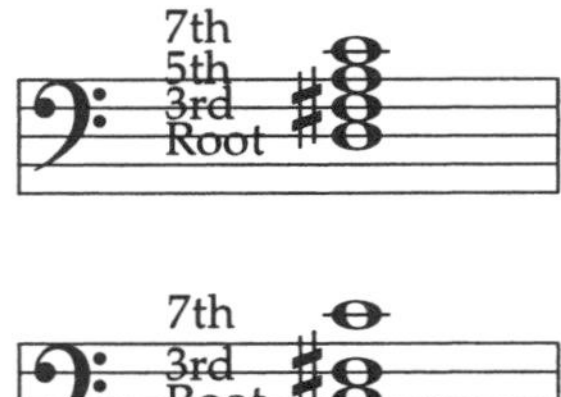

The D7 chord in root position (the root is on the bottom) is used in *The Holly and the Ivy* with the 5th omitted for ease in playing.

THE HOLLY AND THE IVY

DISC ONE 8 ♩= 88

Traditional English Carol

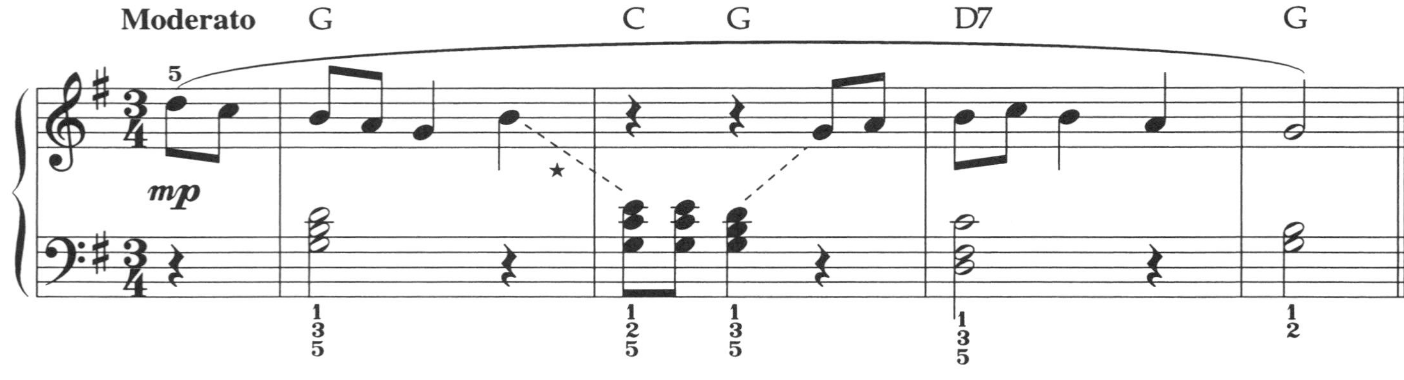

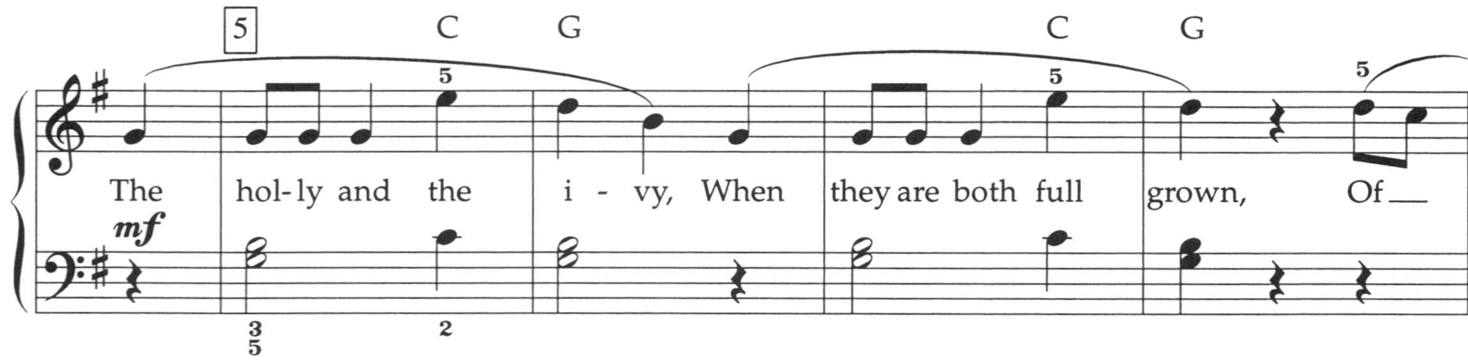

★ A dotted line between staves shows that the melody line crosses from one hand to another temporarily. The melody notes should be played louder than notes in the harmony.

17

C G D7 G

play-ing of the mer-ry or - gan, Sweet sing-ing in the choir.

1 2 5 1 3 5 1 2

21

mf *r.h.* 1 1 1 *8va*

5 5 5 2

l.h. *l.h.*

Edvard Grieg (1843-1907), Norwegian composer, is best known for his piano miniatures, songs, and incidental music to plays. His compositional style is indicative of Norwegian folk songs. *Morning Mood* comes from the popular symphonic suite *Peer Gynt Suite No. 1*, op. 46. The original music, written for Henrik Ibsen's play in 1875, contained twenty-three songs. A re-orchestrated version with only eight songs in two suites was completed in 1886. The first suite is the most well-known.

MORNING MOOD

DISC ONE 9 ♩= 96

Edvard Grieg

Moderato

Peter Ilyich Tchaikovsky (1840-1893), Russian composer, was born in the country town of Votkinsk, the son of a mining inspector. He studied at the School of Jurisprudence before beginning a serious study of music at the age of twenty-one at the St. Petersburg Conservatory. His music is well-loved for its expressive, sensitive melodies. Among his compositions are the ballets *Swan Lake, Sleeping Beauty,* and *The Nutcracker*, the symphonic poem *Romeo and Juliet*, an opera, and six symphonies. The following piece is taken from the second movement of Symphony No. 5 in E minor, op. 64, which took Tchaikovsky over ten years to write.

THEME FROM SYMPHONY NO. 5

Peter Ilyich Tchaikovsky

Andante

Technic

Technical exercises are designed to help develop hand and finger coordination, and to develop ease, control, and facility at the keyboard. Use the technic exercises as a warm up to your daily practice. Playing while counting aloud with a metronome will help ensure a steady tempo. When practicing technic exercises throughout this book, play each exercise three times a day, using different tempos:

Slow (♩ = 50 → ♩ = 60) Medium (♩ = 72 → ♩ = 92) Fast (♩ = 96 → ♩ = 144)

G SCALE ETUDE

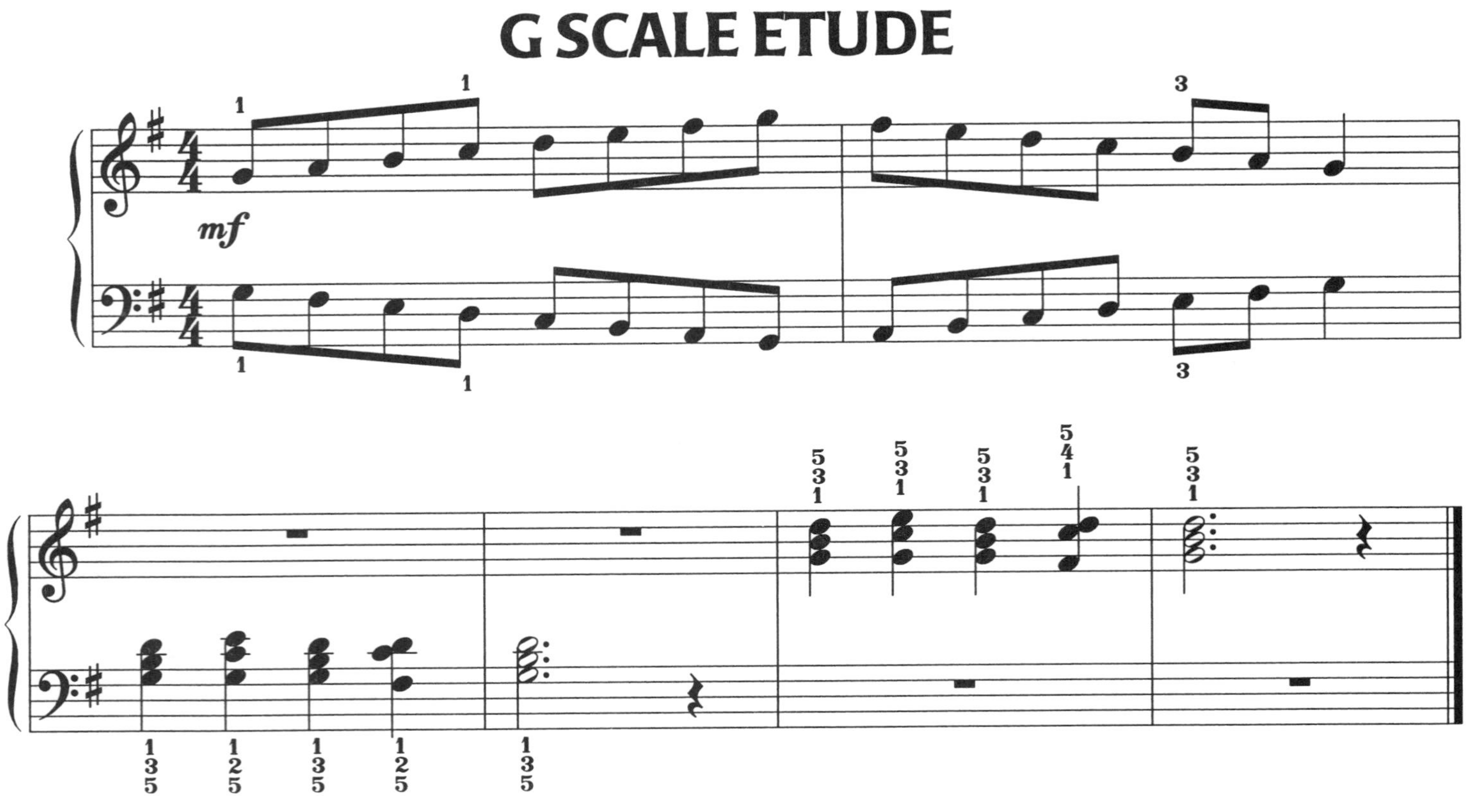

ON THE TREADMILL

Technic

Common Time C

The symbol C, which stands for Common Time, is another way to indicate the $\frac{4}{4}$ time signature.

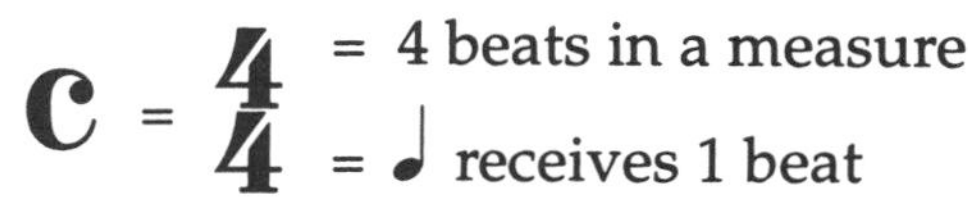

FINGER EXTENSION STUDY

from *The Virtuoso Pianist*

Charles-Louis Hanon

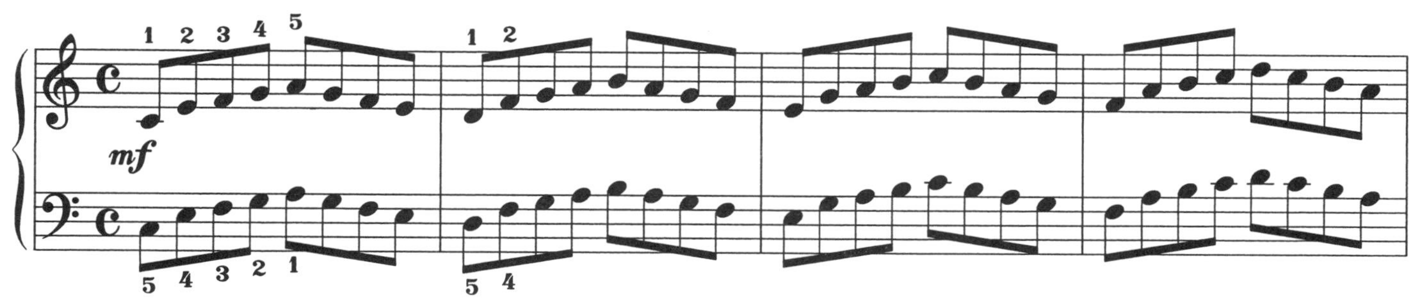

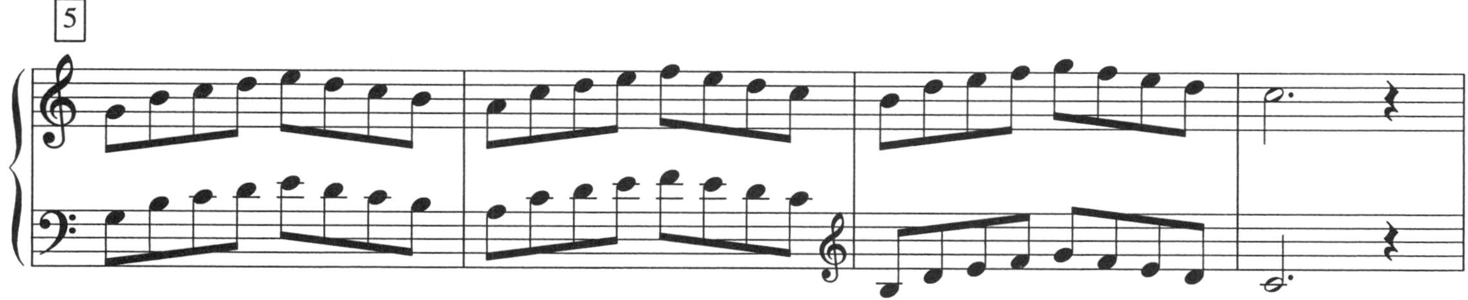

Challenge Piece

Felix Le Couppey (1811-1887), French composer, was born in Paris. He studied at the Paris Conservatoire, where, at the age of fourteen, he won the first Piano Forte prize ever given. Three years later he won the prize for harmony and accompaniment. It was during this year that Le Couppey began teaching at the Paris Conservatoire in the position of assistant teacher of harmony. Throughout his life, he continued teaching there in a variety of positions. He taught solfege, harmony, accompaniment, and piano. *Musette* is one example of the many valuable teaching pieces he wrote for his students.

Cut Time ¢

The symbol ¢, which stands for Cut Time, is another way to indicate the $\frac{2}{2}$ time signature.

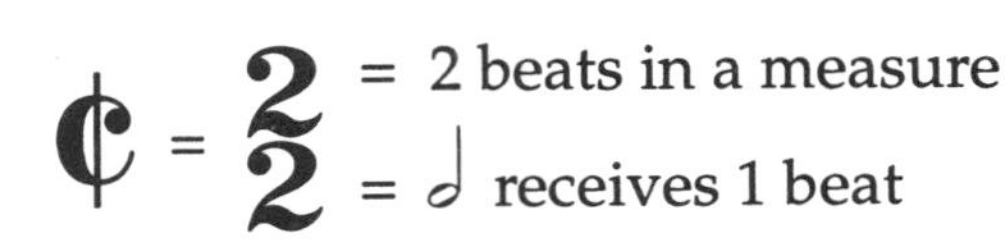

MUSETTE

from *Twenty-Five Very Easy Studies*, op. 17

Felix Le Couppey

★ **Ritmico**

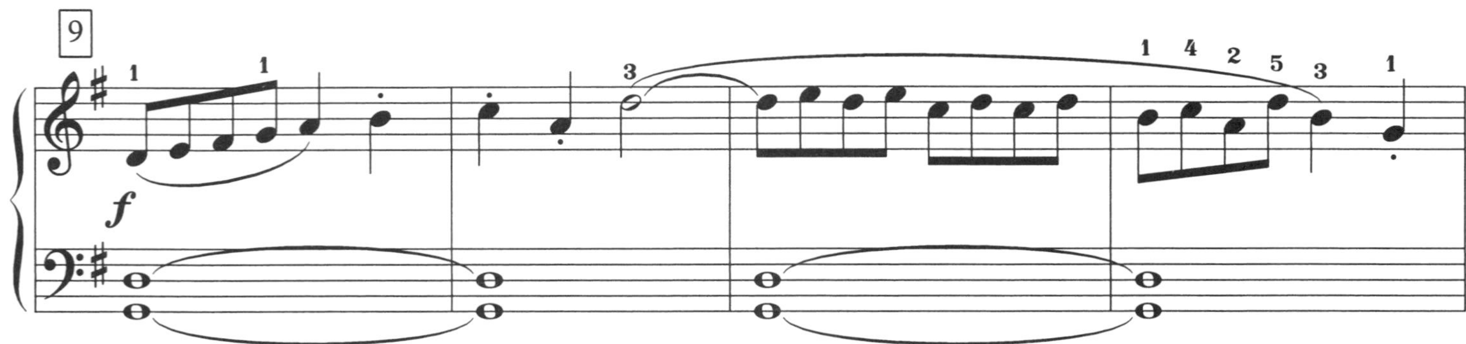

★ The term **Ritmico** means rhythmic, or to play in strict rhythm with a steady beat. To improve precision on this piece, the student can practice with a metronome: 𝅗𝅥 = 60, or subdivide the beat at ♩ = 120.

13
mf
17
p
21
mp
25

Review

A. Write the names of the intervals (2nd, 3rd, 4th, 5th, 6th, 7th, or 8th) in the boxes provided.
B. Write the letter names of the notes in the blanks.
C. Play the notes in the correct place on the keyboard.

D. Identify the following as either half or whole steps.

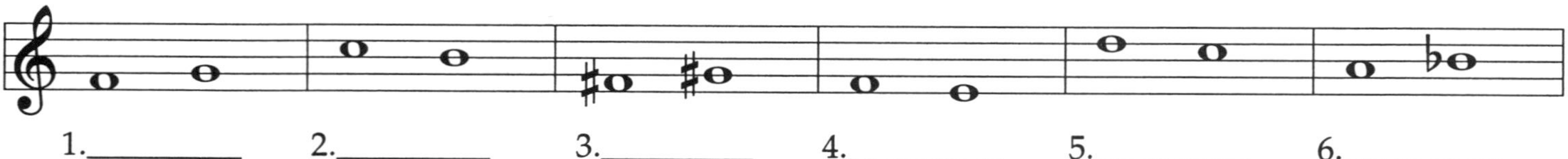

1.________ 2.________ 3.________ 4.________ 5.________ 6.________

The **root** is the note from which a chord originates.
The **root** is the letter which names a chord.

A **triad** is a three-note chord. A **root position triad** is a triad in its most basic form. All notes are stacked in intervals of 3rds, beginning with the root located on the bottom.

A **inversion** is a different arrangement of notes in a triad. The shaded notes indicate the roots in the inversion shown below.

- When a triad is inverted, the root is the top note of the interval of a 4th.

C Chord 

- When a seventh chord is inverted, the root is the top note of the interval of a 2nd.

D7 Chord 

E. Write the G Major scale ascending and descending. Circle the half steps.
F. Write the primary chords in the root position.

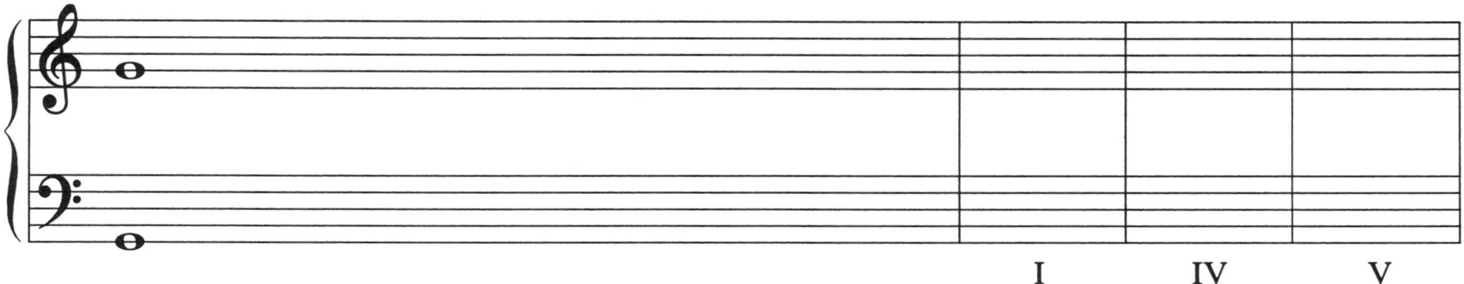

G. In the Key of G:

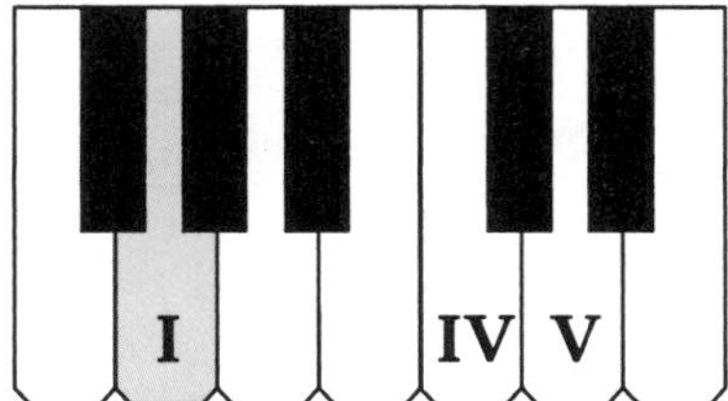

1. The tonic note is G.
2. The root of the tonic chord (I) is ________.

3. The subdominant note is ___________.
4. The root of the subdominant chord (IV) is _________.

5. The dominant note is .
6. The root of the dominant chord (V) is .

H. Write the chord symbols (G, C, or D7) in the boxes provided.
I. Play the chords in the correct place on the keyboard.

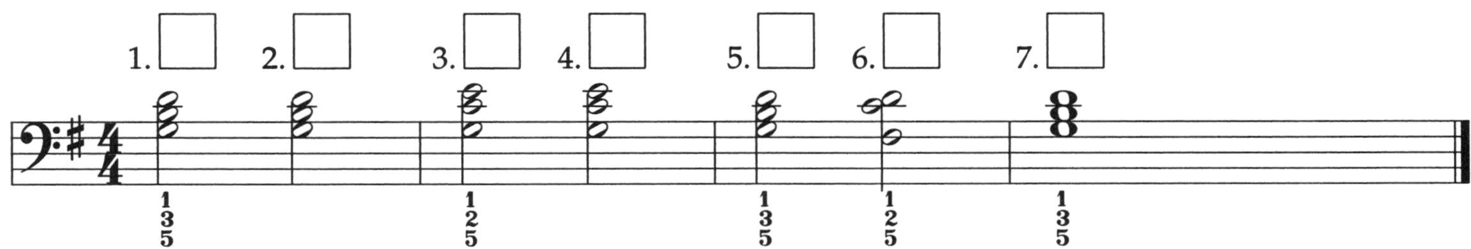

J. Harmonize
Add your own choice of L.H. chords (G, C, or D7) to the following R.H. melody line. Write chord symbols in the boxes provided.

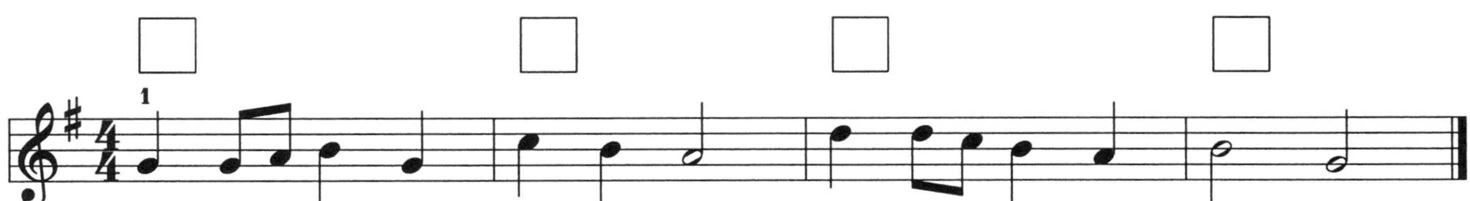

Chapter 2

Reading in E Minor

NEW CONCEPTS	
◆ E Harmonic Minor Scale and Chords	◆ Syncopation
◆ Accent >	◆ Sforzando *sfz*

REVIEW CONCEPTS	
◆ Broken Chord Bass	◆ Major and Minor Triads

The waltz, a dance characterized by a step-slide-step pattern in triple meter, has enjoyed a hold on the popular imagination for over two hundred years. From its beginnings in the exuberant German dances of the 1750s to the height of its development in the sophisticated nineteenth century ballrooms of Vienna, to the musicals and popular songs of the twentieth century, the waltz has exerted a powerful influence on music history.

The origin of the waltz is unclear, but seems to have evolved from the country dances popular in the alpine regions of Europe in the mid-eighteenth century. *Walzen*, the German word meaning 'to turn,' describes the gliding, whirling steps of these dances. The agile and spirited steps of couples in a close embrace, in contrast to the elegant and aristocratic *minuet*, became smoother as the country dances evolved into ballroom dances. Composers like Joseph Lanner and the elder Johann Strauss in Vienna in the 1820s had a major impact on the waltz. The waltz was expanded by these composers who wrote sixteen rather than eight measure sections, increased the tempo, and added an introduction and a coda (ending) to recapitulate the main ideas. The waltz, in its newer, expanded version, became a musical composition in its own right during this time. Johann Strauss, Jr. became known as the "waltz king" for bringing the waltz to the height of its popularity as a dance form and musical composition in the 1860s. *Laughing Song* is one of his most famous waltz melodies from the operetta *Die Fledermaus*.

LAUGHING SONG

Waltz tempo

Johann Strauss, Jr.

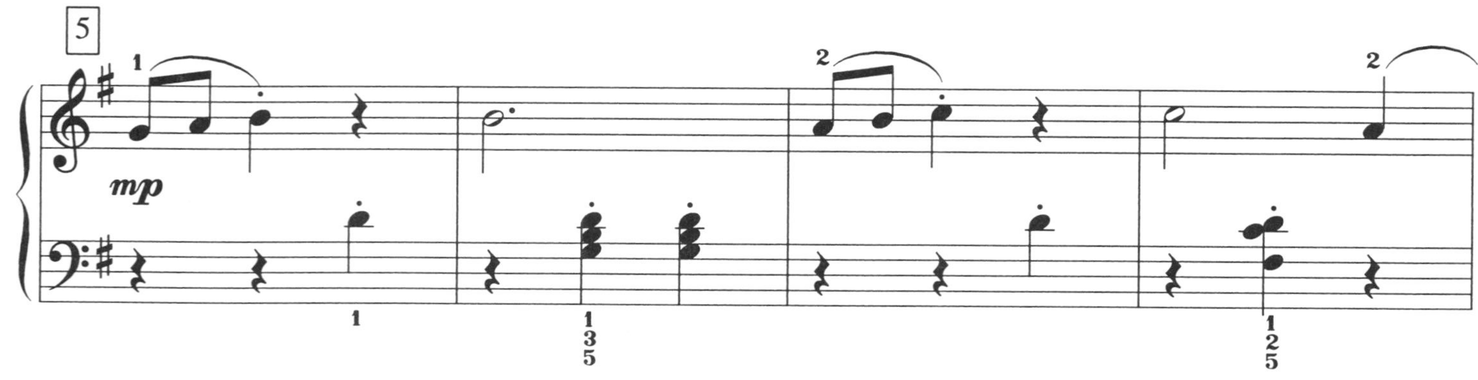

9
3
1
5
mf
mp
5

13
1
2
1
1

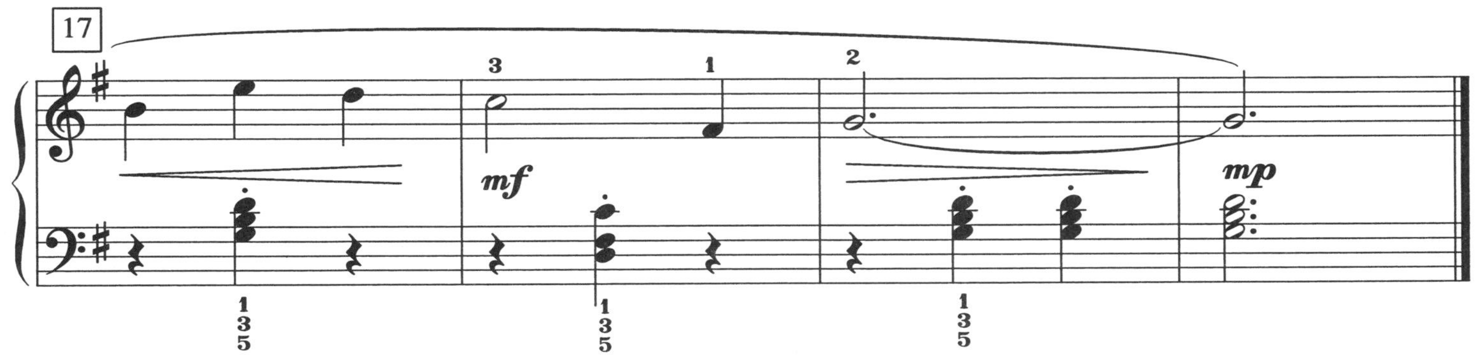
17
3
1
2
mf
mp
1
3
5
1
3
5
1
3
5

Broken Chord Bass

ON TOP OF OLD SMOKY

Moderato

Traditional Folk Song

mf

C F

On top of Old Smok - y, All
court - in's a pleas - ure, And

5

C F C

cov - ered with snow, I
flirt - in' is grief, A

9

G7

lost my true lov - er, For
false - heart - ed lov - er, Is

13

C F 1.C 2.

court - in' too slow. For
worse than a thief.

Broken Chord Bass

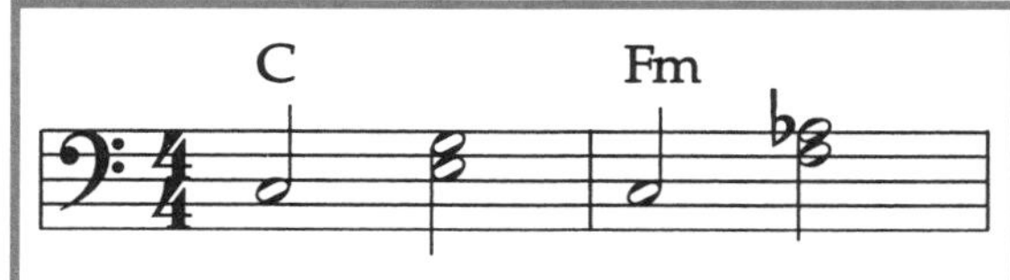

LIGHTS OVER EGYPT

DISC ONE 17 ♩= 96

Moderato

C Fm C
5 2 3
mf
5 1 3 1 2 1 3

5
Fm C
5 1 4 2

9
1 1
f–p

13
Fm C
5 3 5
mf

19
Fm C Fm C
1 4 4
dim. rit. pp
5
8va

Major and Minor Triads

A **Major triad** is made up of a:
Major 3rd (four half steps) and a
minor 3rd (three half steps)

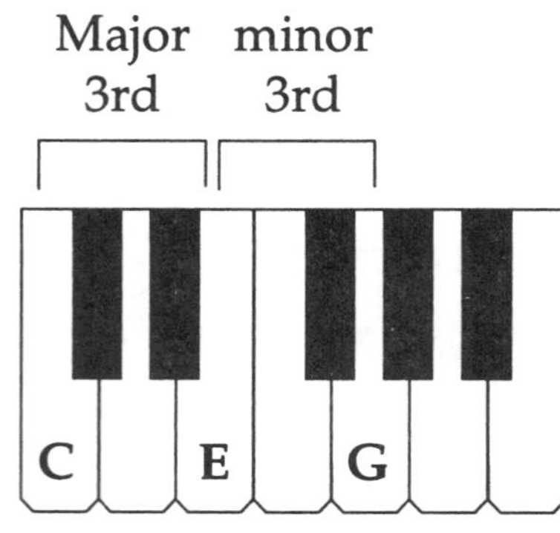

A **minor triad** is made up of a:
minor 3rd (three half steps) and a
Major 3rd (four half steps)

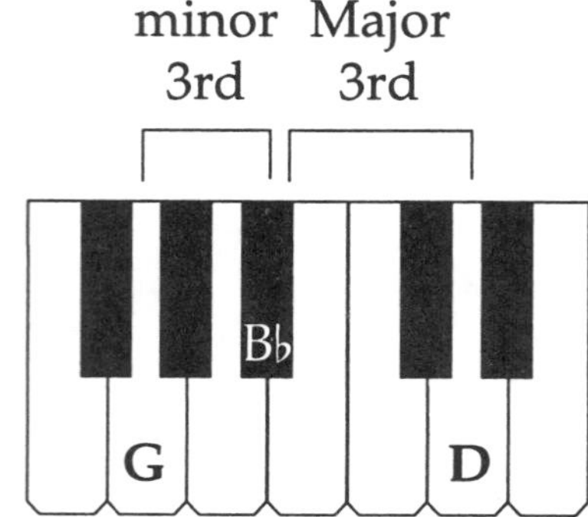

From every Major triad, a minor triad may be formed by lowering the middle note one half step.

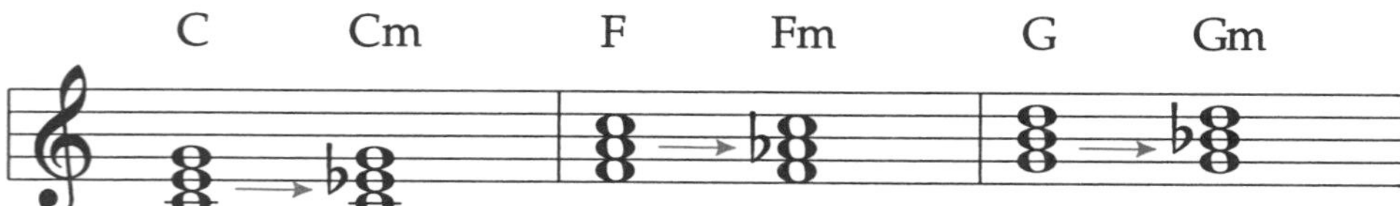

Review

Name the following Major and minor triads.
Notice that some chords are blocked and others are broken.

YORK AVENUE BLUES

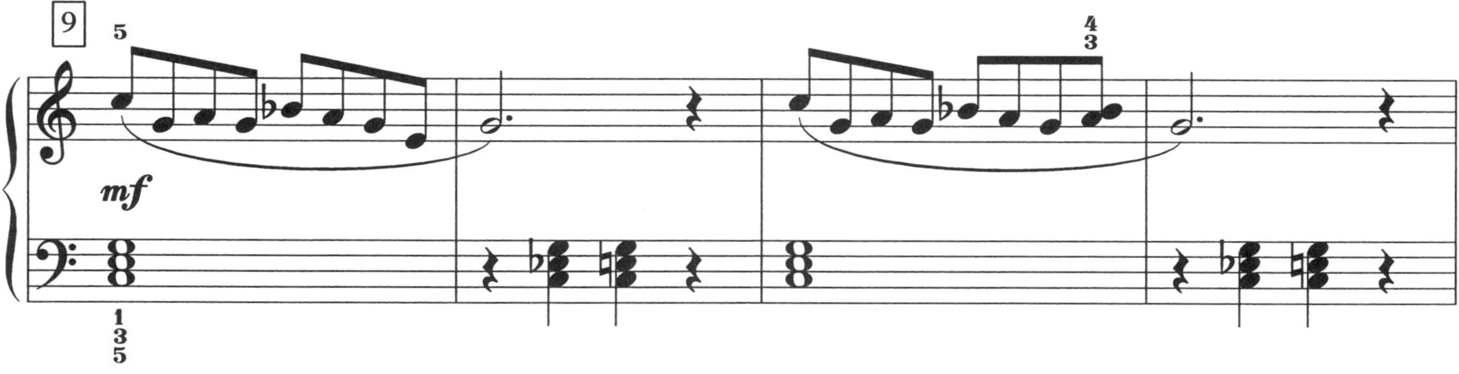

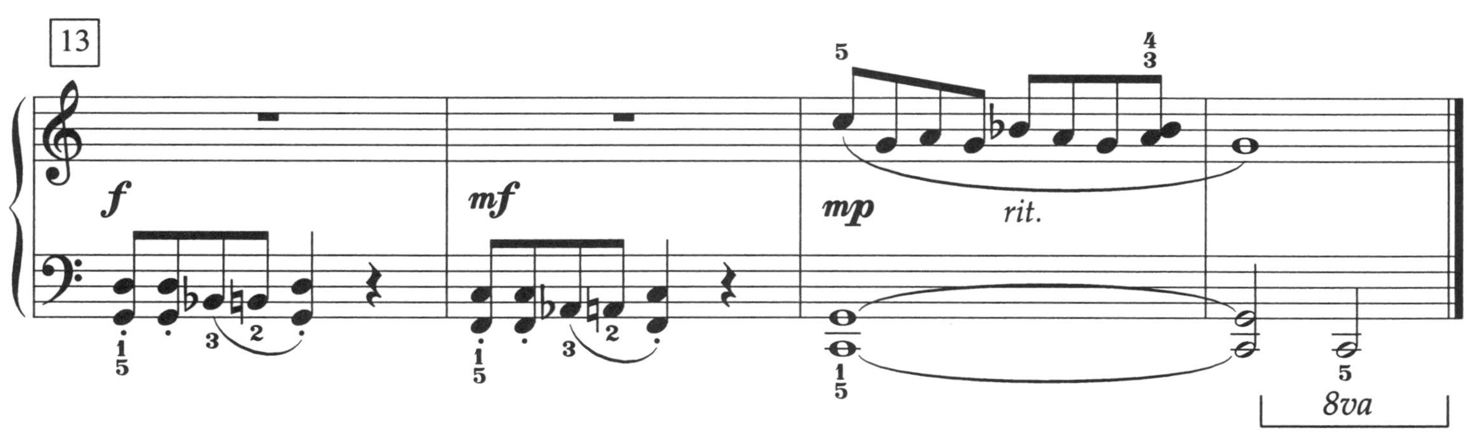

OCEAN VIEW

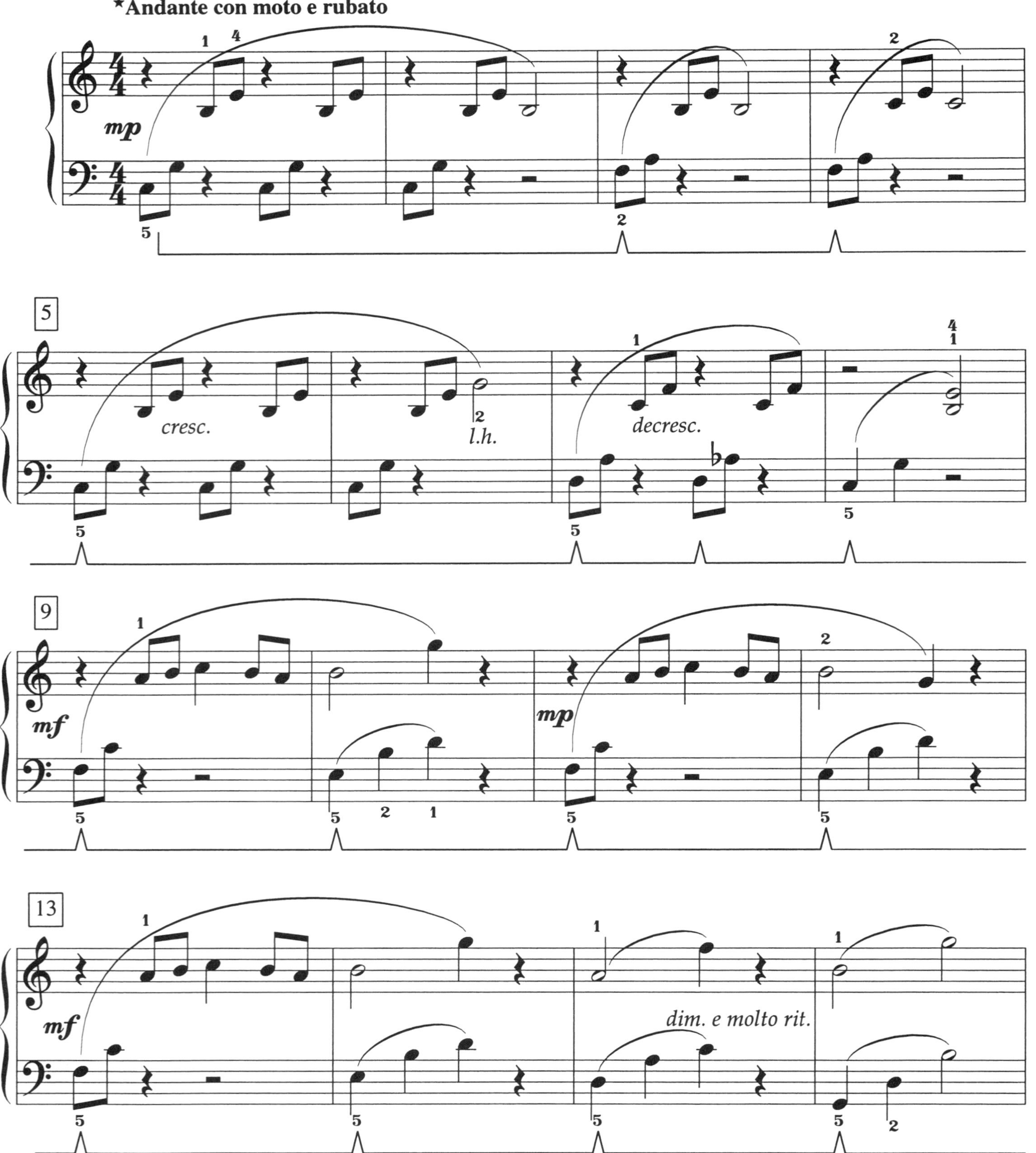

★ The term **Andante con moto** means slowly, but with motion; the term **Rubato** means that time is "borrowed," or that some tones are held longer than their actual values, while others are curtailed, in order to allow more freedom and spontaneity.

17
a tempo
mp
21
cresc.
l.h.
decresc.
25
r.h.
mf
l.h.
29
mp
33
p
molto rit.
l.h.
pp
8va

E Harmonic Minor Scale

For each Major key there is a **relative minor**. The same key signature is used for both keys. The relative minor scale uses the 6th tone of the Major scale for its starting tone. There are three types of minor scales. The most common form is the **harmonic minor**. The harmonic minor scale uses the same tones as the Major scale, with one exception: the **7th tone** in the harmonic minor scale **is raised one half step**. E minor is relative to G Major; both keys have one sharp (F♯).

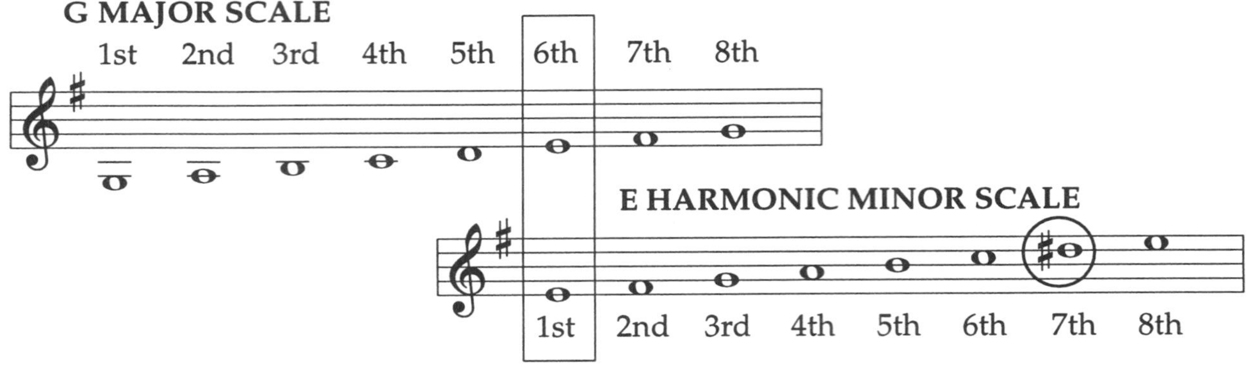

Primary Chords in the Key of E Minor

In a minor key, the i and iv chords are minor. The V chord is Major due to the raised 7th tone in the harmonic minor scale.

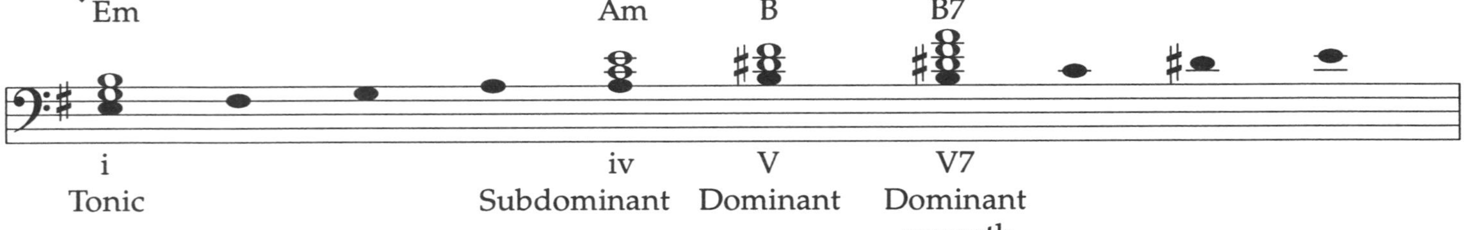

E HARMONIC MINOR SCALE AND CHORDS

Play hands separately first. Memorize the fingering.

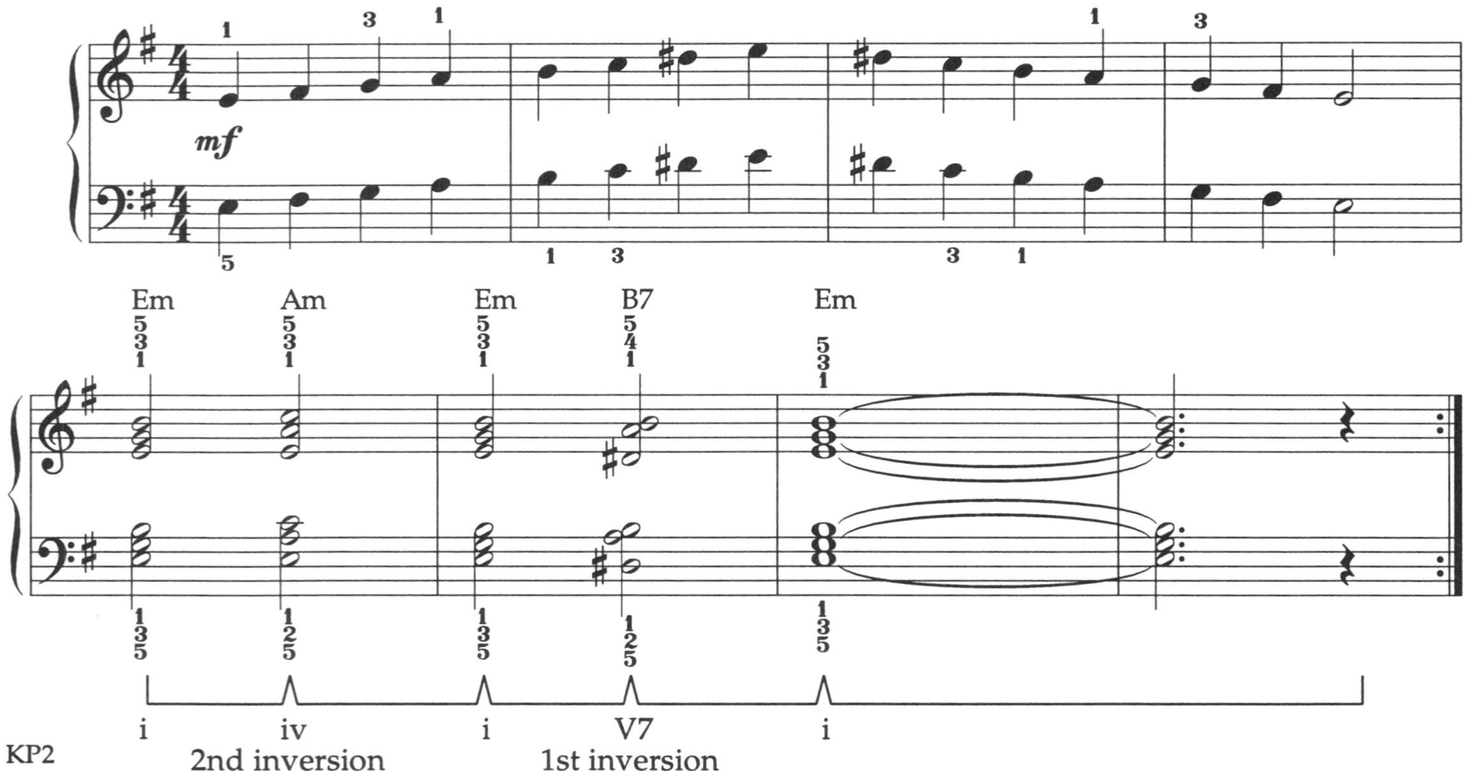

HOUSE OF THE RISING SUN

Moderato

Traditional American Folk Song

mp

3 1

1 1

5 Em B7 Em

mf

5 2

5 5 2 5

9 D7 G

5

5 5

13 Em B7 Em

1 3 5

5 5 1 2

17 B7 Em

5 5 5

Syncopation

Syncopation means to stress or accent weak beats. The most common way this is done is by placing a long note on a weak beat or a weak part of a beat, creating a rhythmic pattern that is SHORT-LONG-SHORT.

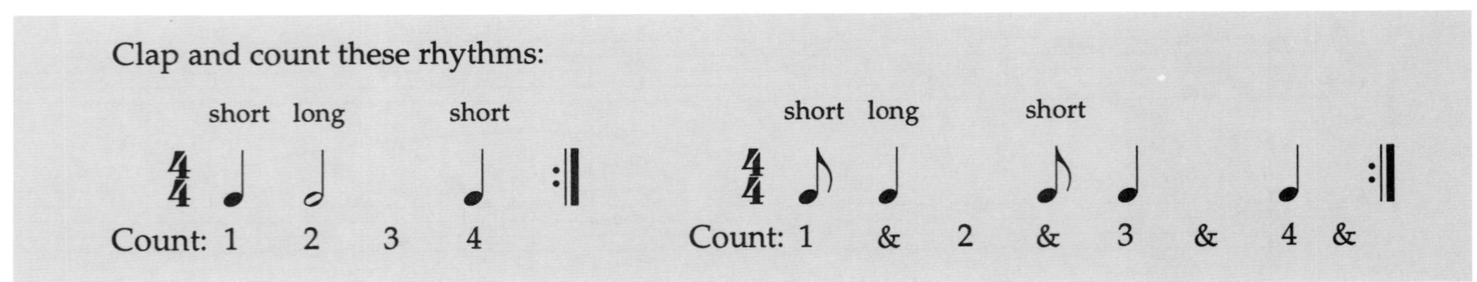

SYNCOPATED ETUDE

DISC ONE 23
♩= 76

Moderato

mp

5

mf

9

f

13

mf

Accent

The symbol > is an **accent** mark. When placed over or under a note, it indicates to stress or accent the note.

HELLO! MY BABY

SAKURA

(CHERRY BLOSSOM SONG)

Japanese Folk Song

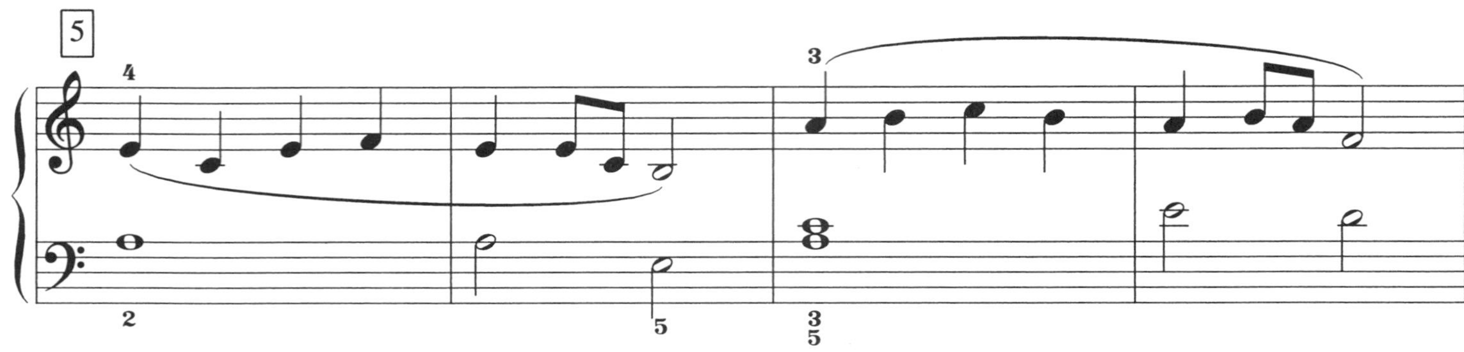

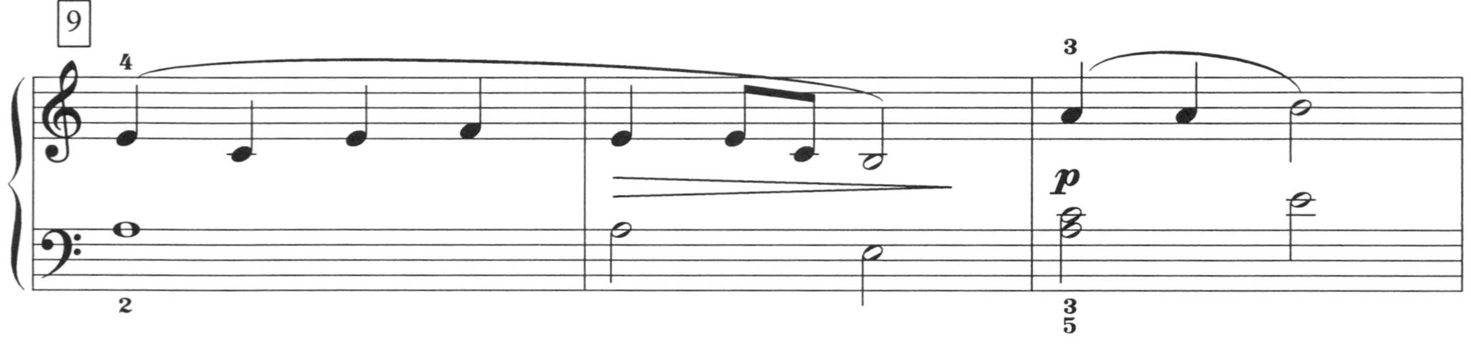

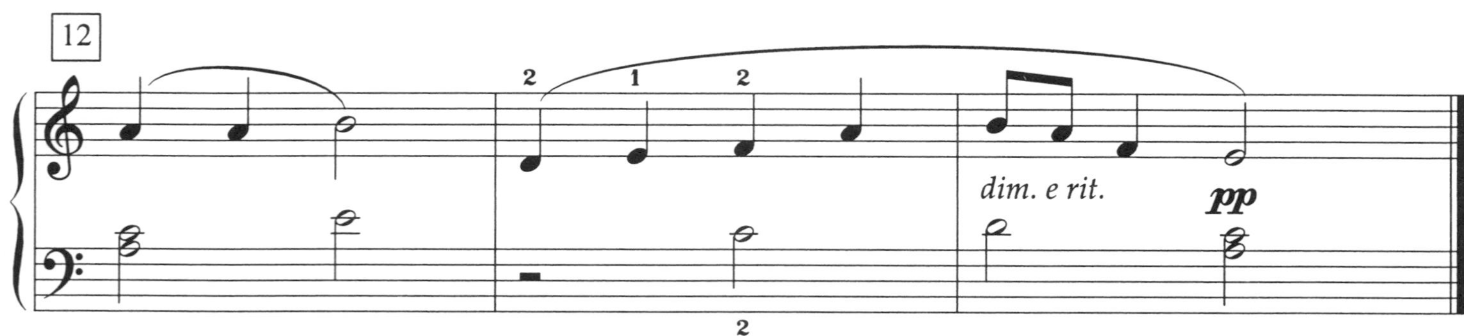

Technic

Note: In measure 17 of this piece, there is a **finger substitution** in the left hand. The dash indicates to continue holding the note with L.H. 5 while switching to L.H. 1. This will allow the hand to stretch down to the low E smoothly with L.H. 5.

ETUDE IN E MINOR

Challenge Piece

Syncopation means to stress or accent weak beats.

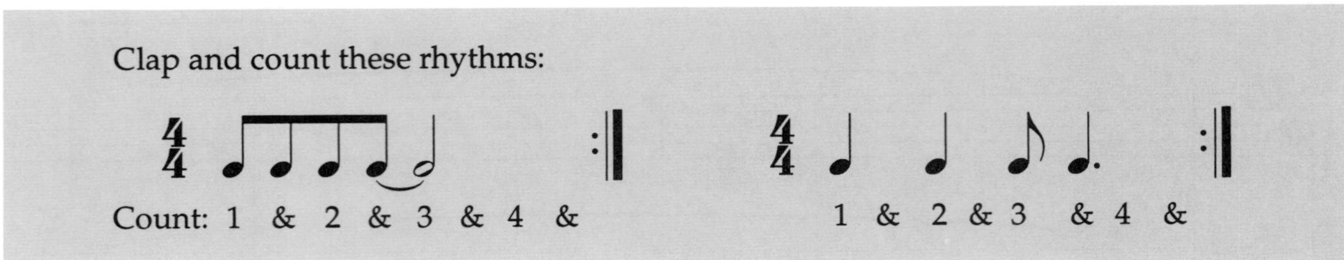

Sforzando

The marking ***sfz*** is an abbreviation for the term sforzando, which means to play with a sudden accent.

FRANKIE AND JOHNNY

Traditional Blues

Moderato

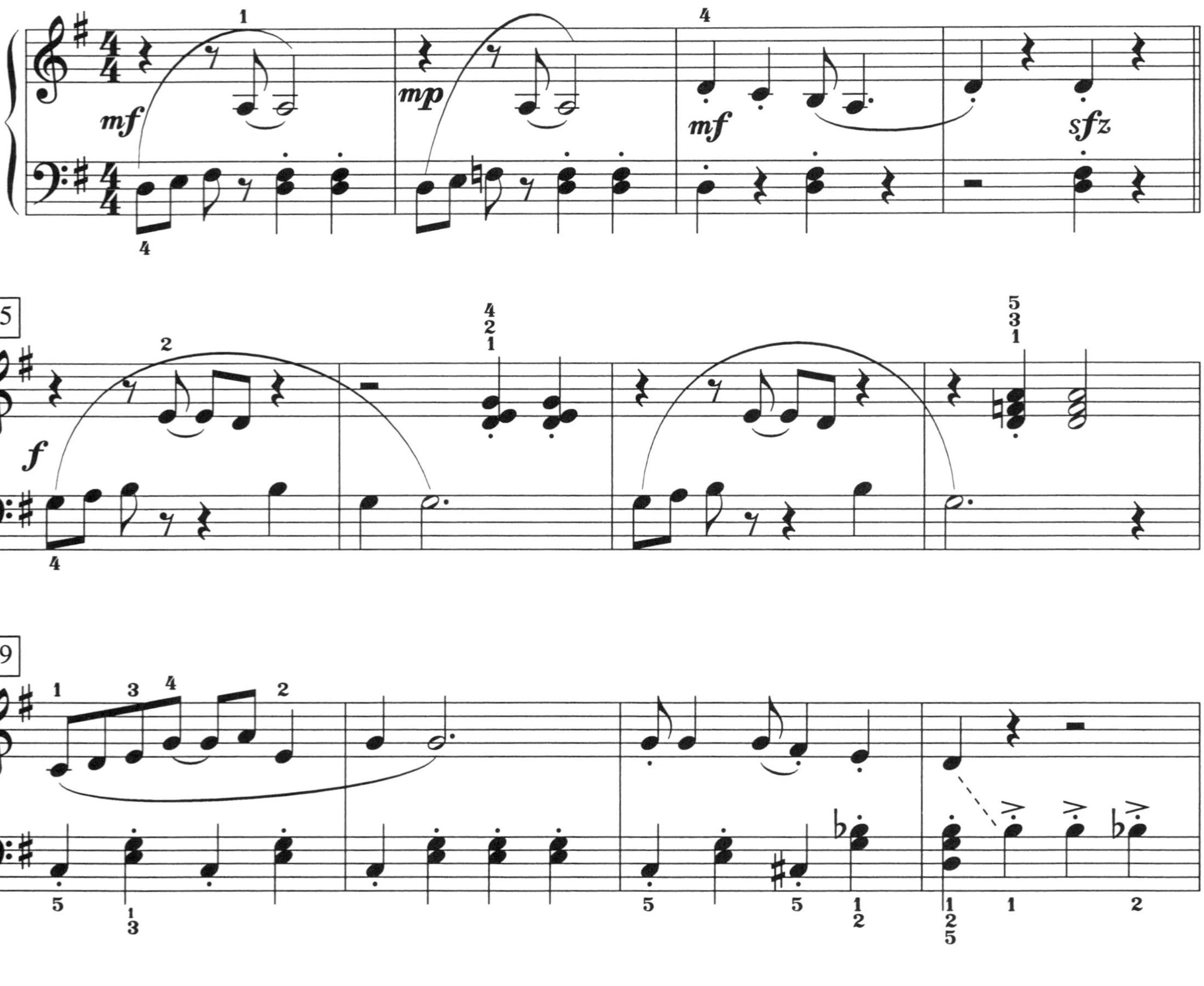

13
17
21
25
rit.
mf
f
pp

Review

A. Match each item with the correct definition or term.

a. 

b. syncopation

c. 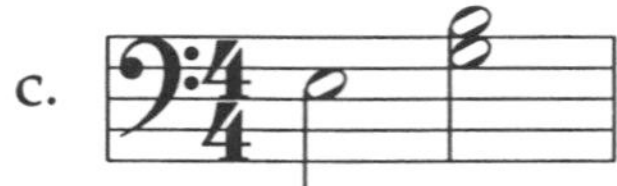

d. ritmico

e. 𝄴

f. rubato

g. triad

h. 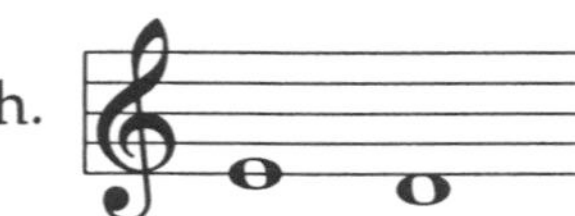

i.

j. 𝄵

k. 

l. 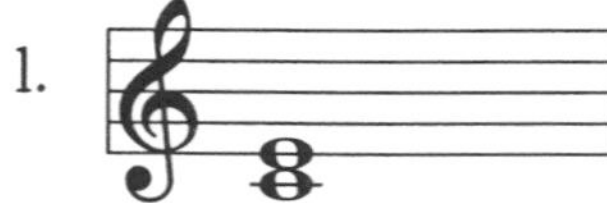

1. _____ whole step

2. _____ time is "borrowed," or some notes are held longer than their actual values, while others are curtailed, in order to allow more freedom and spontaneity

3. _____ common time $\frac{4}{4}$

4. _____ broken chord bass

5. _____ Major 3rd (four half steps)

6. _____ minor 3rd (three half steps)

7. _____ to stress or accent weak beats

8. _____ broken chord bass

9. _____ a three-note chord

10. _____ half step

11. _____ cut time $\frac{2}{2}$

12. _____ rhythmic, or to play in strict rhythm with a steady beat

B. Write the E harmonic minor scale ascending and descending. Circle the half steps.
C. Write the primary chords in root position.

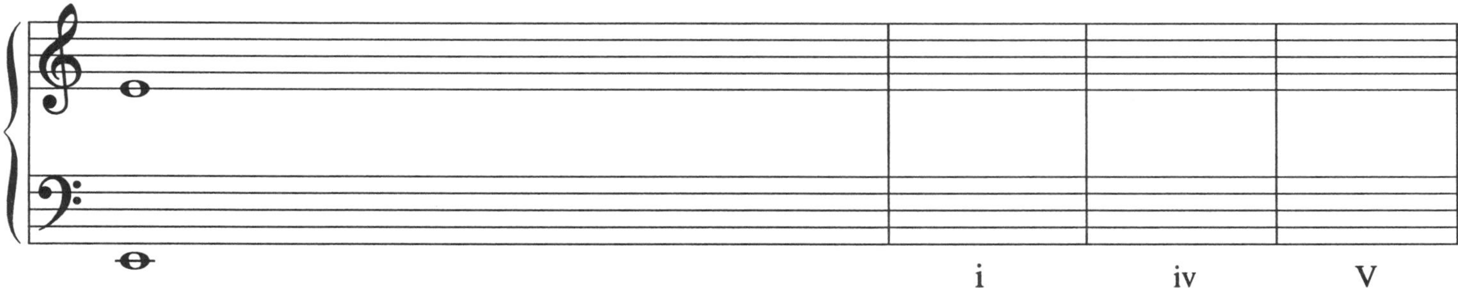

D. In the Key of E minor:

1. Write the key signature: 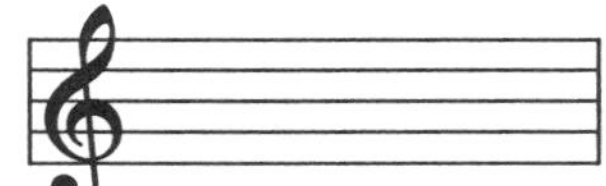

2. The tonic note is E .
3. The root of the tonic chord (i) is_____.

4. The subdominant note is _____.
5. The root of the subdominant chord (iv) is_____.

6. The dominant note is_____.
7. The root of the dominant chord (V) is_____.

8. The tonic and subdominant chords are Major/minor. (circle one)
9. The dominant chord is Major/minor. (circle one)

i iv V

E. Write the chord symbols (Em, Am, or B7) in the boxes provided.
F. Play the chords in the correct place on the keyboard.

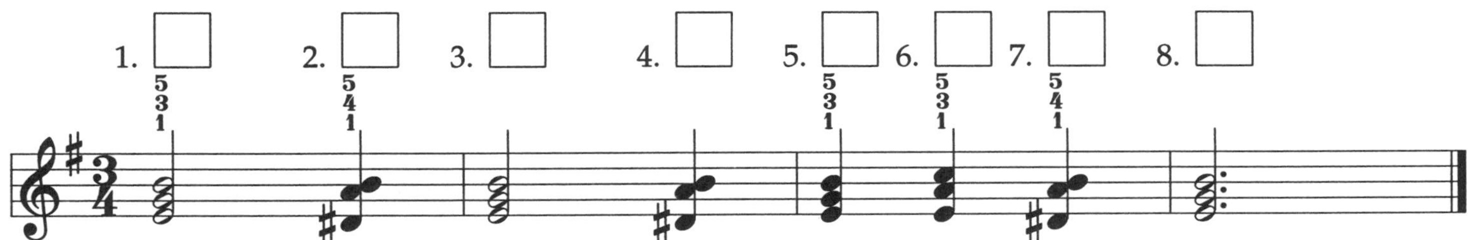

G. Name the following Major and minor triads.

Chapter 3

Reading in F Major and D Minor

NEW CONCEPTS

- 6/8 Time Signature
- Waltz Bass
- F Major Scale and Chords
- D Harmonic Minor Scale and Chords

REVIEW CONCEPTS

- D.C. al Coda 𝄌

6 = 6 beats in a measure
8 = ♪ receives 1 beat

NOTES		RESTS
♪	1 beat	𝄾
♩	2 beats	𝄽
♩.	3 beats	𝄽.
𝅗𝅥.	6 beats	𝄼

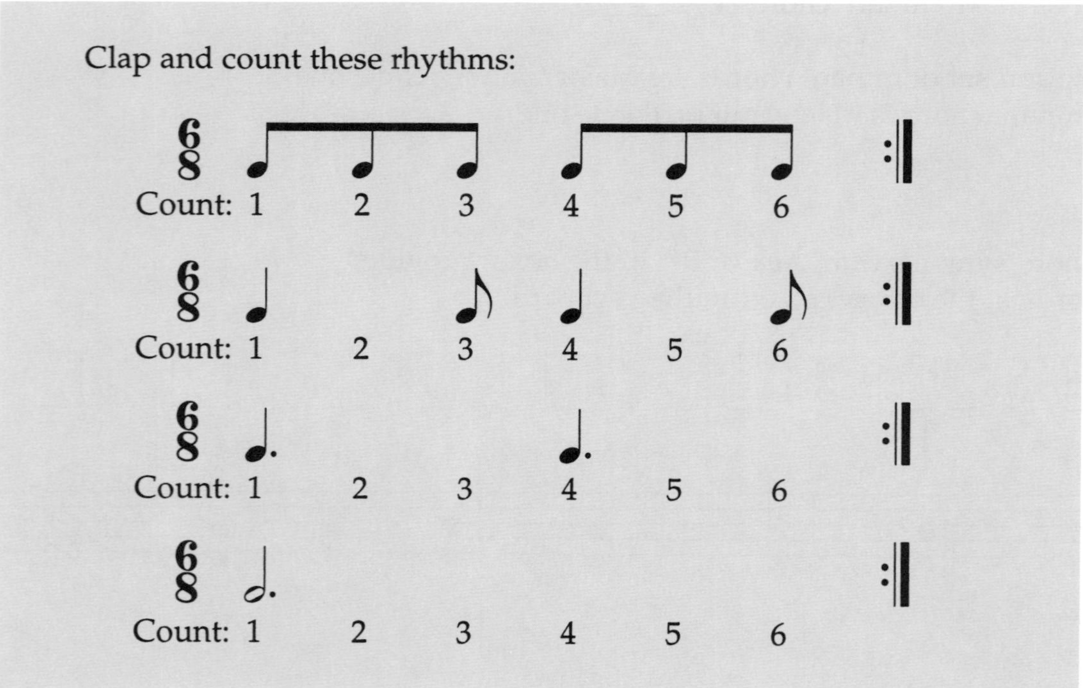

WARM UP

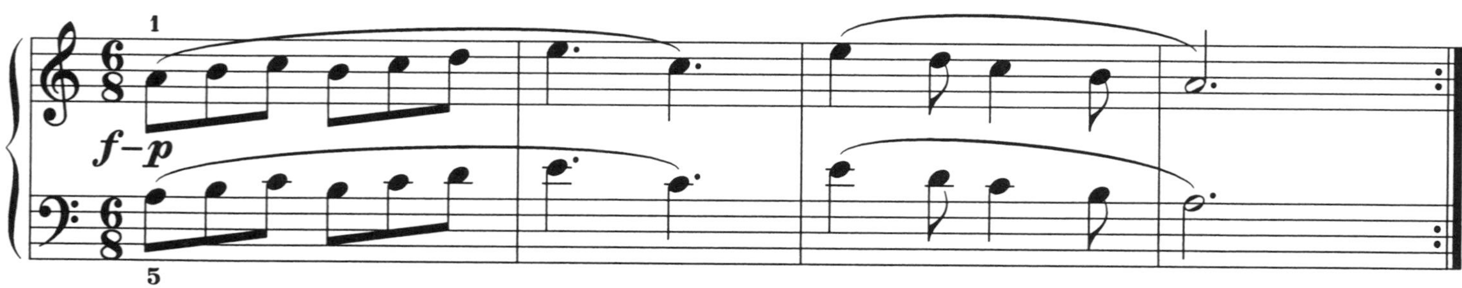

D.C. al Coda means to return to the beginning and play until the directions or the *Coda* sign ⊕ indicate to skip to the *Coda*, which ends the piece.

PRELUDE IN A MINOR

DISC ONE 30
♪ = 96

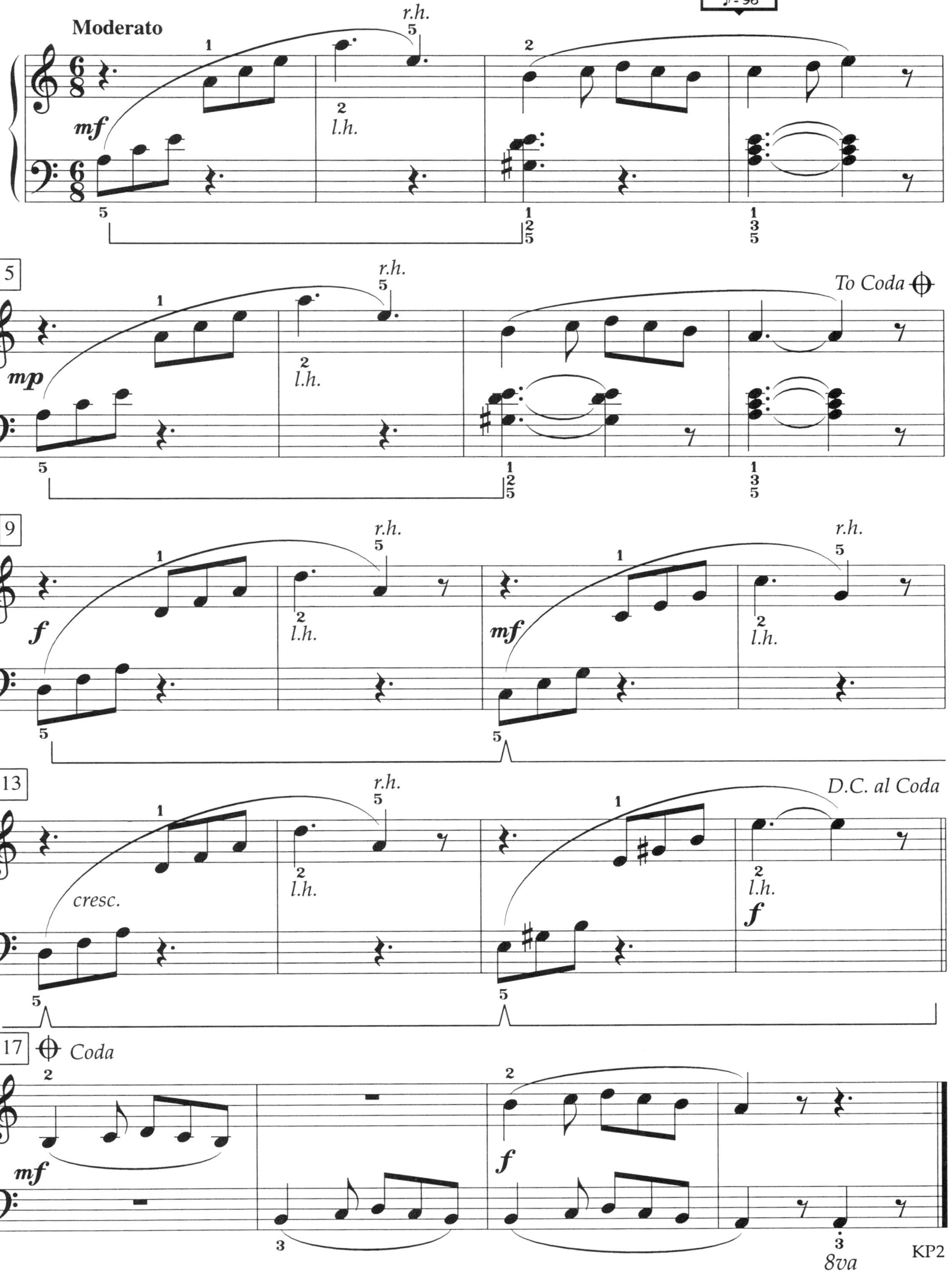

Moderato

r.h. l.h. mf mp f mf cresc.

To Coda ⊕

D.C. al Coda

⊕ Coda

8va

F Major Scale

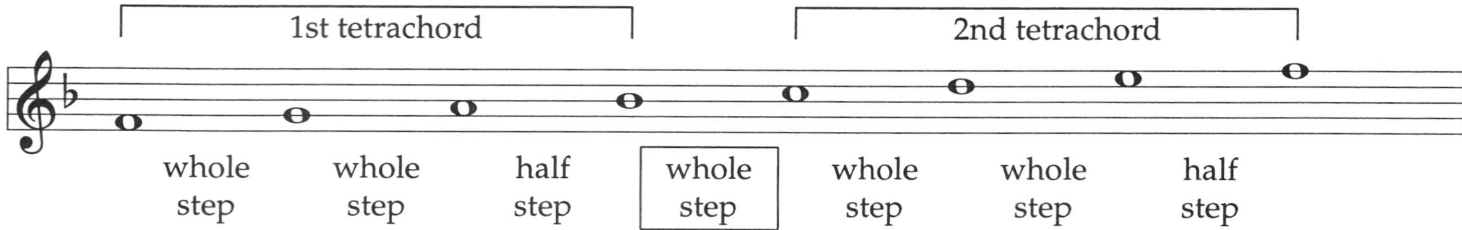

Primary Chords in the Key of F Major

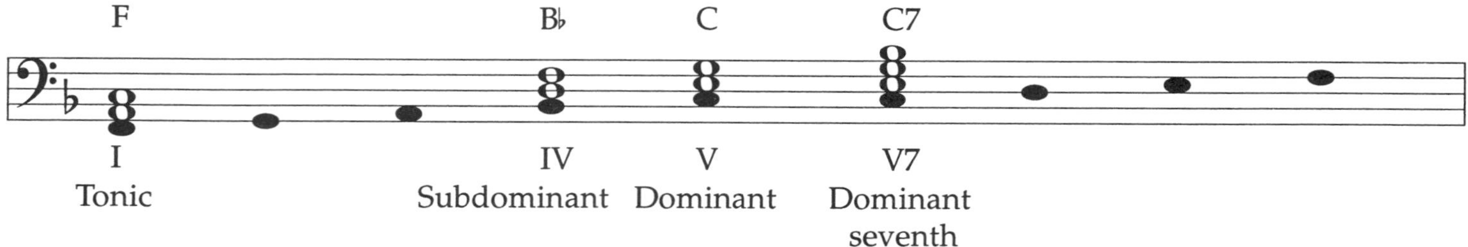

F MAJOR SCALE AND CHORDS

Play hands separately first. Memorize the fingering.

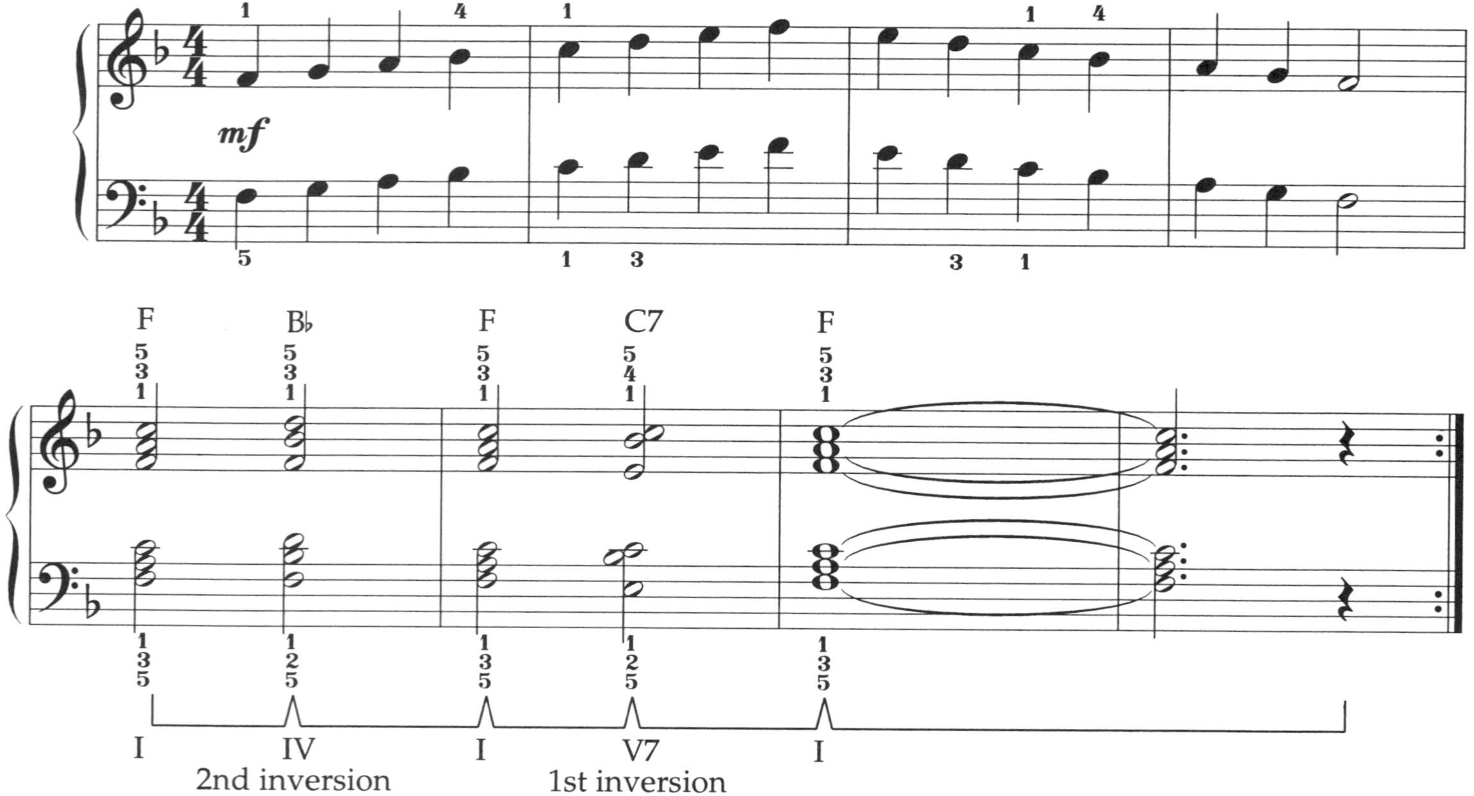

SCOTTISH BAGPIPES

Scottish Folk Song

*Vivo

mf

5

f

9

1.

13

2.

dim.

* The term **Vivo** means lively.

SUMMER WHIRLWIND

DISC ONE 34 ♩= 88

Allegretto

5 5 5 4 2

mf *leggiero 2 l.h. 2 rit.

5 a tempo

1 2 1 1

f

1 3 5 1 2 5

9

1 2 1

mf

* The term **leggiero** means to play lightly.

rit.
8va

Franz Lehar (1879-1948), Austrian composer and conductor, was the son of a military bandmaster who composed dances and marches. Throughout his childhood Lehar lived in many towns across Hungary as his father was transferred between posts. The life Lehar experienced in these different towns allowed him to develop a proficiency in languages, musical versatility, and a cosmopolitan nature that later influenced his compositions. He studied violin very early, composed his first *lied* (song) at eleven, and began studying music at the Prague Conservatory at twelve. Lehar became popular in Vienna both conducting and playing in various infantry regiments in the army. His *Gold and Silver Waltz*, composed in 1902, earned him international recognition. Lehar focused his efforts on composing operettas and became the leading operetta composer of the twentieth century. He is remembered for reviving the genre as a form of entertainment. In 1905, Lehar composed the operetta *The Merry Widow*, which became a world success. *The Merry Widow Waltz* is one of Lehar's most famous melodies.

Waltz Bass

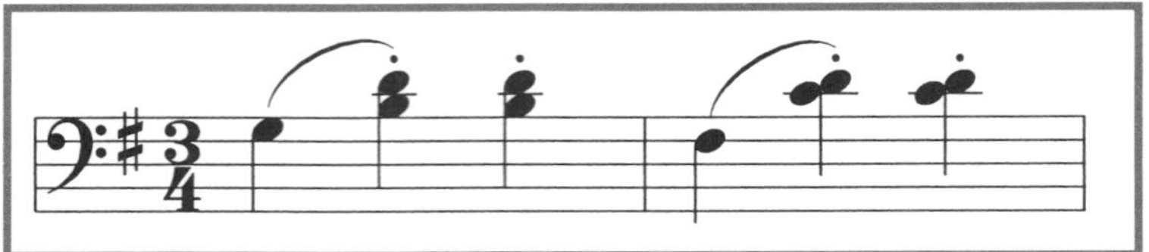

THE MERRY WIDOW WALTZ

Franz Lehar

13
17
mf
21
25
mp
29
p

D Harmonic Minor Scale

For each Major key there is a **relative minor**. The same key signature is used for both keys. The **harmonic minor** scale uses the same tones as the Major scale, with one exception: the 7th tone in the harmonic minor scale is raised one half step. D minor is relative to F Major; both keys have one flat (B♭).

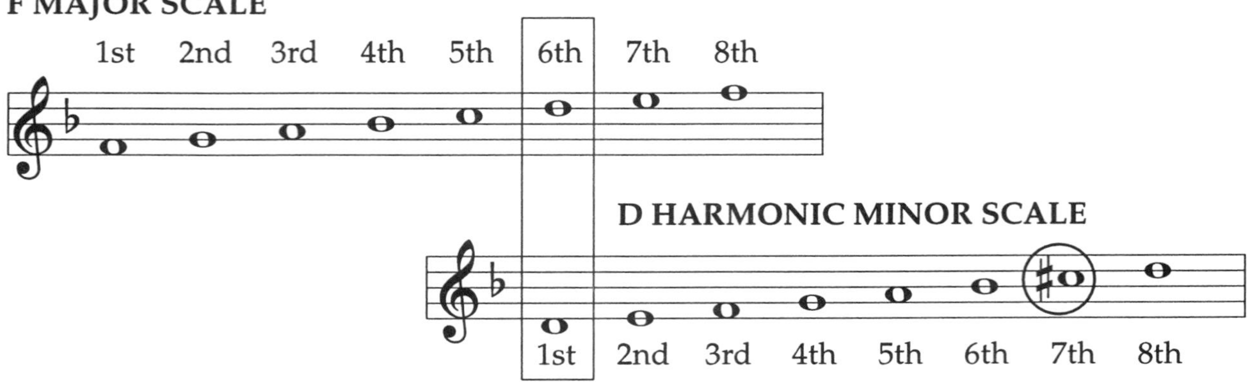

Primary Chords in the Key of D Minor

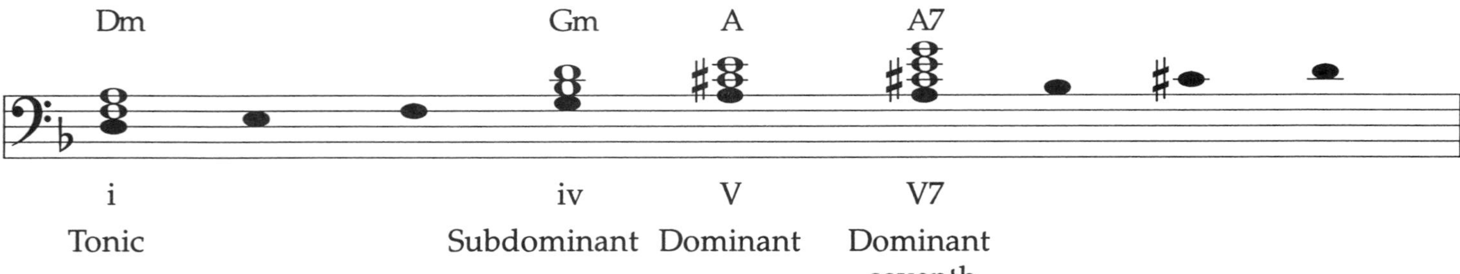

D HARMONIC MINOR SCALE AND CHORDS

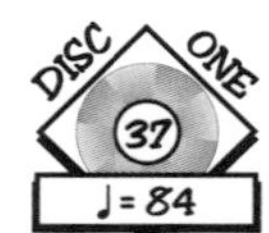

Play hands separately first. Memorize the fingering.

THE MINSTREL'S SONG

DISC ONE 38 ♩= 80

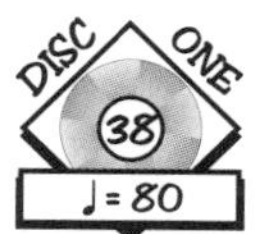

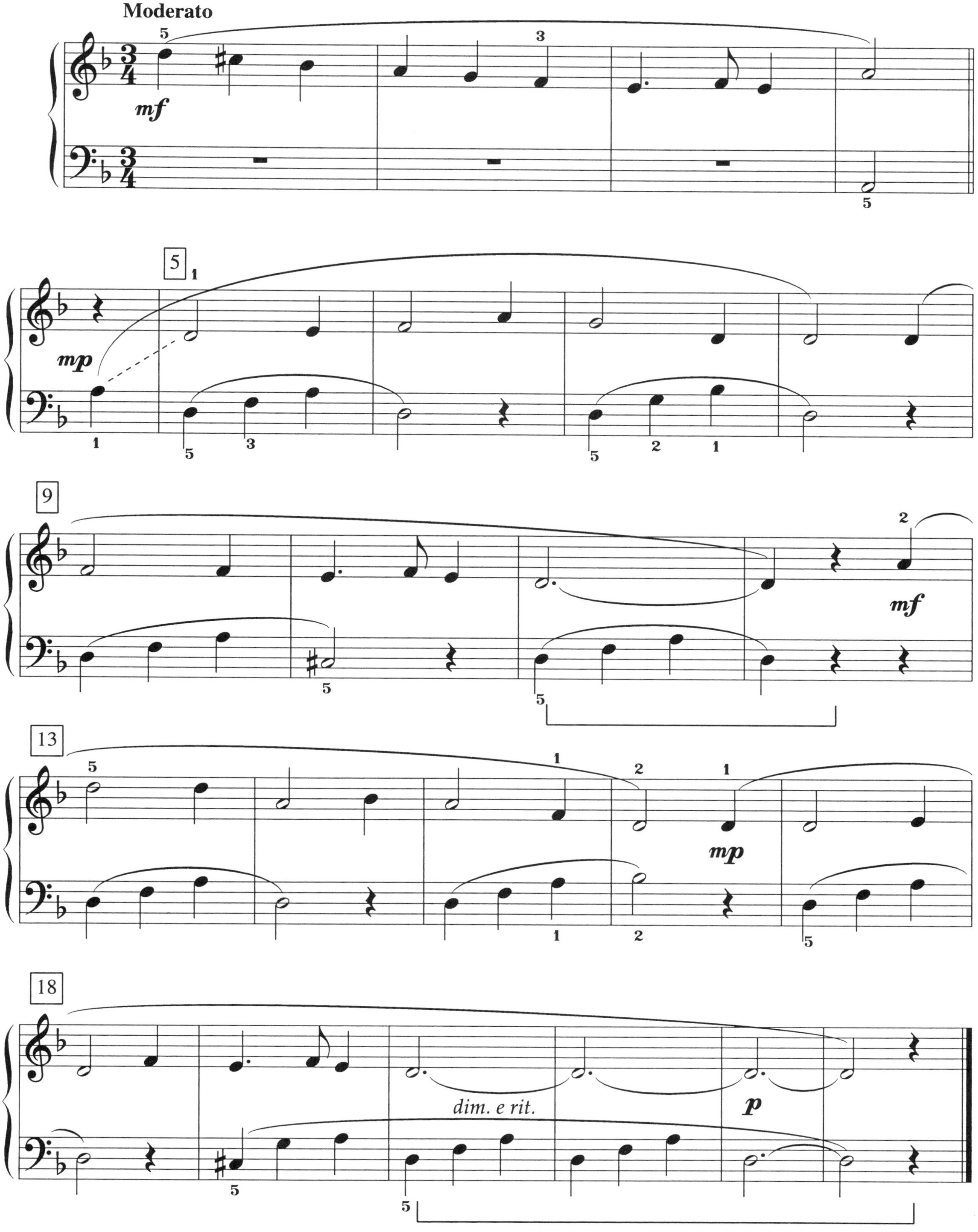
Moderato
mf
5
mp
9
mf
13
mp
18
dim. e rit.
p

Cornelius Gurlitt (1820-1901), German organist and composer, was born in Altona into an artistic family. Gurlitt studied piano with Johann Peter Reinecke and Christoph Weyse, and as a young man he traveled throughout Europe meeting many great composers, including Robert Schumann. Well-respected as a musician, he was appointed organist and music director at the Altona Cathedral and held these positions for thirty-four years. Gurlitt also taught at the Hamburg Conservatory. He composed several sonatas for violin and cello, as well as two operettas and two operas; his four-act opera *Scheik Hassan* was never performed. He is best known and remembered for his numerous piano miniatures, mostly teaching pieces, which reflect the influence of Schumann. This piece is an example of one of Gurlitt's teaching pieces that can be considered a left-hand etude (study), because the melody is in the left hand.

Note: To achieve a good sound, balance the hands by playing the left hand melody louder and the right hand chords softer. In cases such as the etude below, where there are many repeated right hand chords, it is helpful to keep the fingers curved and very close to the keys to maintain dynamic control.

ETUDE

DISC ONE 39 ♩= 80

Cornelius Gurlitt

*Allegro non troppo

mp mf

4

* The term **Allegro non troppo** means fast, but not too fast.

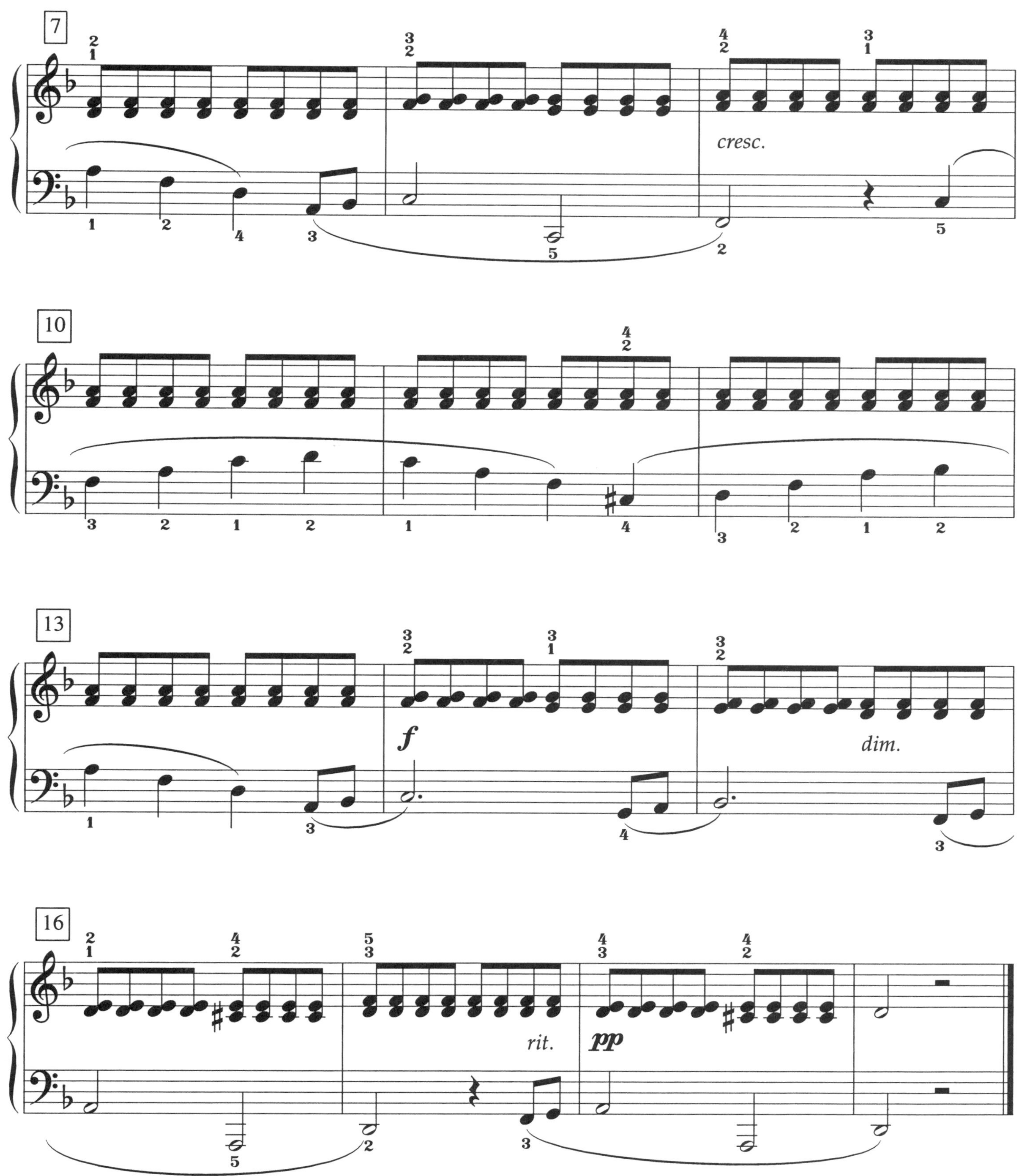

7
cresc.
10
13
dim.
16
rit.
pp

JOE TURNER

Traditional Blues
Adaptation

Note: Often in jazz, eighth notes are played "long-short," as demonstrated on the CD accompaniment. This is called "swinging" the eighth notes.

VENETIAN SONG

Italian Air

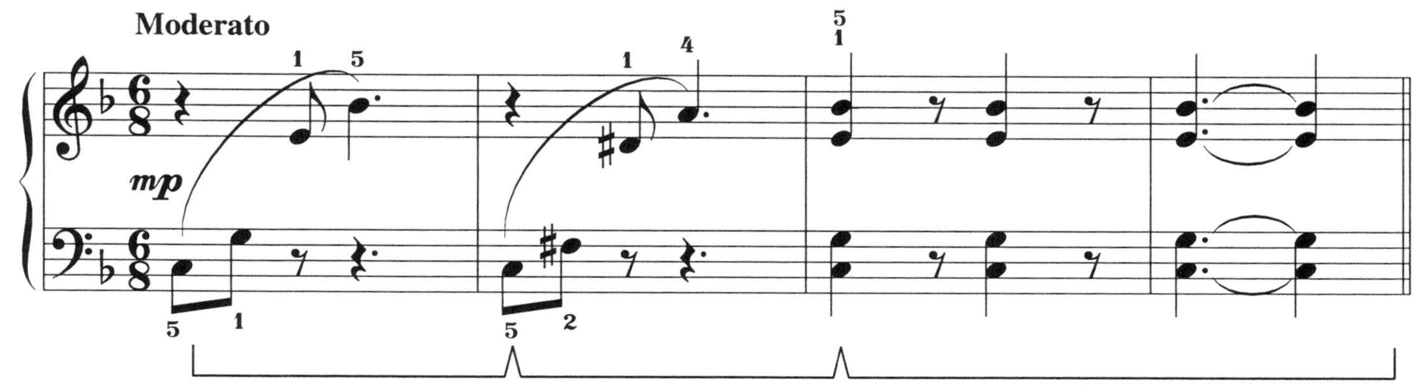

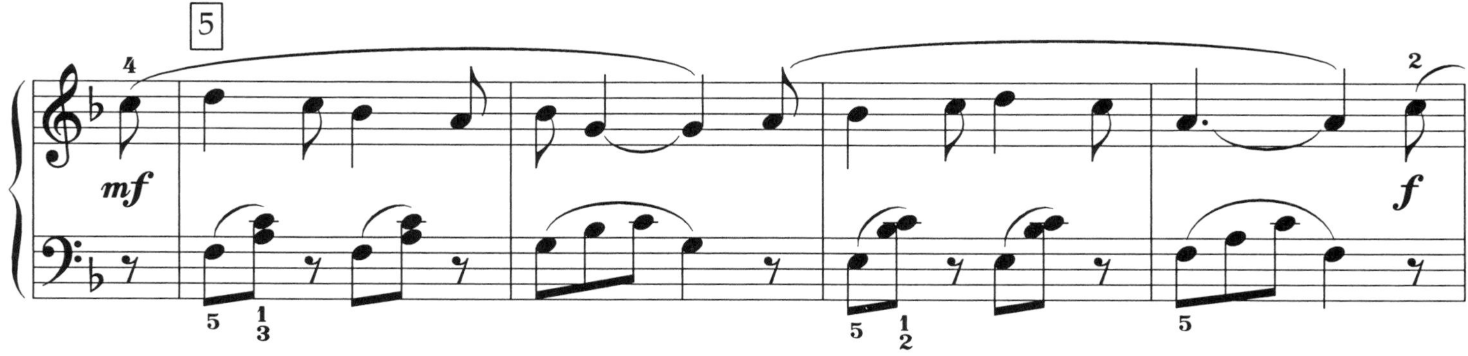

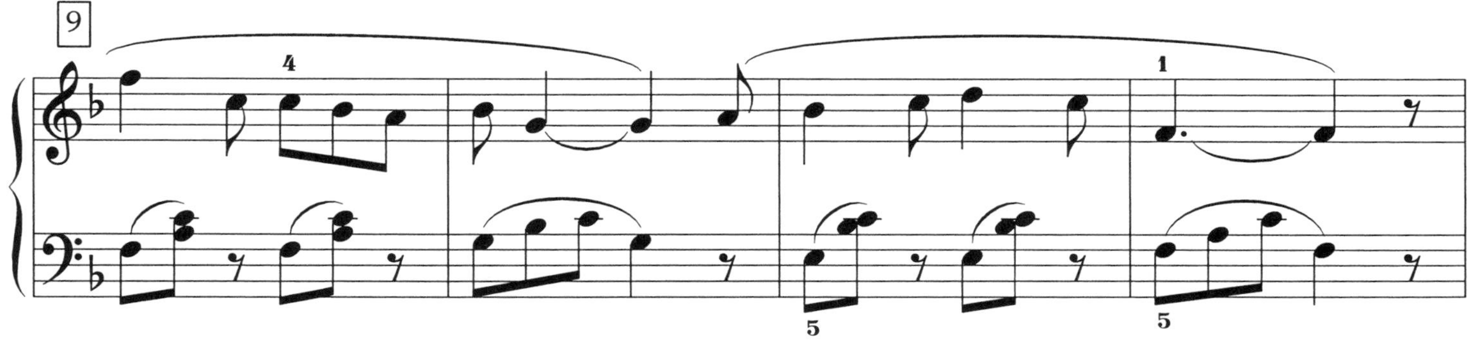

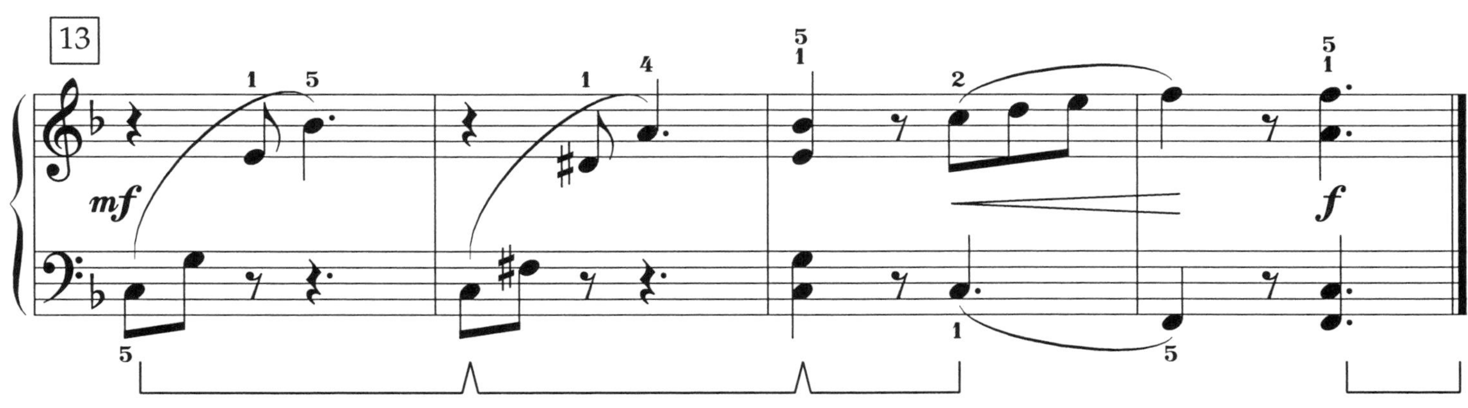

WALTZ

Op. 39, No. 15

Johannes Brahms

Technic

FINGER EXTENSION STUDY

from *The Virtuoso Pianist*

Charles-Louis Hanon

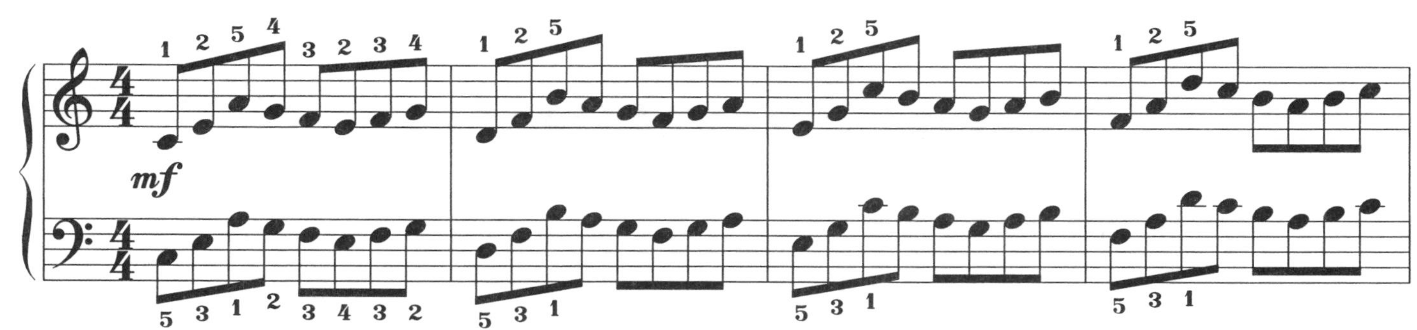

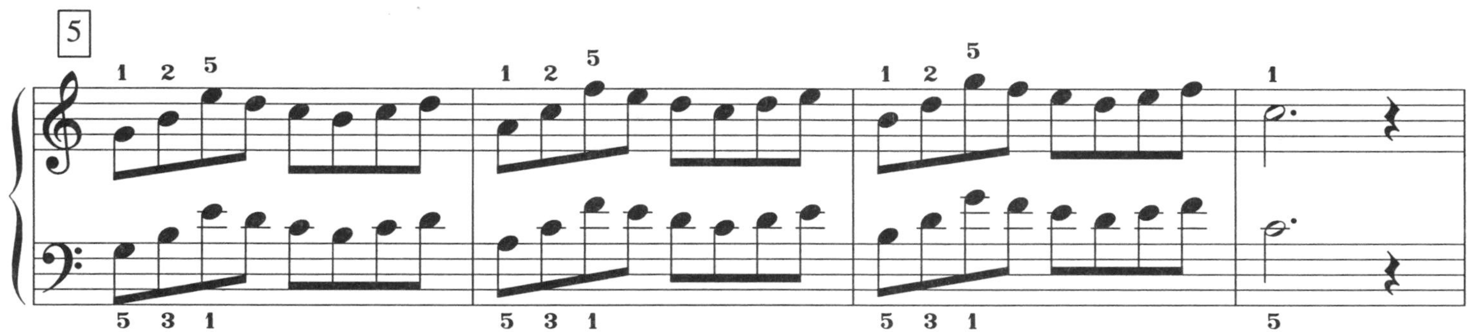

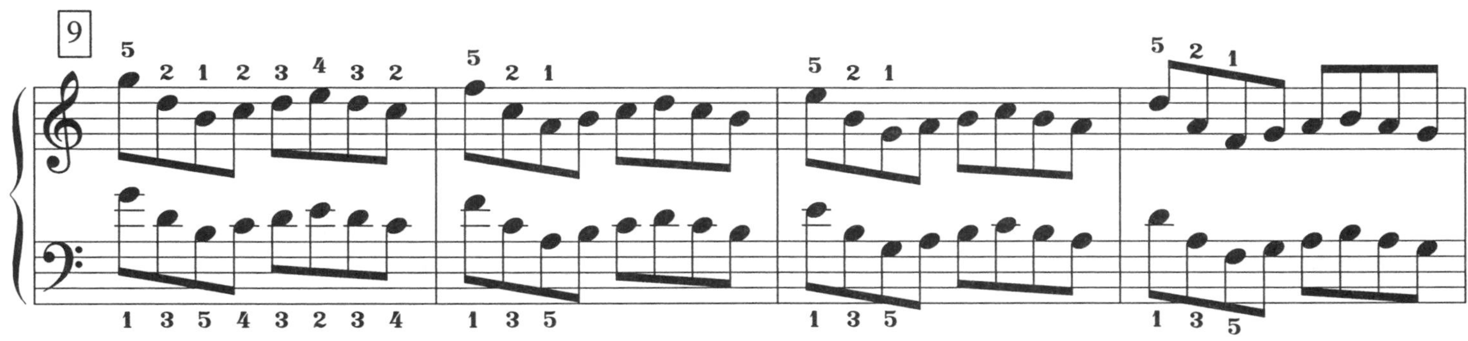

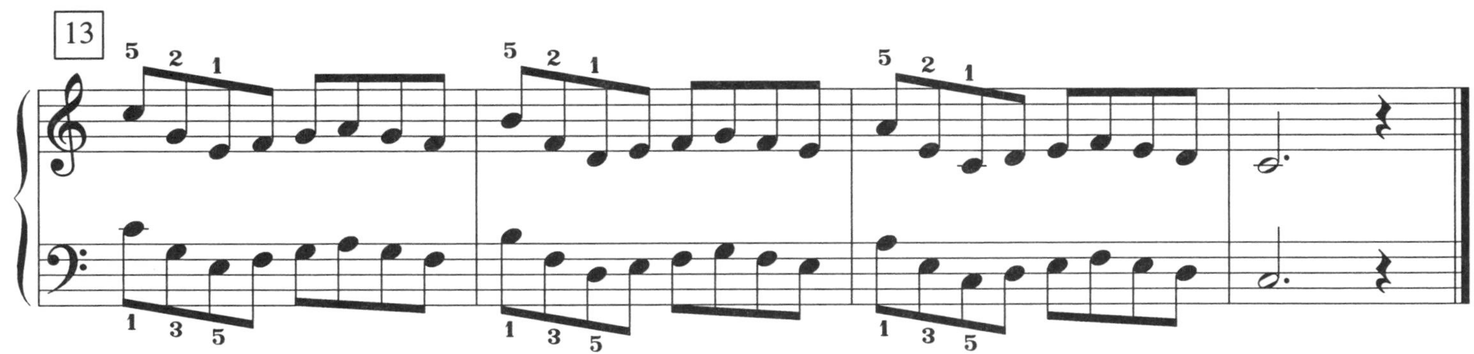

Challenge Piece

Note: Measures 1-3 use the same notes in three different octaves on the keyboard.

HEARTS FROM HEAVEN

Andante con rubato

8va

mp *l.h.*

rit.

5 *a tempo*

mf

9 8va

mp

13
mf
17
mp
dim. e rit.
p
a tempo
21
mf
25
8va
mp
dim. e molto rit.
pp

Review

A. Write the number of beats each note receives in $\frac{6}{8}$.

1. ____ 2. ____ 3. ____ 4. ____ 5. ____ 6. ____ 7. ____ 8. ____

B. Add barlines to complete each measure.

C. Add one note to complete each measure.

D. Add one rest to complete each measure.

E. Match each item with the correct definition or term.

a. Allegro non troppo	1. _____ lively
b.	2. _____ minor
c. Vivo	3. _____ key of G Major or E minor
d. *leggiero*	4. _____ Major
e. 	5. _____ walking tempo
f. m	6. _____ upbeat
g. Andante	7. _____ lightly
h. 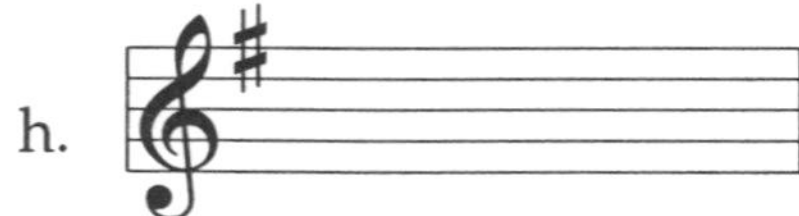	8. _____ the same as
i. M	9. _____ waltz bass
j. *simile*	10. _____ fast, but not too fast

F. Write the F Major scale ascending and descending. Circle the half steps.
G. Write the primary chords in root position.

H. In the Key of F Major:

1. Write the key signature: 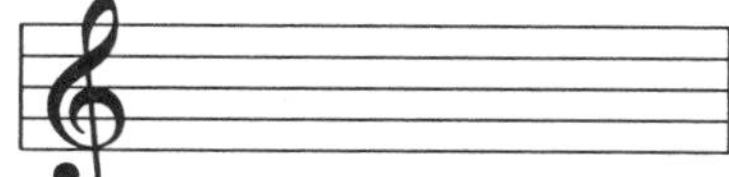

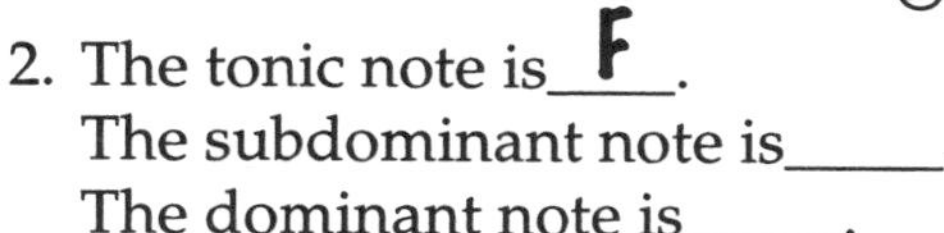

2. The tonic note is F.
   The subdominant note is_____.
   The dominant note is_____.

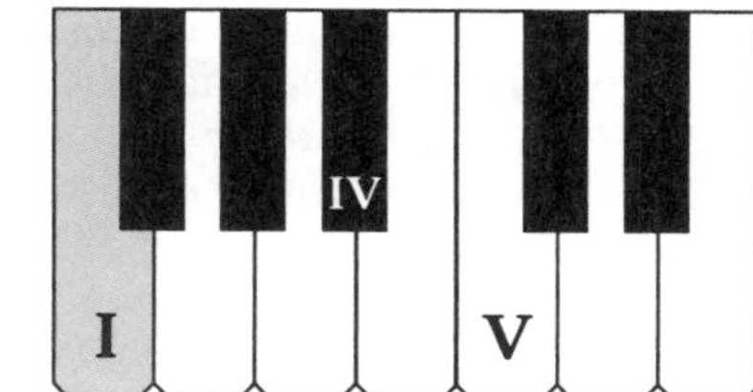

3. The root of the tonic chord (I) is_____.
   The root of the subdominant chord (IV) is_____.
   The root of the dominant seventh chord (V7) is_____.

4. The I, IV, and V chords are Major/minor. (circle one)

I. Write the D harmonic minor scale ascending and descending. Circle the half steps.
J. Write the primary chords in root position.

K. In the Key of D minor:

1. Write the key signature: 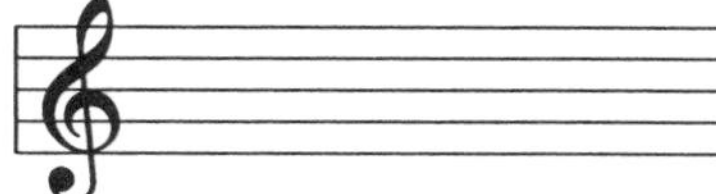

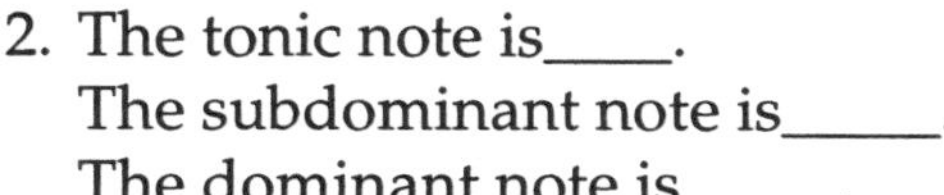

2. The tonic note is____.
   The subdominant note is_____.
   The dominant note is_____.

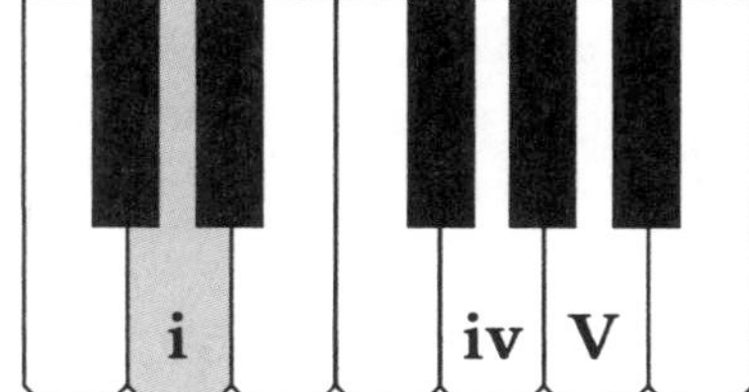

3. The root of the tonic chord (i) is_____.
   The root of the subdominant chord (iv) is_____.
   The root of the dominant seventh chord (V7) is_____.

4. The i and iv chords are Major/minor. (circle one)

5. The V chord is Major/minor. (circle one)

Chapter 4
Triads and Inversions

NEW CONCEPTS

- Transposition
- Triplet Rhythm
- $\frac{6}{4}$ Time Signature
- Octave Sign *15ma*

REVIEW CONCEPTS

- Triads and Inversions
- Major and Minor Triads

Stephen Foster (1826-1864), American composer, was born in Lawrence, Pennsylvania, the ninth of ten children in his family. As a child, Foster taught himself to play the flute. In 1841, his family moved to Allegheny, Pennsylvania, where he began composing his first songs. His parents, who noticed his talent, did not approve of his ambitions and provided no encouragement in his musical endeavors. He was sent to work as a bookkeeper for his brother, a grocer in Cincinnati. In 1848, Foster's song *Oh Susannah* became an overnight hit and was sung by the "forty-niners" on their way westward to the California gold fields. *Old Folks at Home* was Foster's next big hit in 1851. Wanting to be known for his serious songs, he signed over his rights for a small fee and the song was published under the name Edwin Christy, of the Christy Minstrels. After his mother died in 1860, he had difficulty composing. He was careless with his money and died, penniless, at the age of thirty-seven. Stephen Foster's legacy of over two hundred songs exemplifies American folk traditions and is part of a great cultural heritage.

OLD FOLKS AT HOME

Words and Music by
Stephen Foster

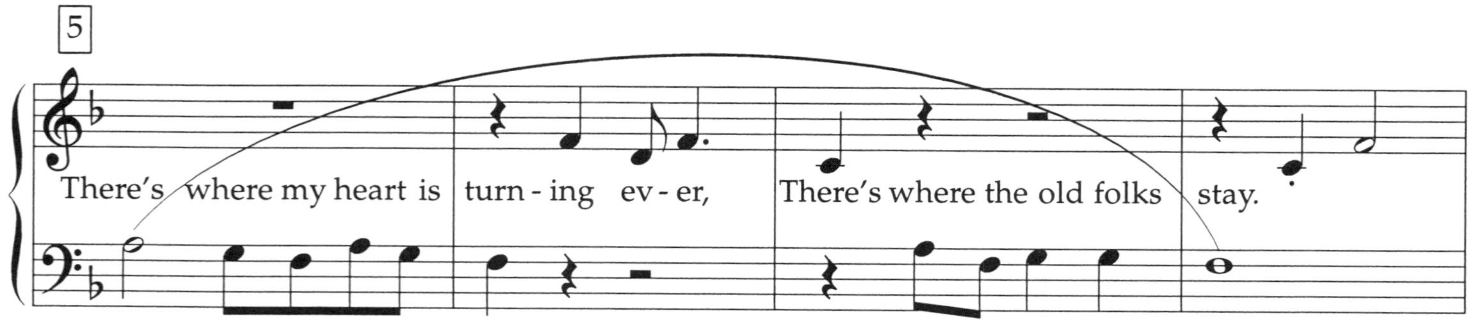

9
All up and down the whole cre - a - tion,
Sad - ly I roam,

13
Still long-ing for the old plan- ta-tion,
And for the old folks at home.

17
f All the world is sad and drear - y,
Ev - ry-where I roam,

21
mf Oh! hon-ey, how my heart grows wear - y,
Far from the old folks at home.

Triads and Inversions

A triad is a three-note chord. A root position triad is a triad in its most basic form. All notes are stacked in intervals of 3rds, beginning with the root located on the bottom.

An inversion is a different arrangement of notes in a triad. The shaded notes indicate the roots in the inversions shown below. When the triad is inverted, the root is the top note of the interval of a 4th.

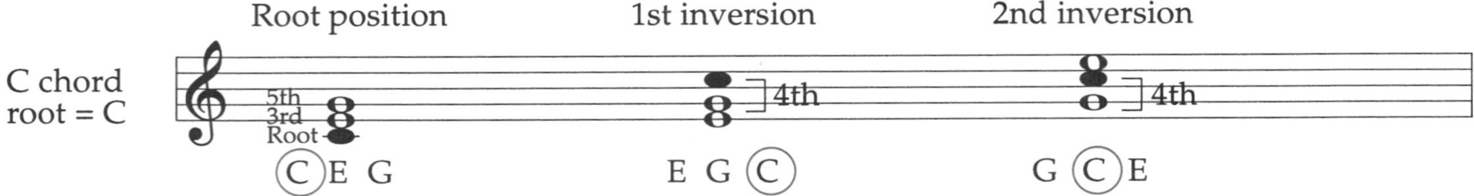

Transposition

To **transpose** means to play in a different key than written. Although different notes are used, the intervals between them are the same. For example, if a chord is in root position in the original key, it will also be in root position in the new key; if a chord is inverted in the original key, it will be in the same inversion in the new key.

C Major

transposed to G Major

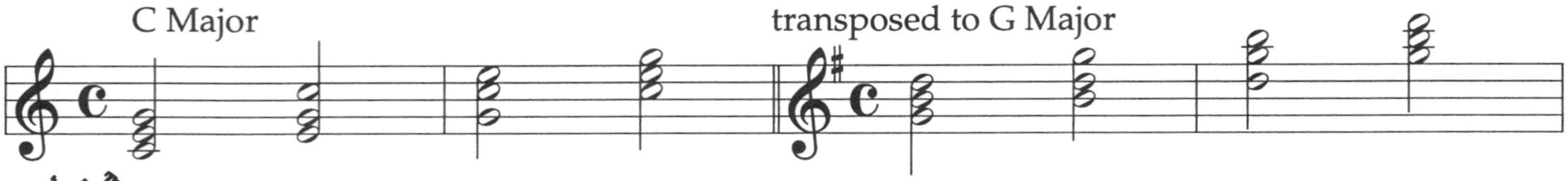

FOLLOW THROUGH

After practicing the following exercises in the keys in which they are written, transpose exercise 1 from C Major to G Major and exercise 2 from A minor to D minor.

1. C

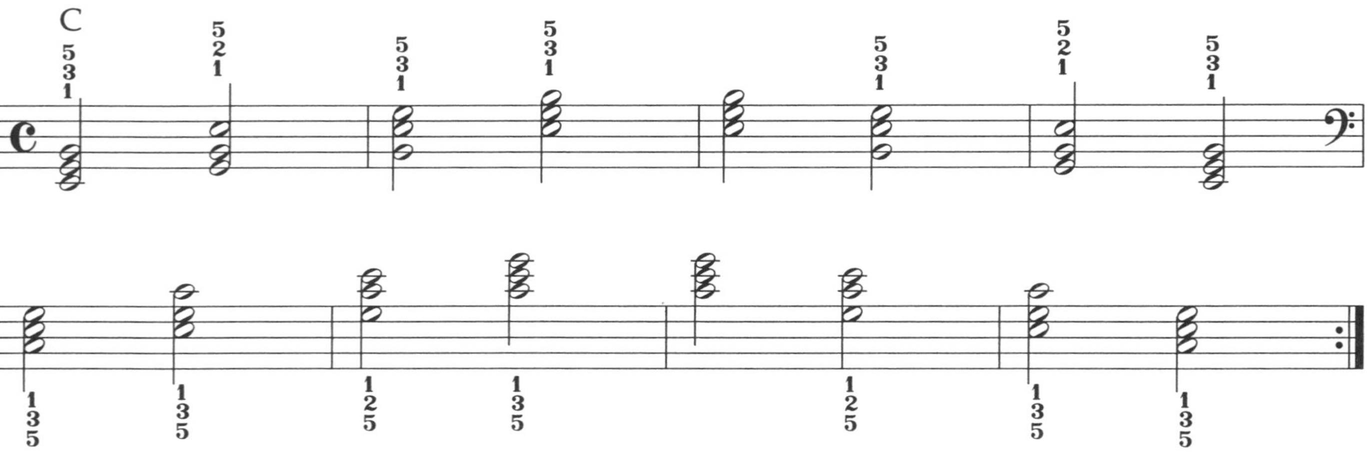

2. Am

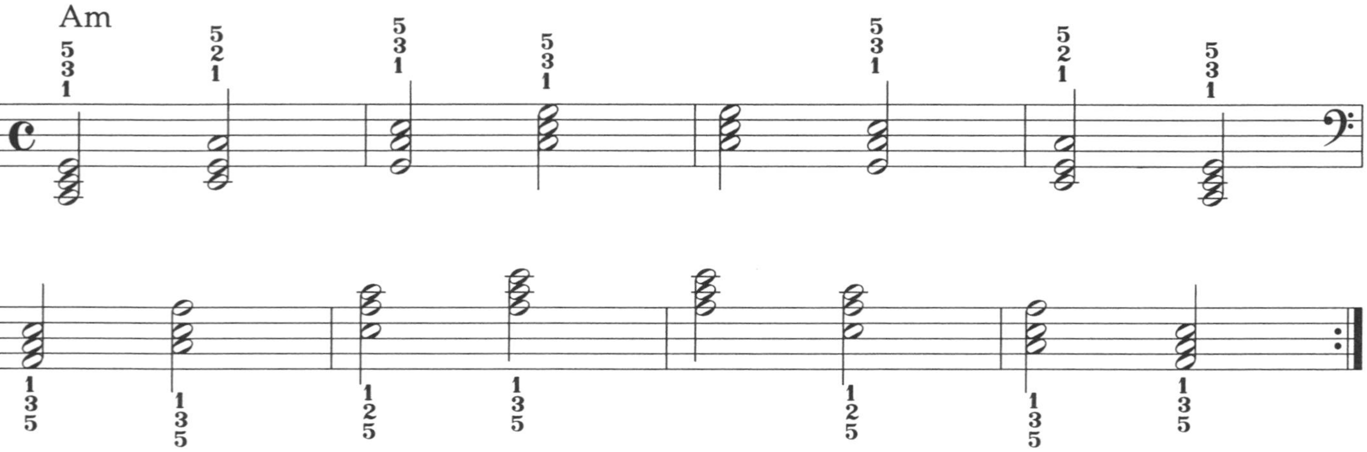

REVEILLE

Traditional Bugle Call

★ The term **Animato** means with animation.

LA JOLLA SUNSET

DISC ONE 49 ♩= 72

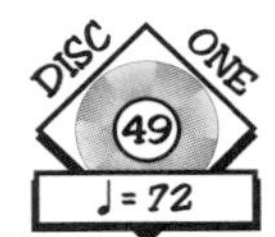

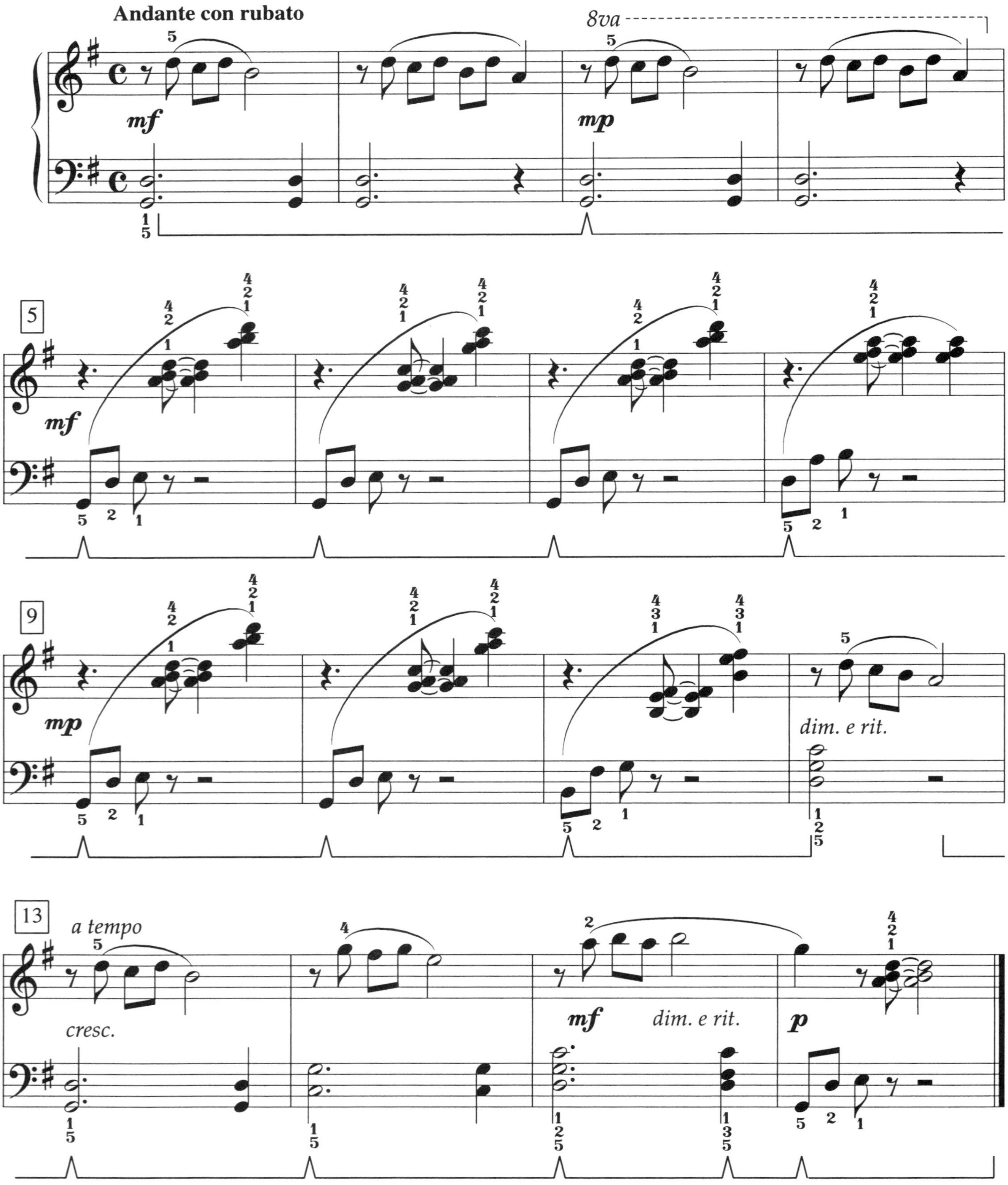
Andante con rubato
8va
mf
mp
5
mf
9
mp
dim. e rit.
13
a tempo
cresc.
mf
dim. e rit.
p

Major and Minor Triads

From every Major triad, a minor triad may be formed by lowering the **3rd** (middle note) one half step.

Moving Down a Half Step:
A sharp note becomes a natural note.

D Major

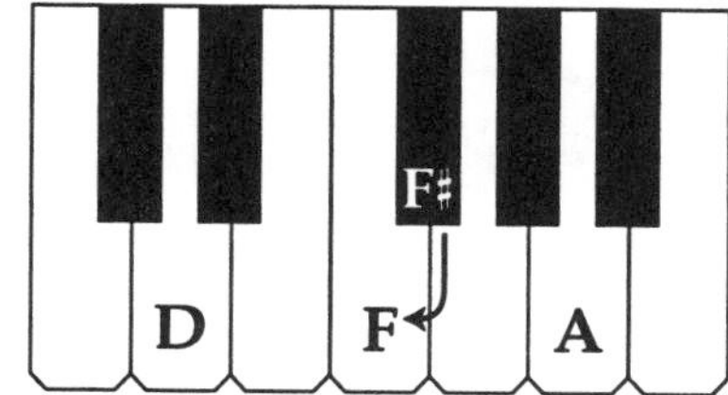

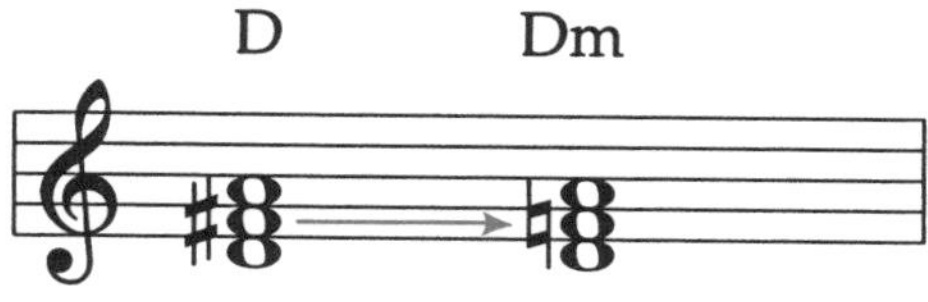

A natural note becomes a flat note.

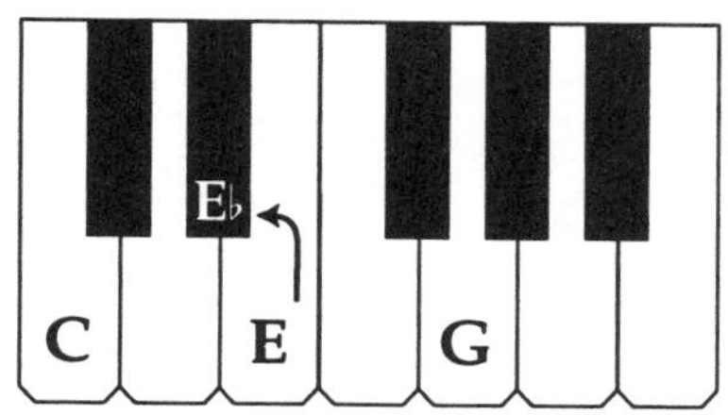

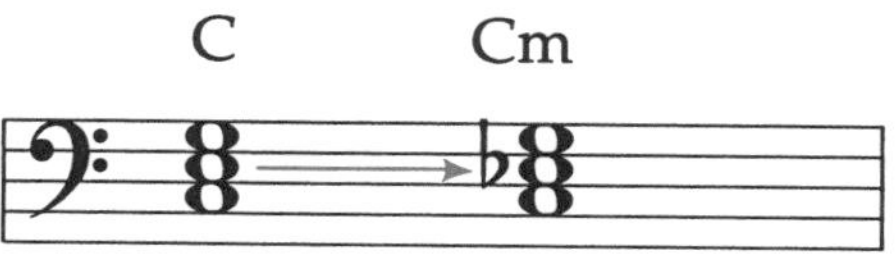

Review

For each example:
- A. Name the given Major triad.
- B. Draw and name the corresponding minor triad.
- C. Play the triads on the keyboard.

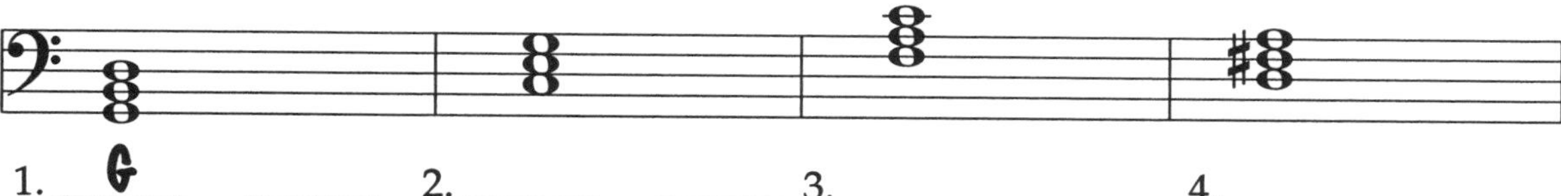

1. G ______ ______ 2. ______ ______ 3. ______ ______ 4. ______ ______

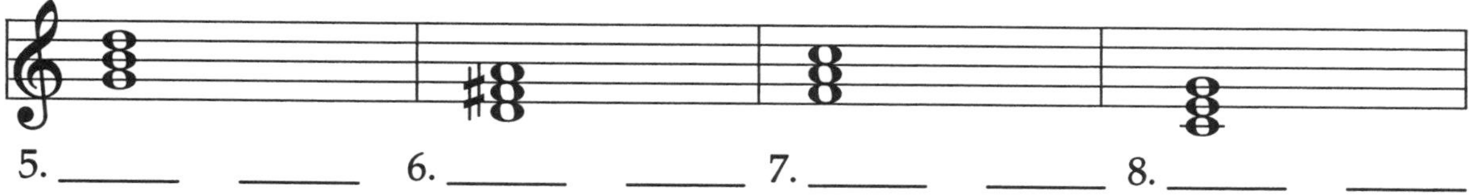

5. ______ ______ 6. ______ ______ 7. ______ ______ 8. ______ ______

D. Name the following Major and minor triads.

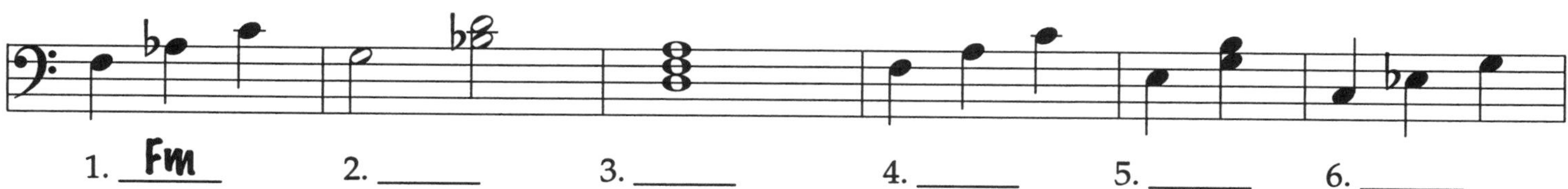

1. Fm 2. ______ 3. ______ 4. ______ 5. ______ 6. ______

Triplet Rhythm 

An eighth note triplet is equal to one quarter note in duration. ♪♪♪ (3) = ♩ = 1 beat
To count triplets, it is helpful to subdivide each beat into three parts.

Clap and count the following rhythm. Use this method or any other one your teacher suggests for counting triplet rhythm.

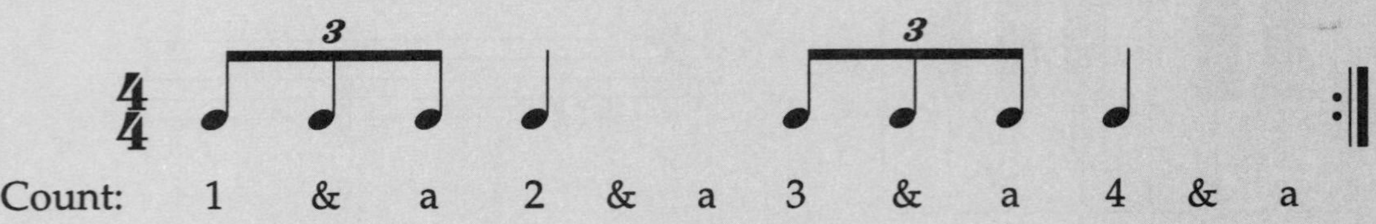

After playing *Warm Up* in the key of C Major, transpose to G Major and F Major.

WARM UP

AUTUMN BREEZE

Moderato con rubato

a tempo

mf *mp* *rit.* *l.h.* *mf*

mp

To Coda

f

mf

D.S. al Coda

Coda

mp *rit.* *r.h.* *dim. e rit.* *l.h.* *l.h.* *pp*

6	= 6 beats in a measure
4	= ♩ receives 1 beat

Notes		Rests
♩	1 beat	𝄽
𝅗𝅥	2 beats	𝄼
𝅗𝅥.	3 beats	𝄼.
𝅗𝅥. ‿ 𝅗𝅥.	6 beats	𝄻

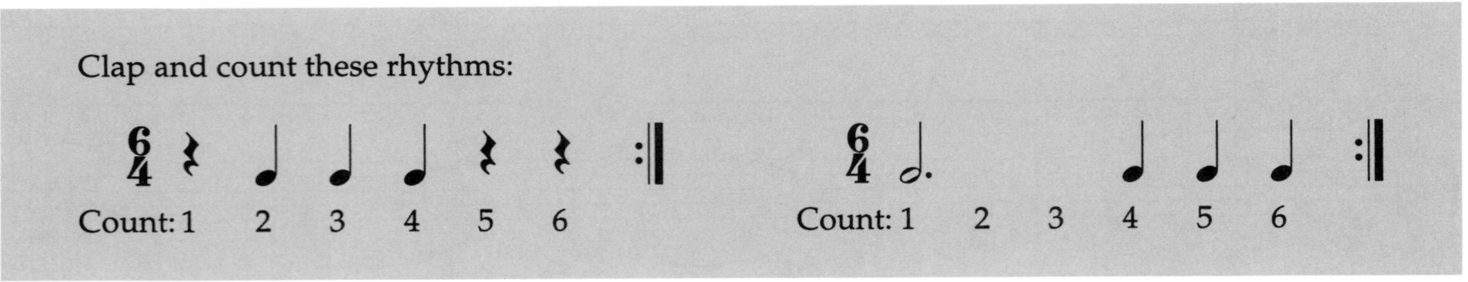

SPANISH FIESTA

* The term **Con Spirito** means with spirit.

13
17
8va
21
25
29
f
p
mf
ff

BAYOU BLUES

Slow blues

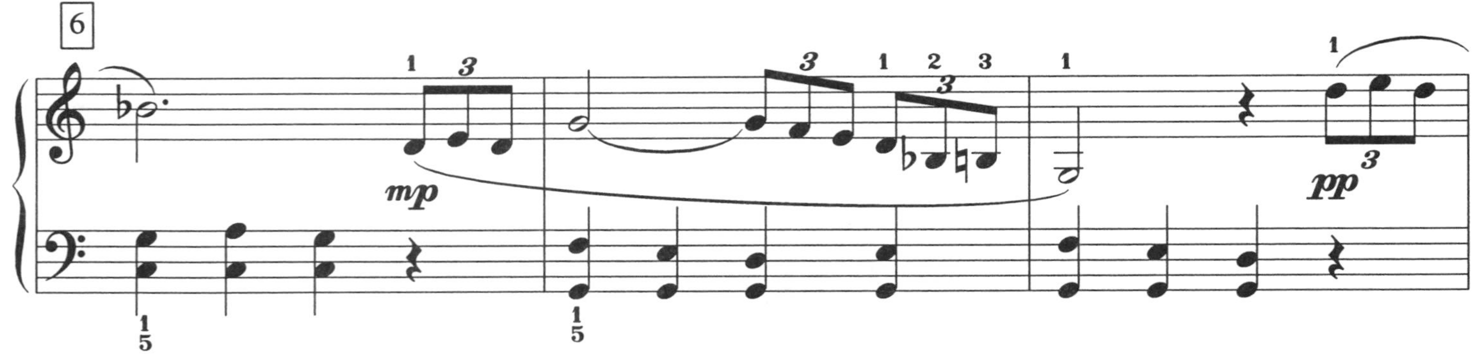

James Hook (1746-1827), English composer, organist, and teacher, was musically gifted from a young age. He performed harpsichord concertos in public when he was six and composed an opera by the age of eight. After his father's death when Hook was eleven, he helped support his family by teaching and performing. He held various positions as organist, composer, and music director at Marylebone Gardens and Vauxhall Gardens and taught piano at The Gough House, a private school for young ladies. He became a prolific composer with a true facility for writing captivating and memorable melodies of all kinds. His compositions include over two thousand songs, as well as odes, cantatas, overtures, concertos, quartets, trios, and many sonatas for keyboard instruments. He also wrote an instruction book, *Guida di Musica*, that contains teaching pieces for piano. The following *Minuet* is a dance in triple meter that uses counterpoint (two or more melodies that are played simultaneously).

MINUET

DISC ONE 53 ♩= 69

James Hook

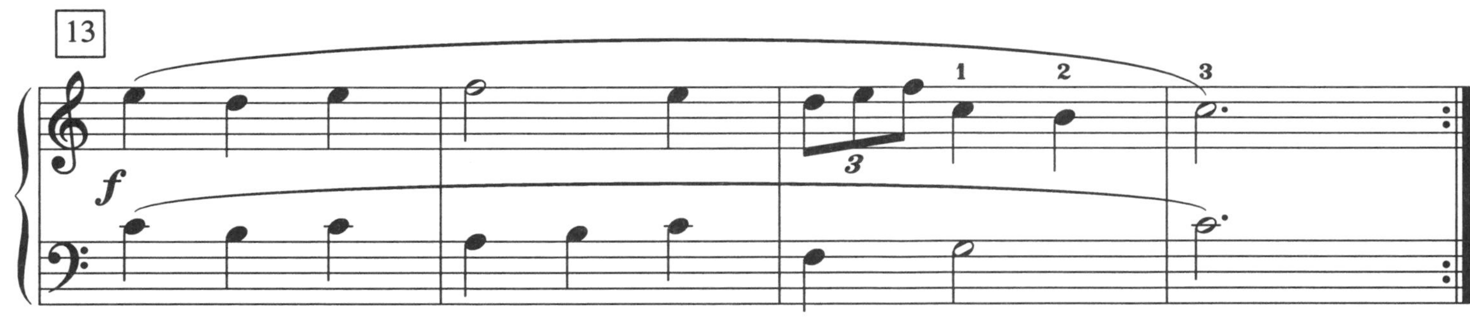

TANGO TIME

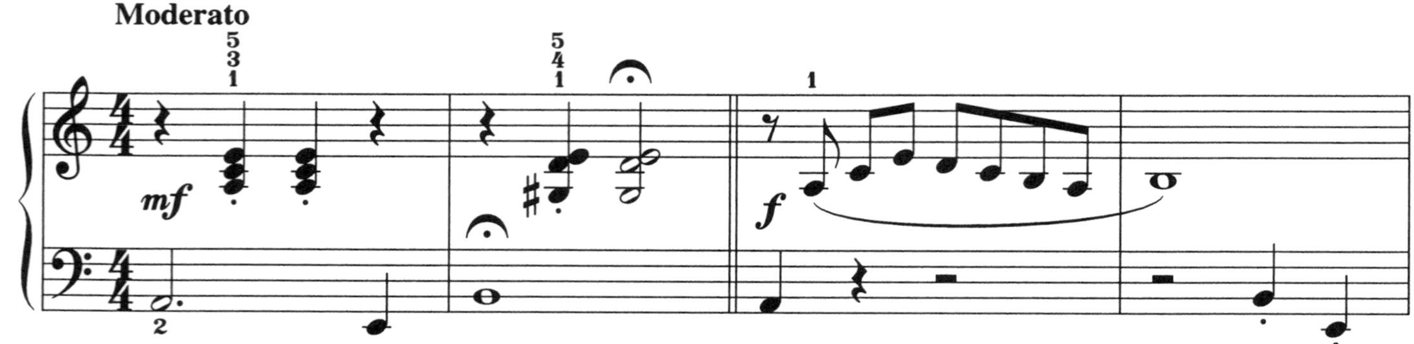

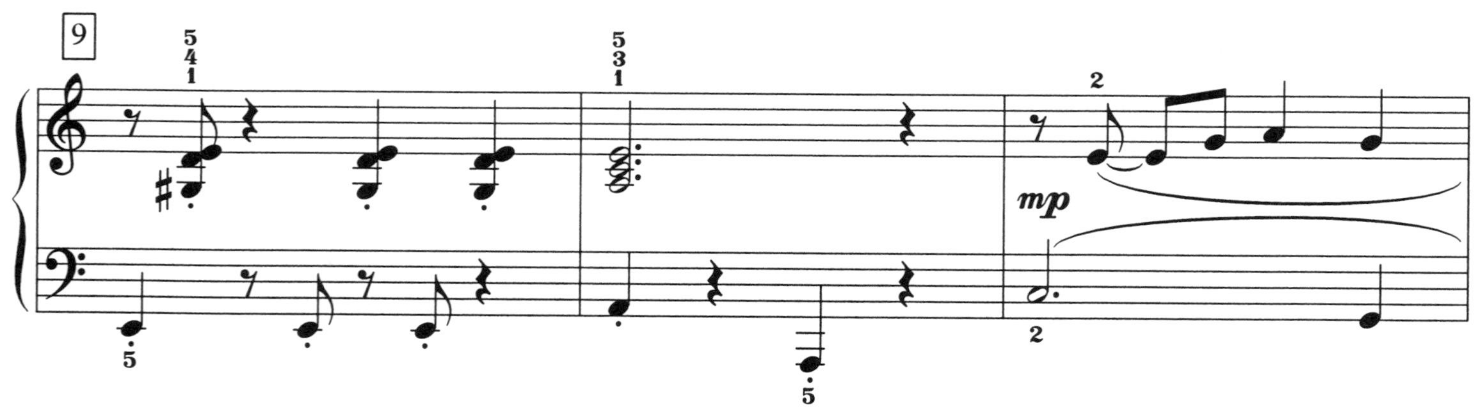

12
mf
f
16
dim.
mp
19
f
23
sfz

Technic

After playing the following exercise in C Major, transpose to the keys of G Major and F Major.

MAJOR TRIADS AND INVERSIONS

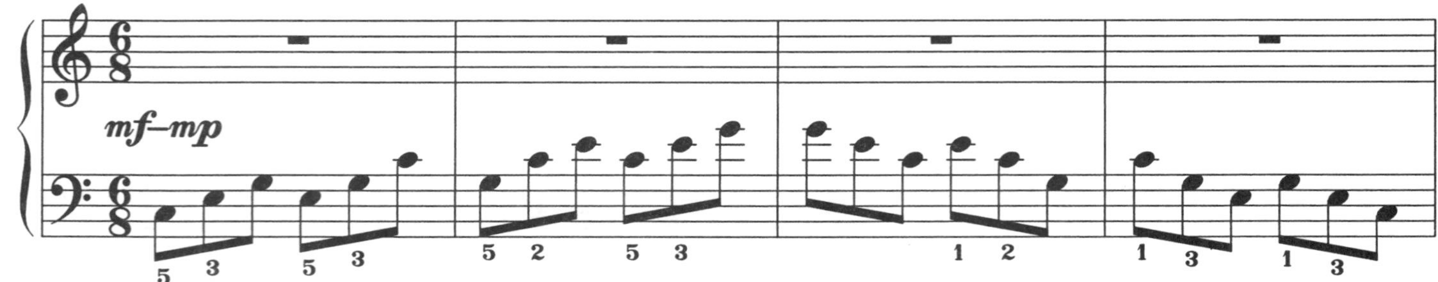

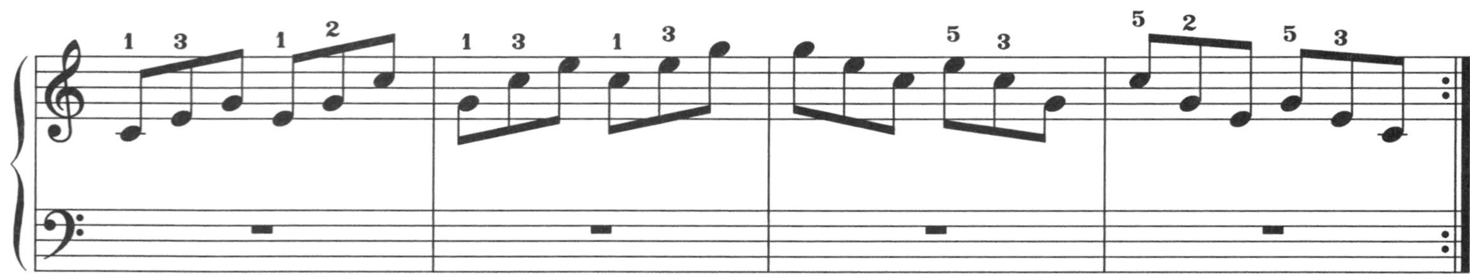

After playing the following exercise in C minor, transpose to the keys of E minor and D minor.

MINOR TRIADS AND INVERSIONS

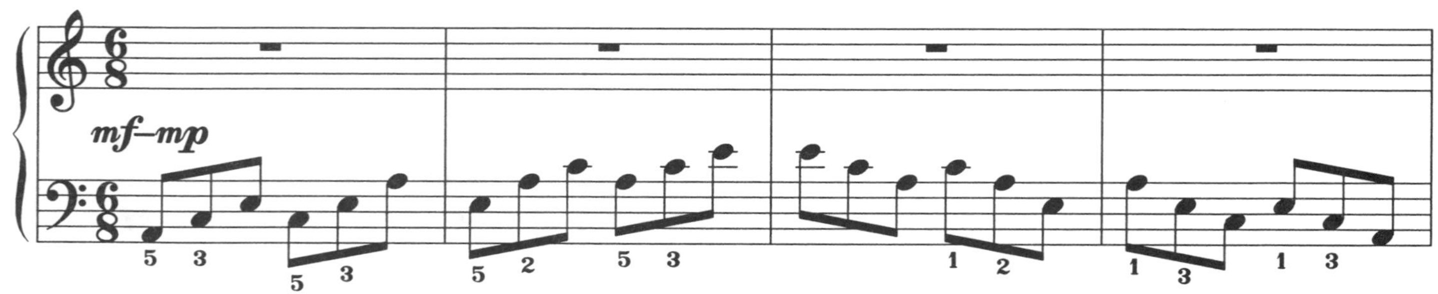

Technic

PLAYING TRIPLETS

ON THE ESCALATOR

Challenge Piece

Octave Sign

When the sign *15ma* is placed over a note(s), play the note(s) **two** octaves higher then written. When the sign *15ma* is placed under a note(s), play the note(s) **two** octaves lower than written.

16
mf
20
p
24
mp
28
31
15ma
8va
r.h
dim.
l.h.
rit.
pp
8va

Review

Any root position triad may be inverted (rearranged) by moving the root to the top or middle. (Note: the root is the top note of the 4th in an inversion.)

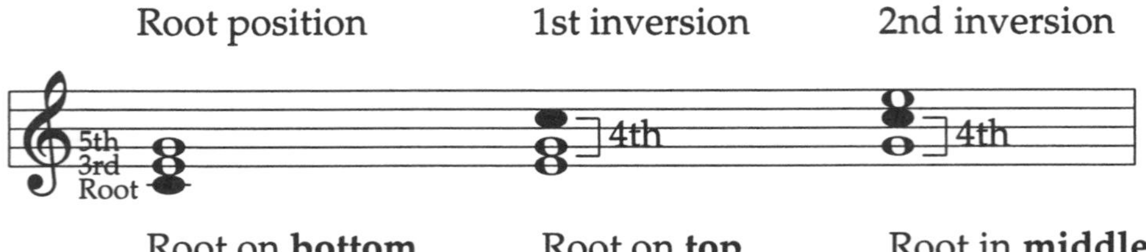

A. Draw the notes for the inversion of these triads, then play the chords.

Root position **1st inversion** **2nd inversion**

1. F Major

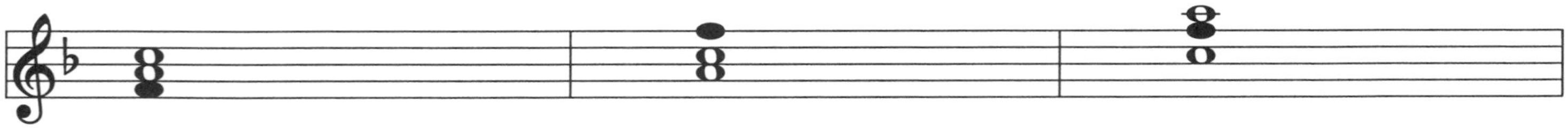

2. D minor

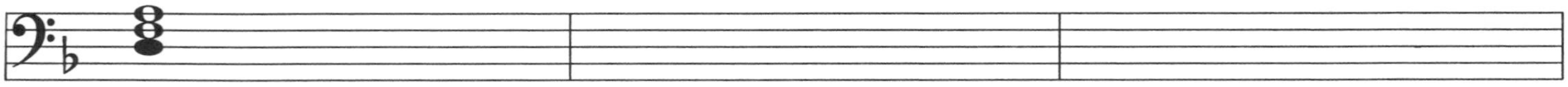

3. C Major

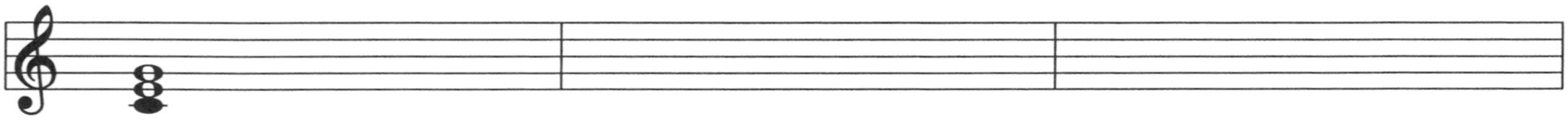

4. A minor

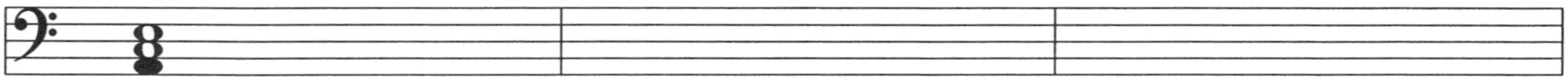

5. G Major

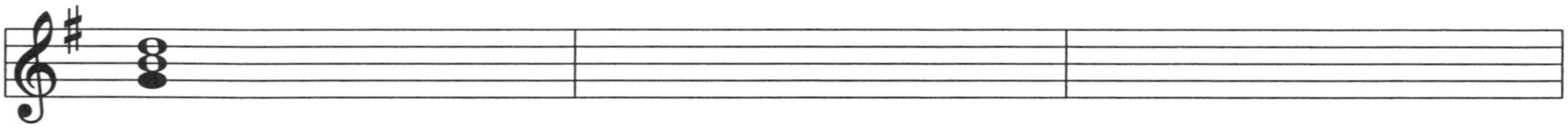

6. E minor

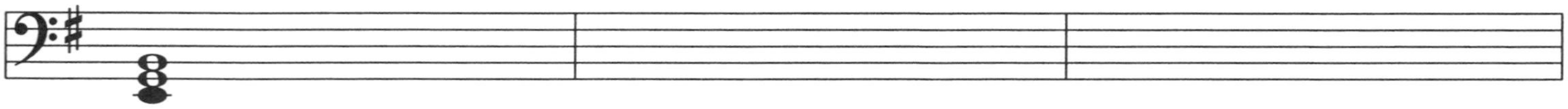

B. In the Key of C Major:

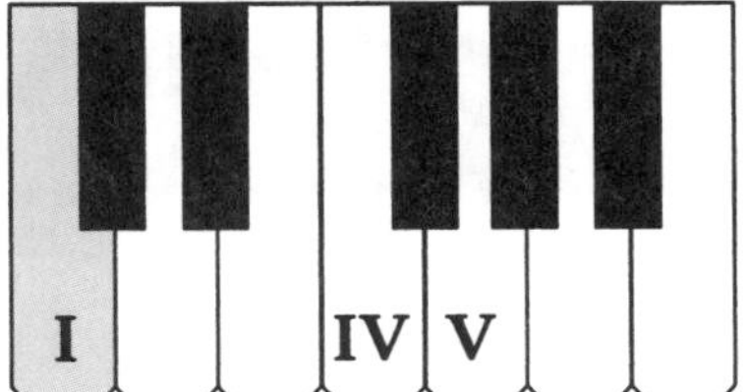

1. The tonic chord (I) is built on C.
   The subdominant chord (IV) is built on ____.
   The dominant chord (V) is built on ___.
2. Write the scale ascending and descending.
3. Write the primary chords (I, IV, V) in root position.

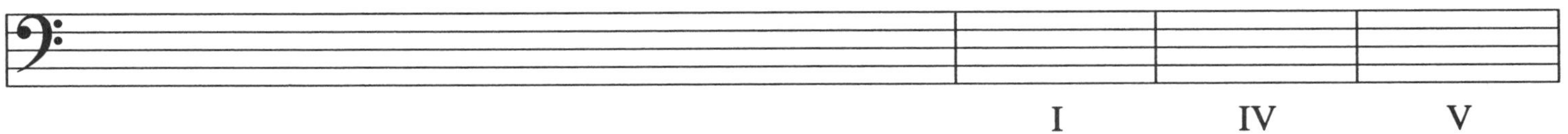

C. In the Key of G Major:

1. Write the key signature: 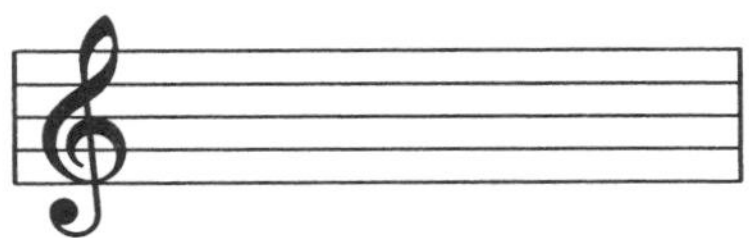

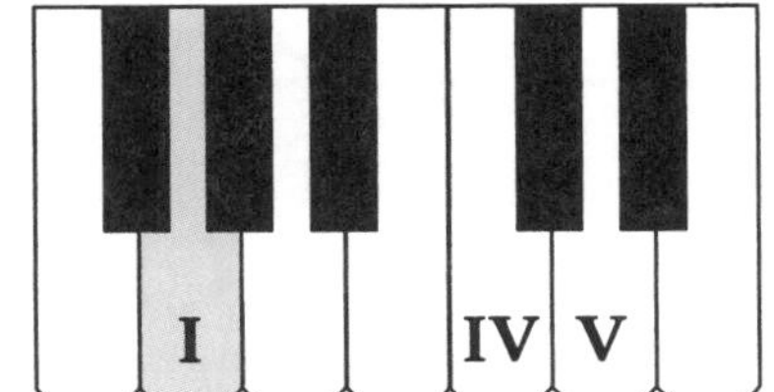

2. The tonic chord (I) is built on ____.
   The subdominant chord (IV) is built on ____.
   The dominant chord (V) is built on ____.
3. Write the scale ascending and descending.
4. Write the primary chords (I, IV, V) in root position.

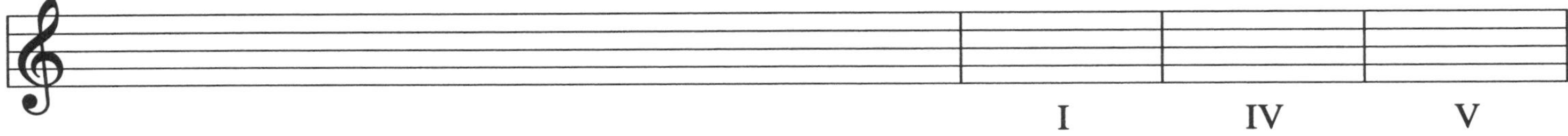

D. In the Key of F Major:

1. Write the key signature: 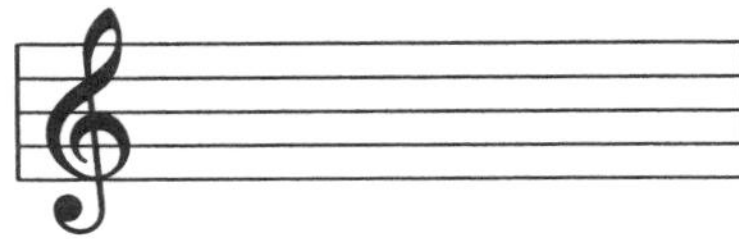

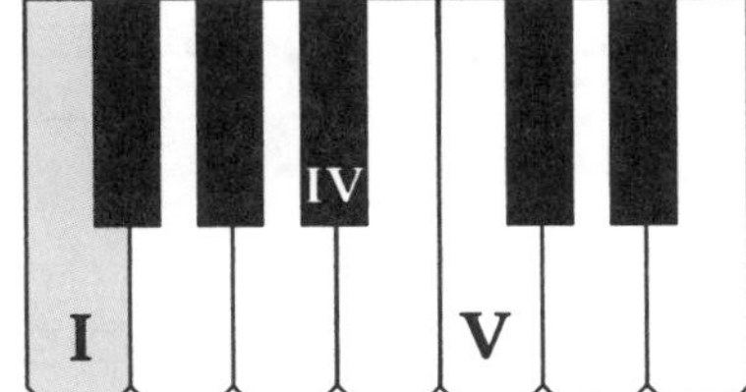

2. The tonic chord (I) is built on ____.
   The subdominant chord (IV) is built on ____.
   The dominant chord (V) is built on ____.
3. Write the scale ascending and descending.
4. Write the primary chords (I, IV, V) in root position.

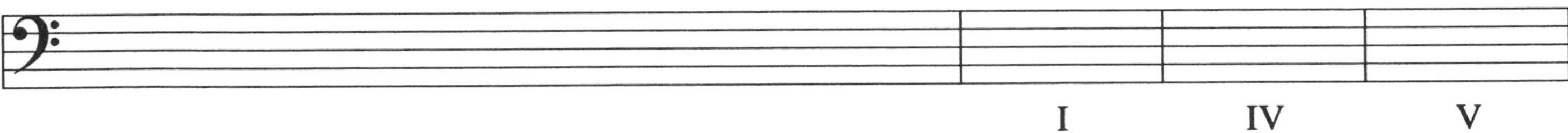

Chapter 5
Group 2 Keys

NEW CONCEPTS

- Boogie Bass Line
- Order of Sharps
- Group 2 Keys: D, A, E
- Identifying Major Sharp Keys
- D Major Scale and Chords

REVIEW CONCEPTS

- Identifying 1st Inversion Triads

Boogie Bass Line

CHASIN' THE BLUES

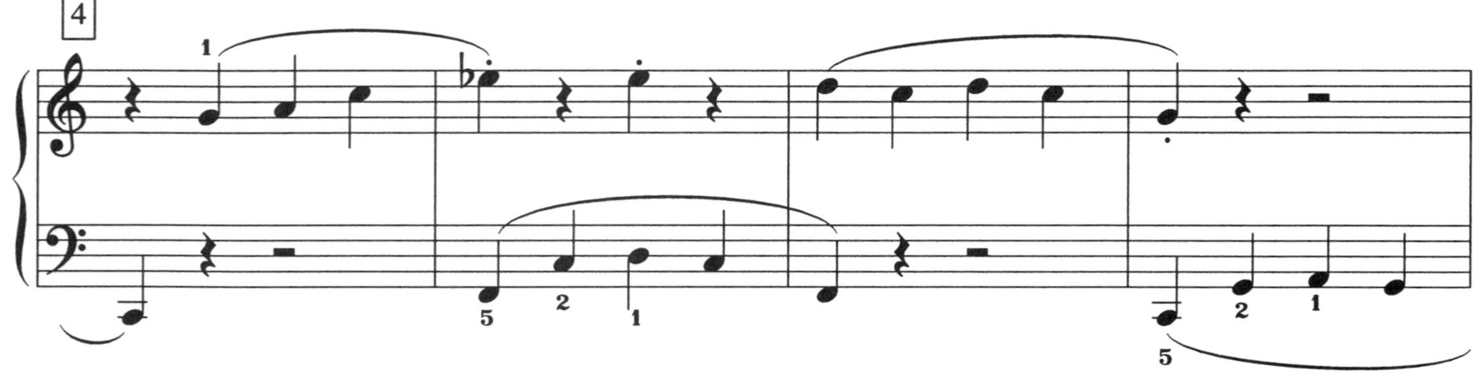

12
To Coda
mf
16
f
mp
21
D.S. al Coda
mf
25
Coda
mp
pp
8va

THE ORDER OF SHARPS

The sharps are always written in the same order on the staff. **Memorize** this order.

Write the order of sharps three times on the staff below.

Identifying Major Sharp Keys

The **key signature** is the sharp(s) or flat(s) located at the beginning of each staff. The **key signature** indicates which notes are sharp or flat throughout the piece. It can also indicate the main tonality or **key** of the piece.

To find a **sharp** key name:

- Locate the last sharp to the right in the key signature.
- Name the next letter in the music alphabet (go up a half step).
- This is the name of the Major key.

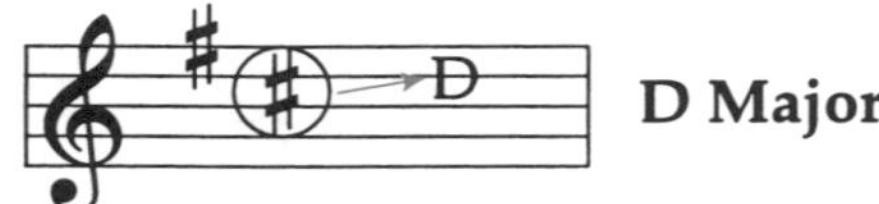

D Major

Name the keys indicated by these key signatures.

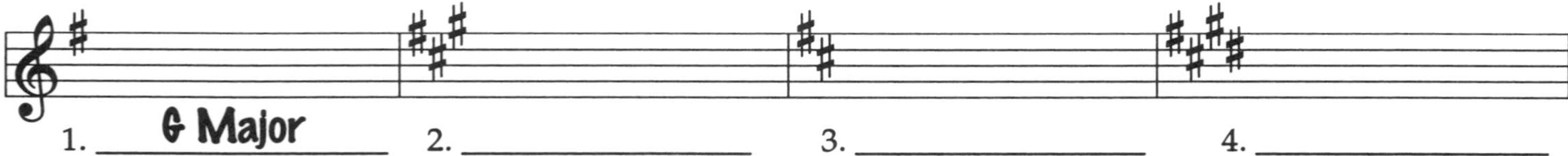

1. G Major
2. __________
3. __________
4. __________

Group 2 Keys: D, A, E

The keys of D, A, and E Major are called the **Group 2 Keys** because they all have the same look and feel in their I chords. Each chord has a **black key** in the middle.

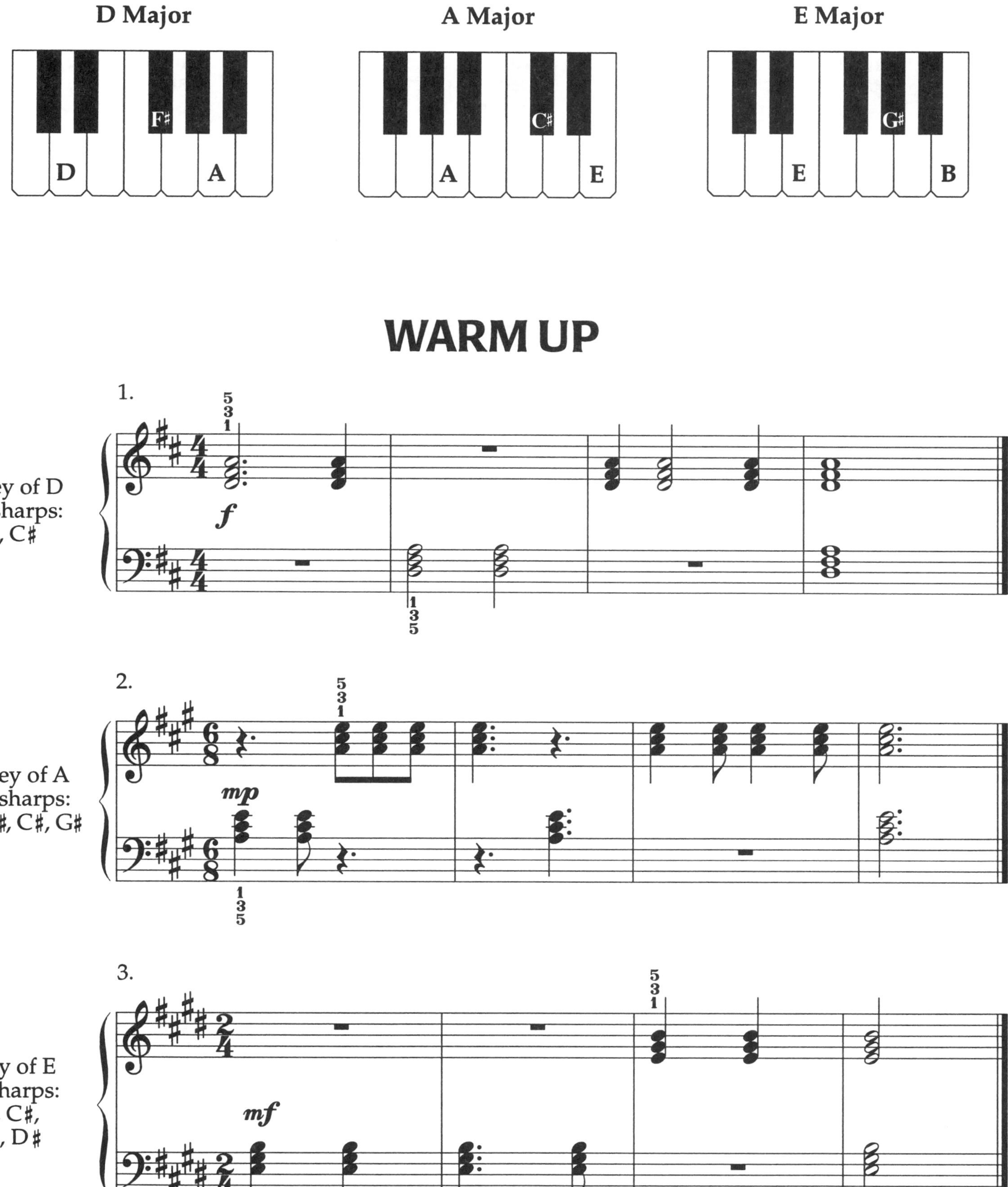

D Major Scale

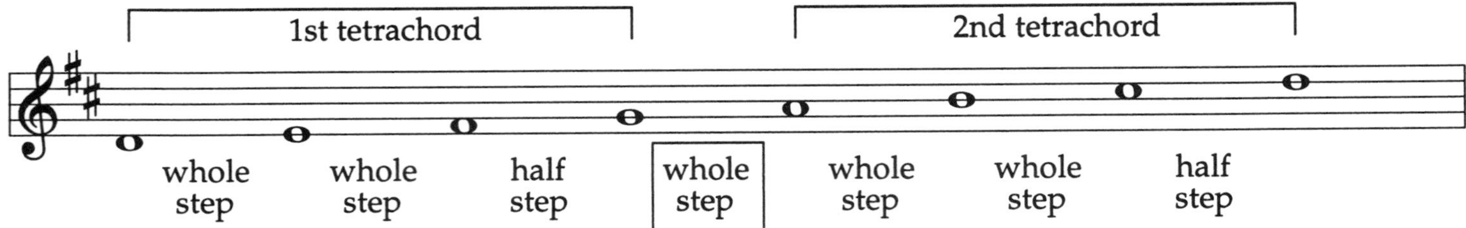

Primary Chords in the Key of D Major

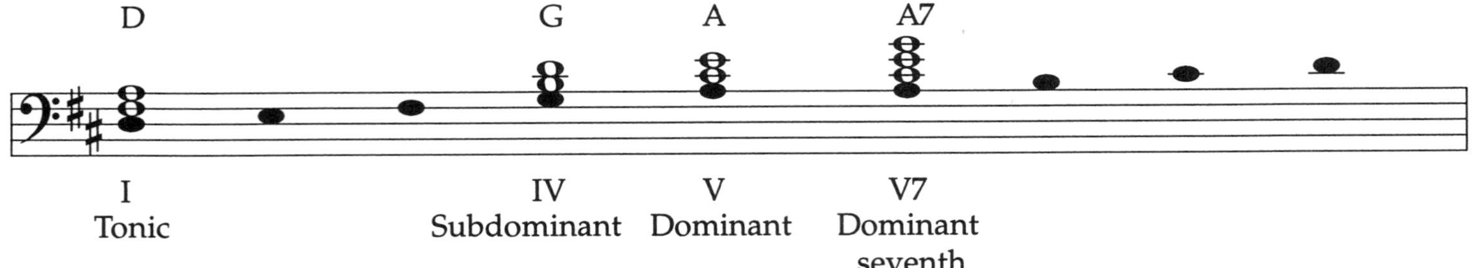

D MAJOR SCALE AND CHORDS

Play hands separately first. Memorize the fingering.

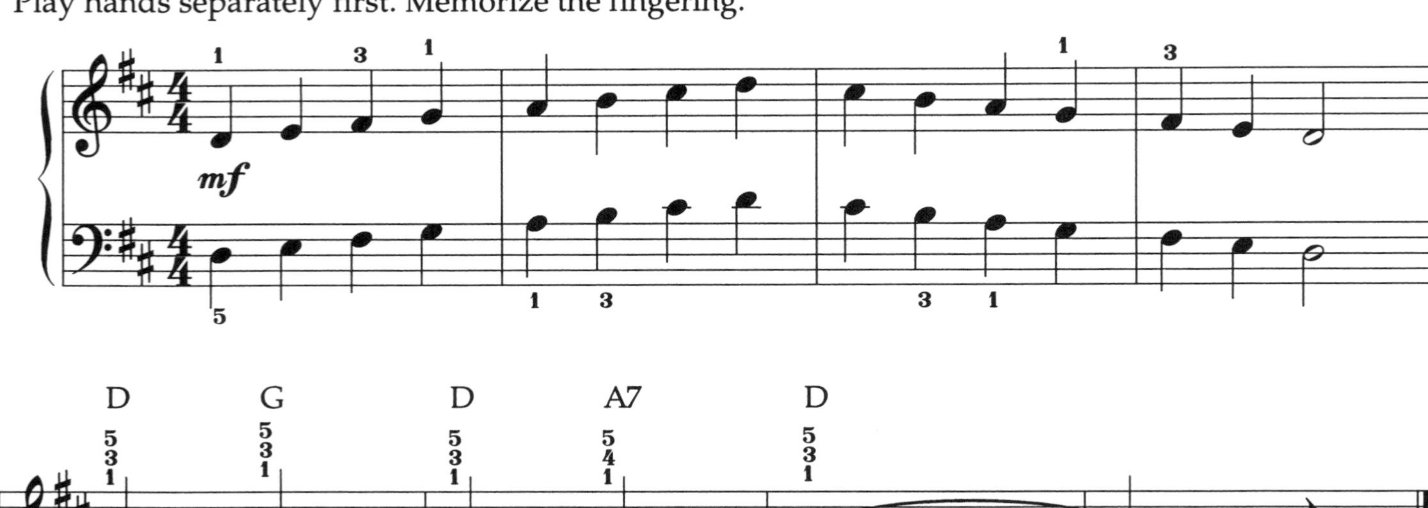

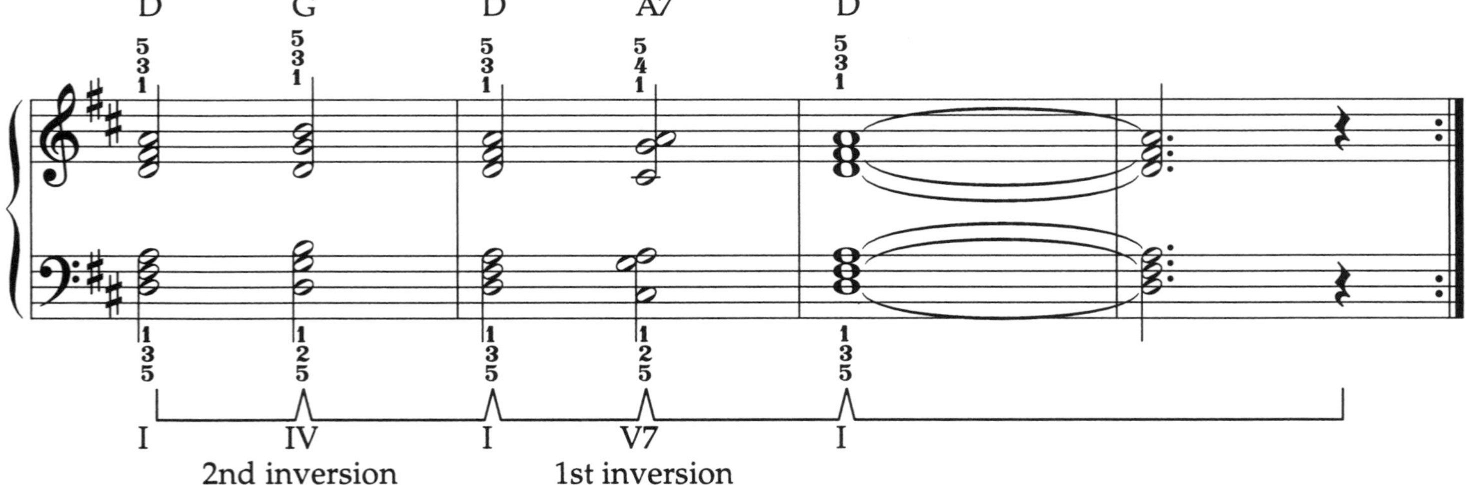

BARBARA ALLEN

Traditional Scottish Folk Song

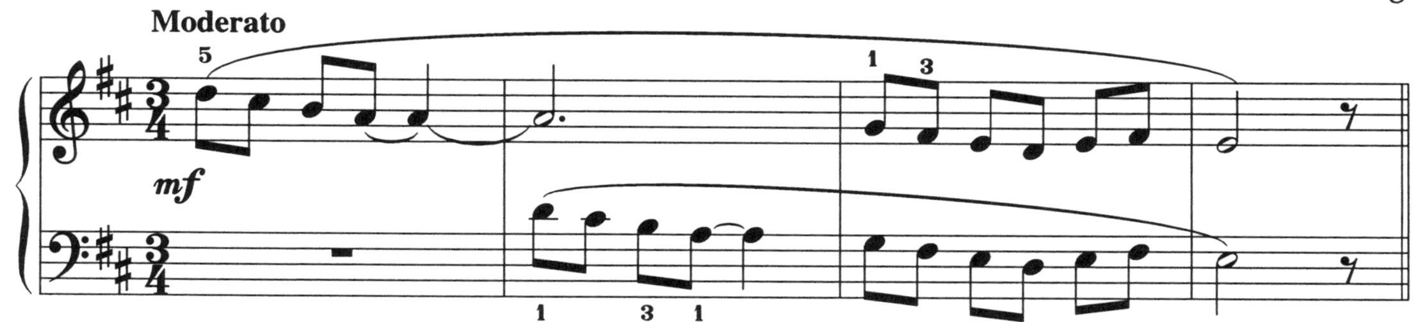

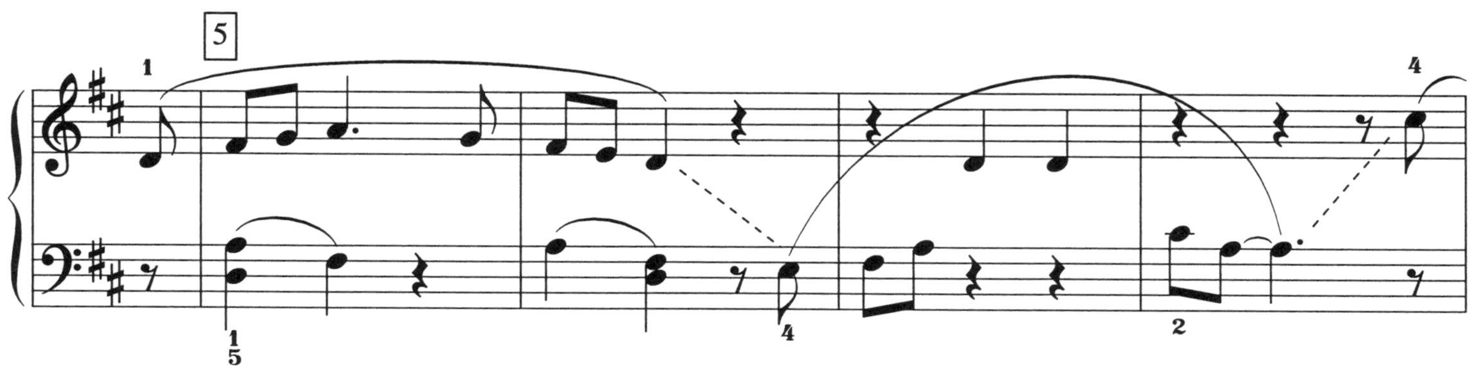

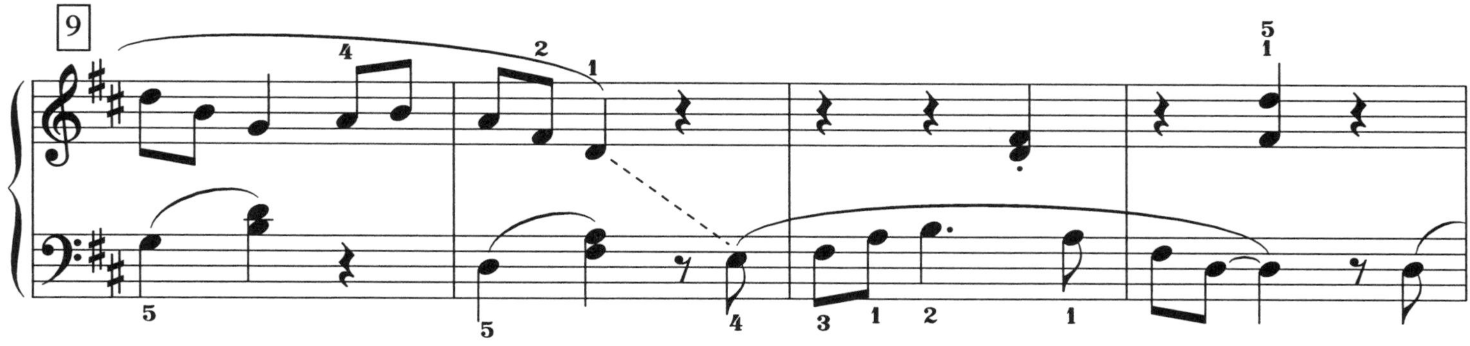

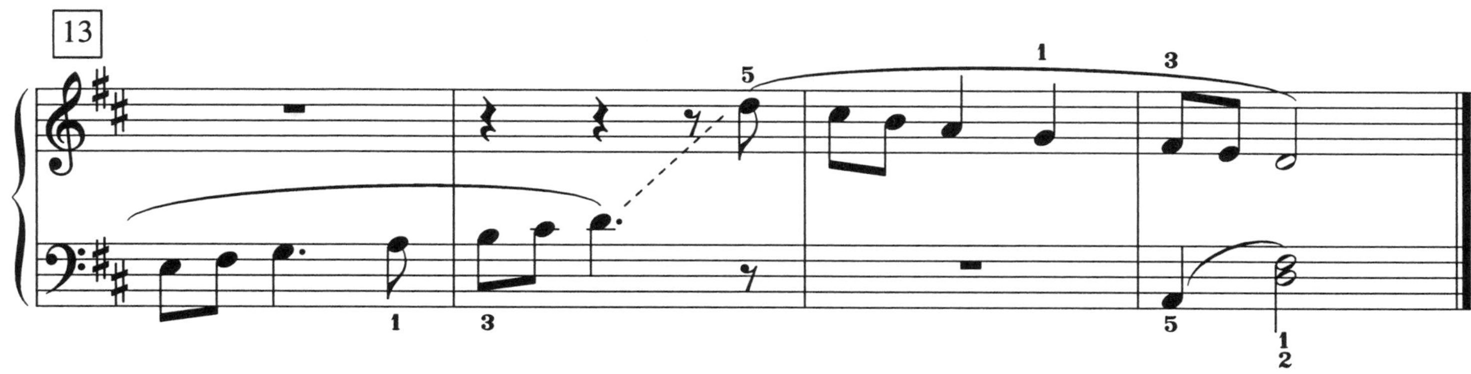

STROLLING DOWN THE MIDWAY

Moderato

mf

5

To Coda ⊕

9

f

13

mp

D.C. al Coda

⊕ *Coda*

17

f

mp

f

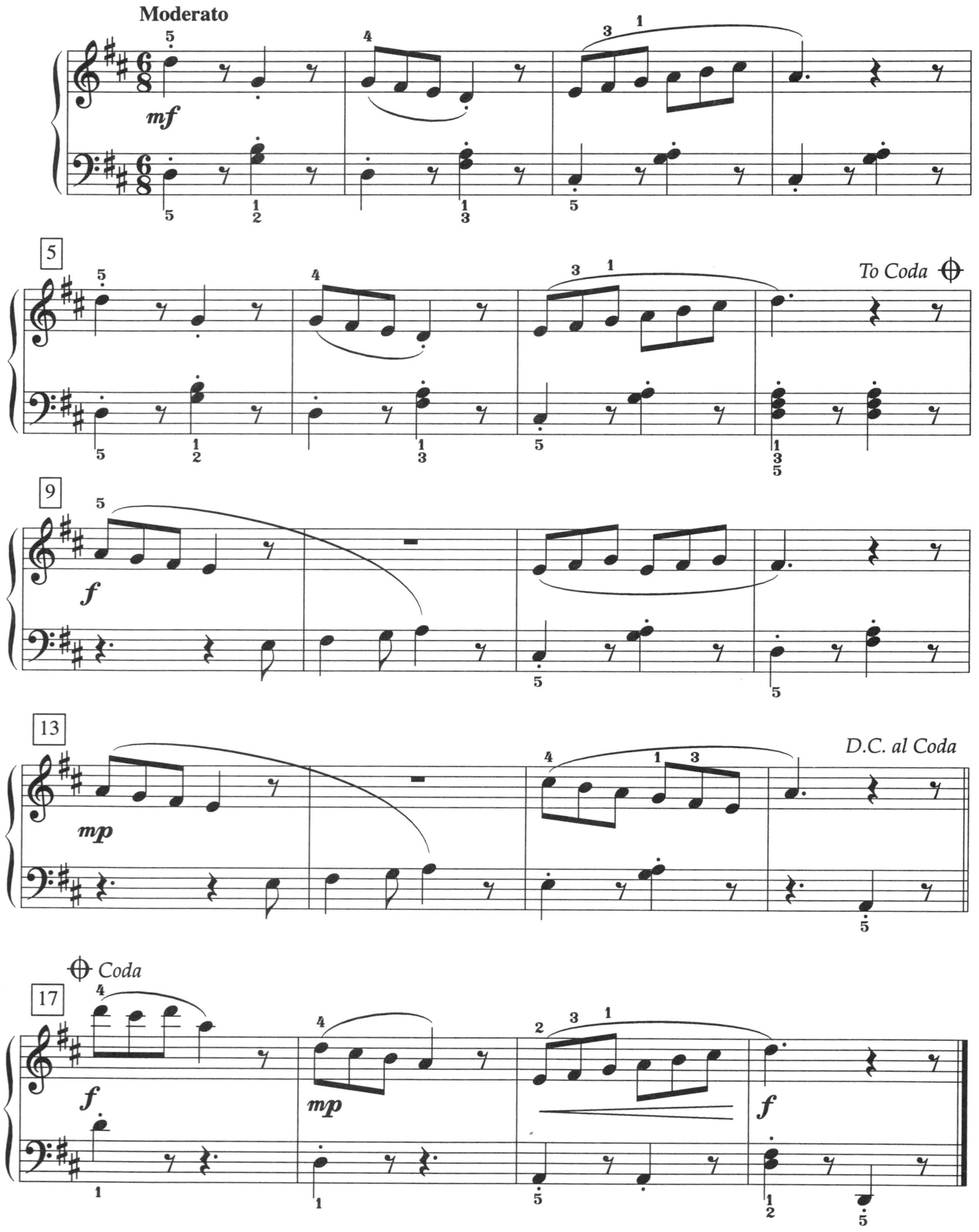

Review

A. Write the order of sharps two times on the staff below.

To identify a Major sharp key:

- Name the last sharp: **F#**
- Name the next letter **up** in the music alphabet: **G**
- The answer is **G Major**

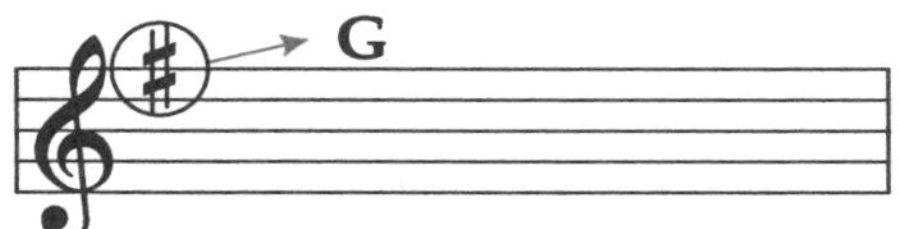

Note: F♯ and C♯ Major need a sharp added to their letter name.

When no sharps or flats appear in the key signature, the Major key name is C.

- Name the last sharp: **E**
- Name the next letter **up** in the music alphabet: **F**
  F is already sharp.
- The answer is **F# Major**

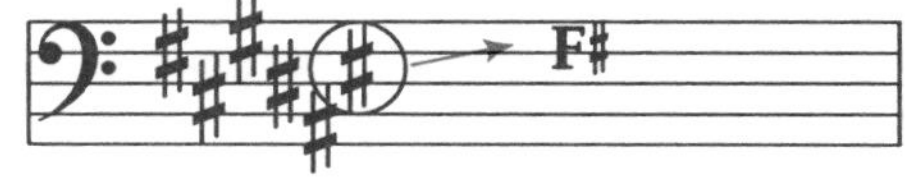

B. Identify the keys indicated by the key signatures below.

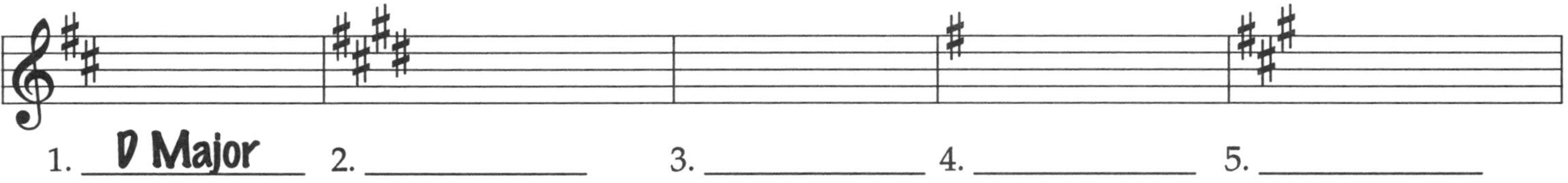

1. D Major 2. ______ 3. ______ 4. ______ 5. ______

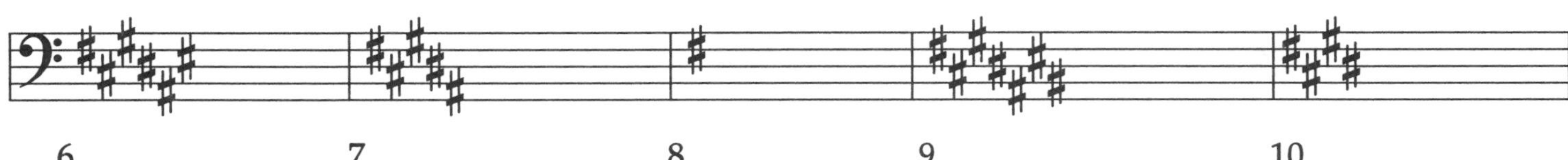

6. ______ 7. ______ 8. ______ 9. ______ 10. ______

Identifying 1st Inversion Triads

In **1st inversion triads**, the root is on top of the triad.

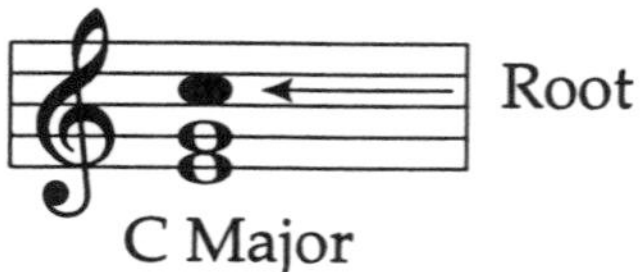

C Major

A minor

G Major

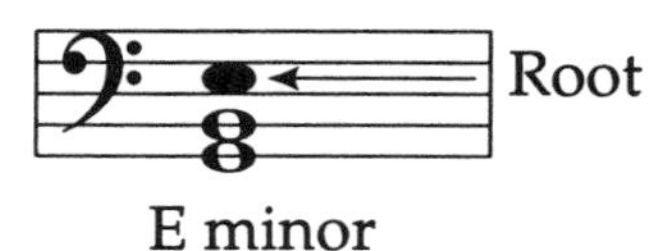

E minor

Review

Write the names of these 1st inversion triads, then play them.

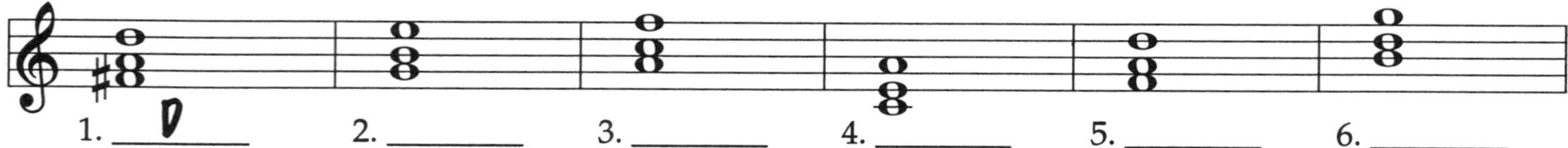

1. D 2. ________ 3. ________ 4. ________ 5. ________ 6. ________

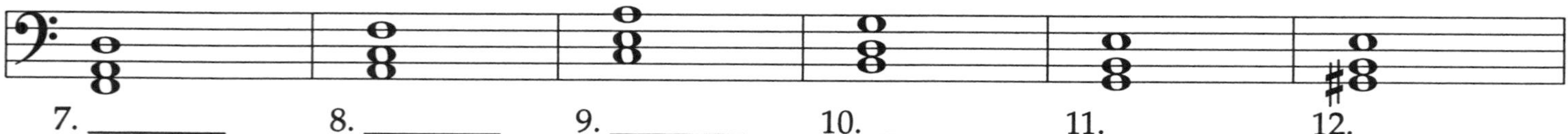

7. ________ 8. ________ 9. ________ 10. ________ 11. ________ 12. ________

1st Inversion Triads

Play these 1st inversion triads. Practice hands separately first.
Play as written, then transpose to G Major and F Major.

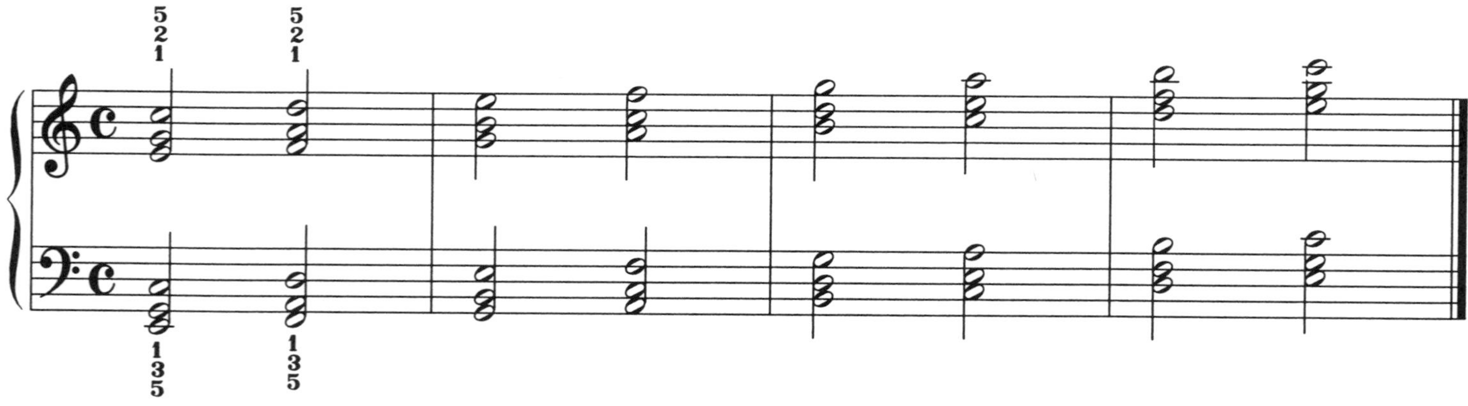

Note: When playing in G Major, remember the F♯'s.
When playing in F Major, remember the B♭'s.

BELLS OF MILAN

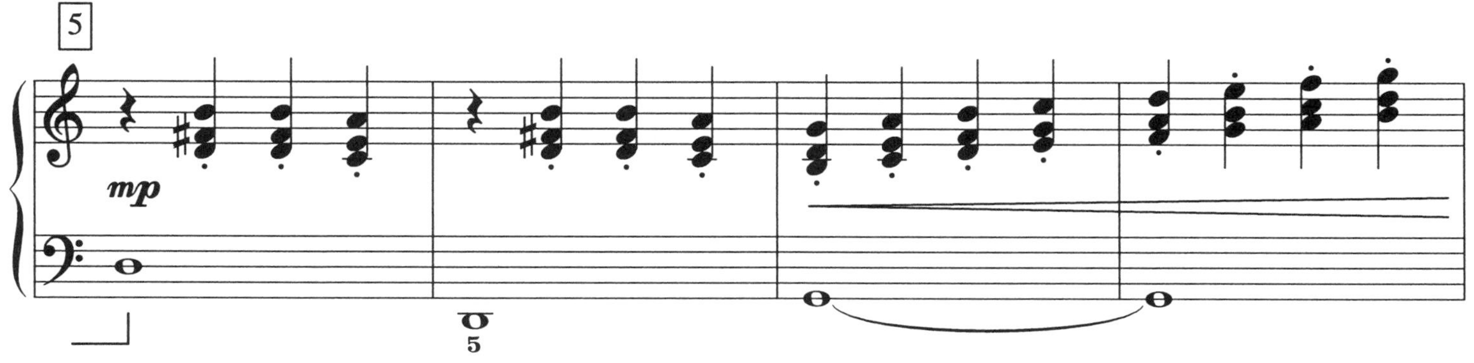

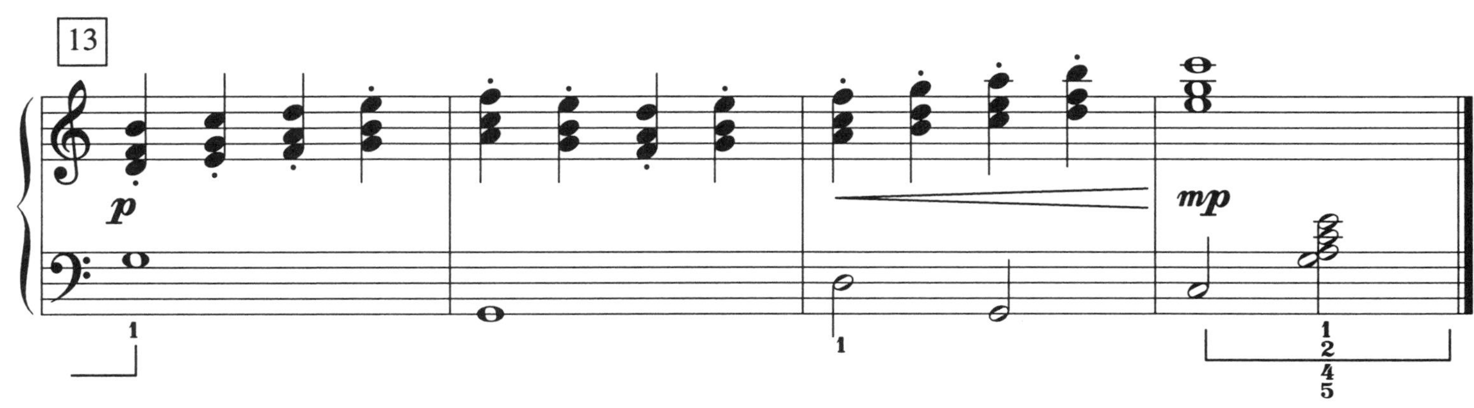

HE'S GOT THE WHOLE WORLD IN HIS HANDS

Traditional African-American Spiritual

2. He's got the little bitty baby in His hands,...
3. He's got you and me, brother, in His hands,...
4. He's got you and me, sister, in His hands,...
5. He's got everybody in His hands,...

Technic

D SCALE ETUDE

D CHORD ETUDE

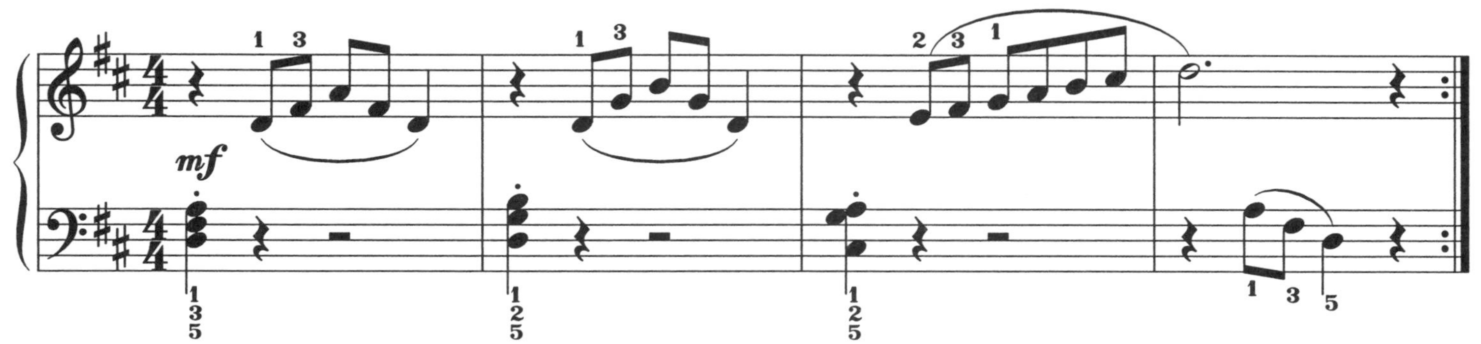

ICE SKATING

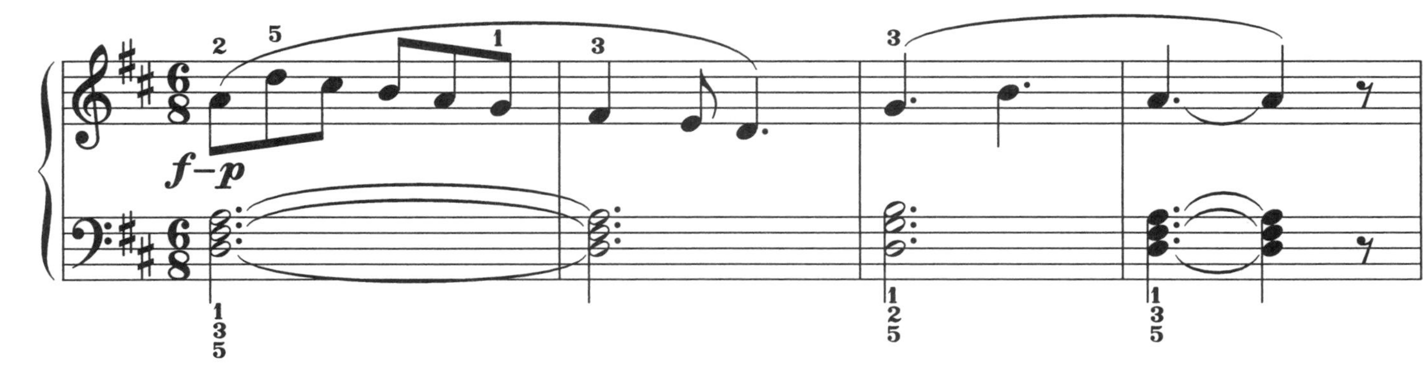

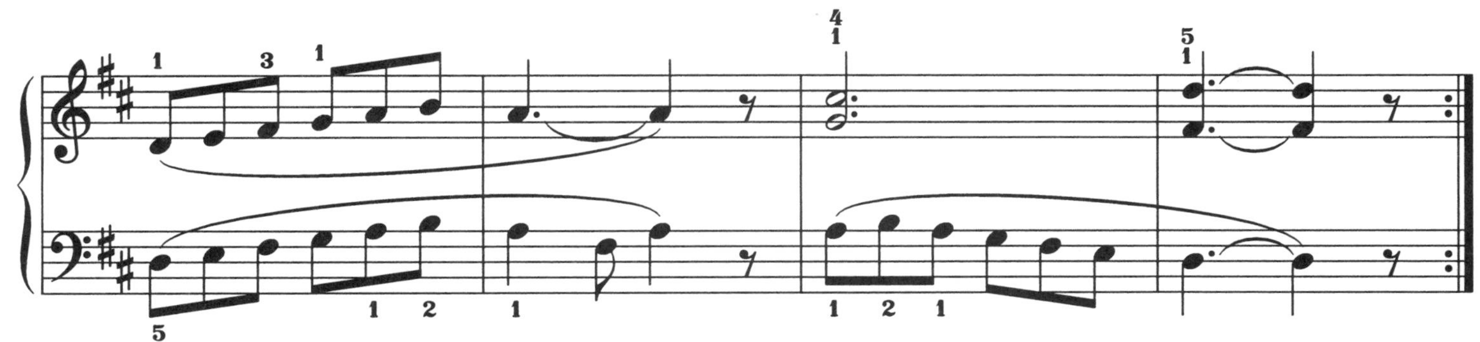

Challenge Piece

MAPLE LEAF RAG

Scott Joplin

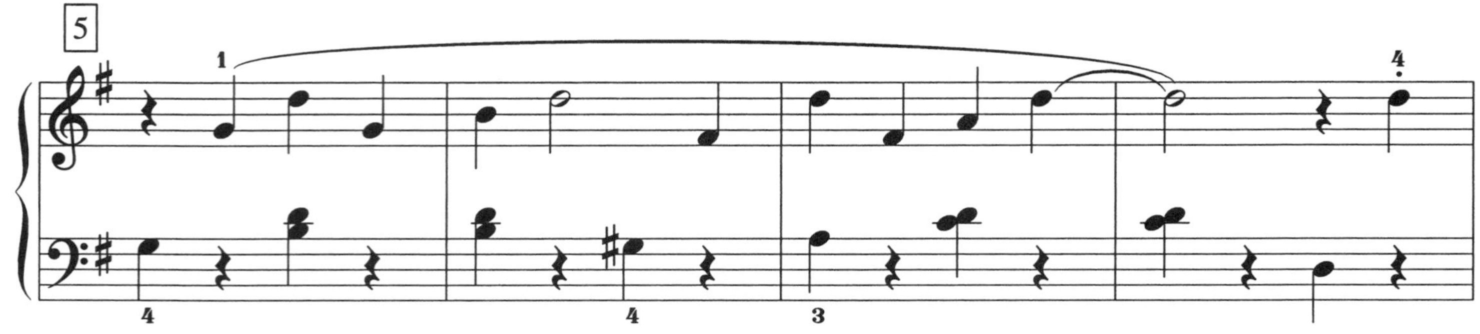

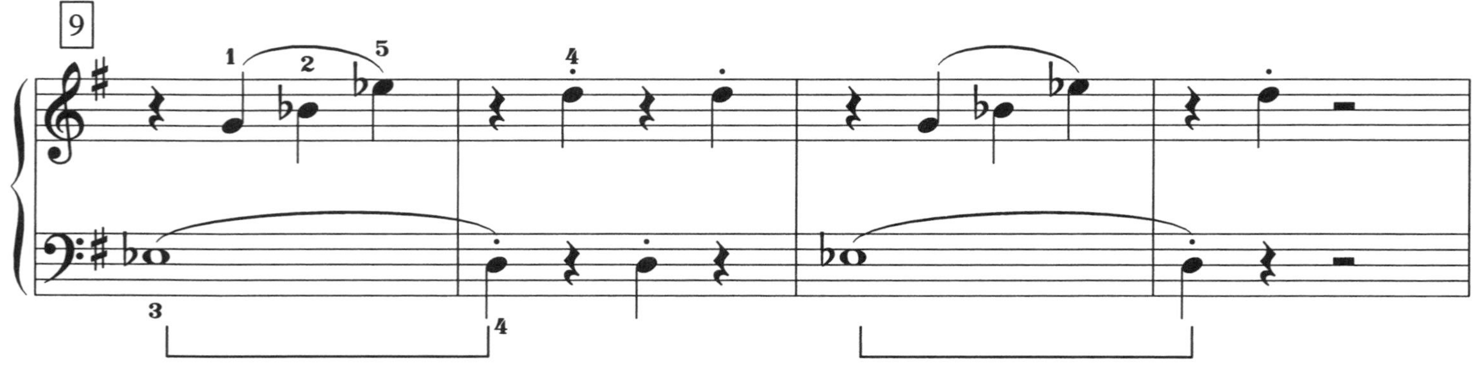

17
(8va)
f
21
25
29
1.
2.

Review

A. Write the order of sharps.

B. Identify the Major keys indicated by the key signatures below.

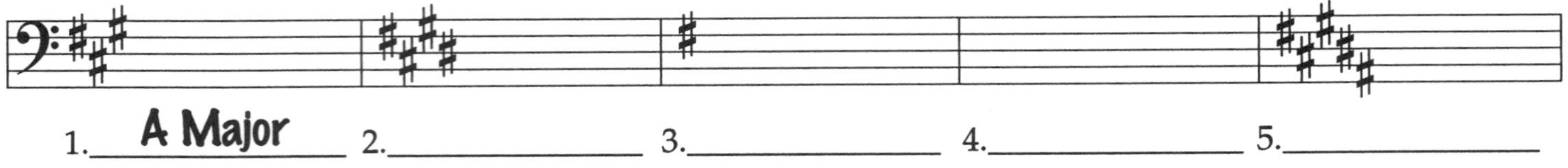

1. A Major 2. ______ 3. ______ 4. ______ 5. ______

6. ______ 7. ______ 8. ______ 9. ______ 10. ______

C. Circle the root of each 1st inversion triad below.
D. Name each chord in the blanks provided.
E. Play the chords on the keyboard.

1. F 2. ______ 3. ______ 4. ______ 5. ______ 6. ______

7. ______ 8. ______ 9. ______ 10. ______ 11. ______ 12. ______

F. Add one note to complete each measure.

G. Write the D scale ascending and descending. Circle the half steps.
H. Write the primary chords in root position.

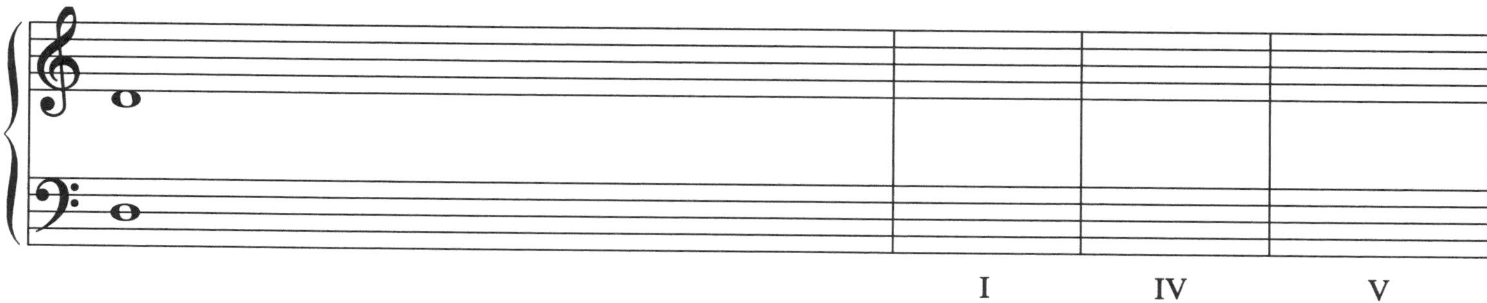

I. Write the chord symbols (D, G, or A7) in the boxes provided, then play the chords.

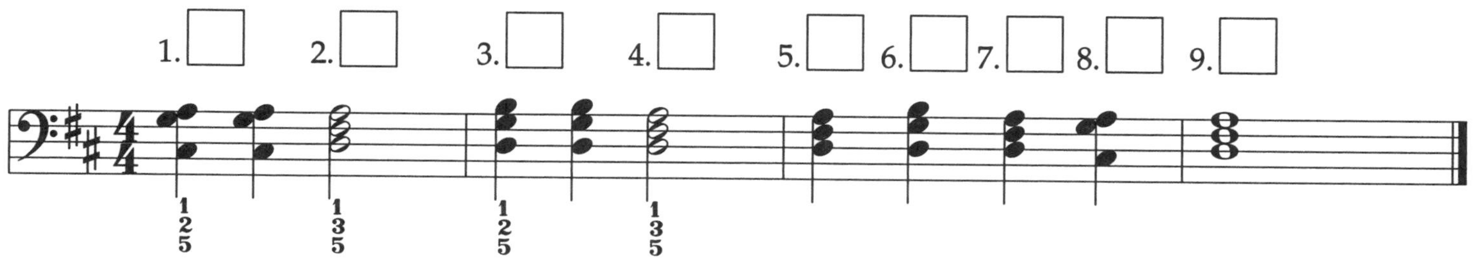

J. Harmonize
Add your own choice of L.H. chords (D, G, or A7) to the following R.H. melody line. Write chord symbols in the boxes provided.

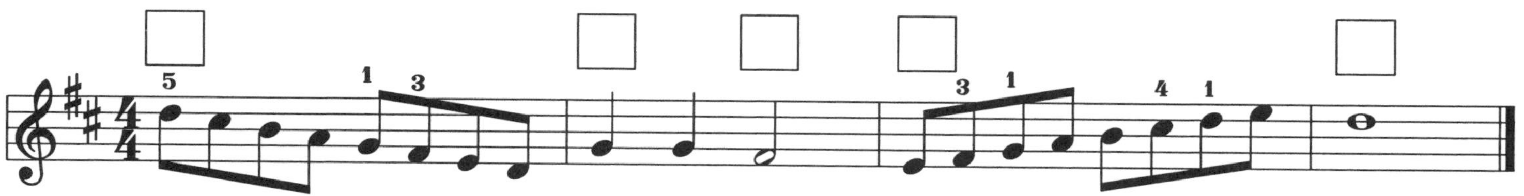

K. Match each item with the correct definition or term.

a.	1. _____fermata
b. *pp*	2. _____pedal sign
c.	3. _____very soft
d.	4. _____accent
e.	5. _____octave sign
f. *8va* --------	6. _____very loud
g. *ff*	7. _____staccato

Chapter 6
Reading in A Major

NEW CONCEPTS

- A Major Scale and Chords
- Sixteenth Notes
- Grace Notes
- New Rhythm

HEART BREAKER

Moderato con rubato

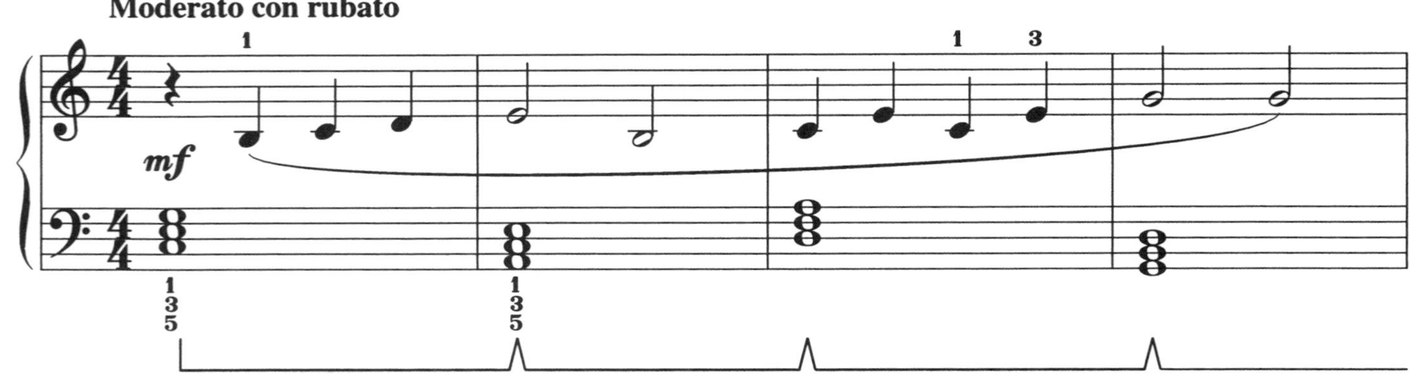

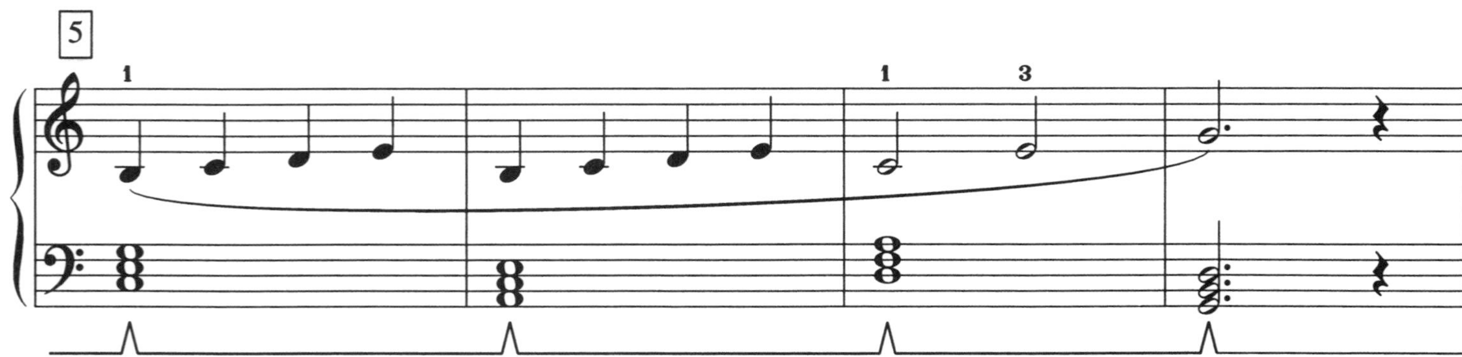

9
2
f
mf
1
3
5
13
1
5
3
mp
17
2
pp
21
1
1
3
5
1
3
5

A Major Scale

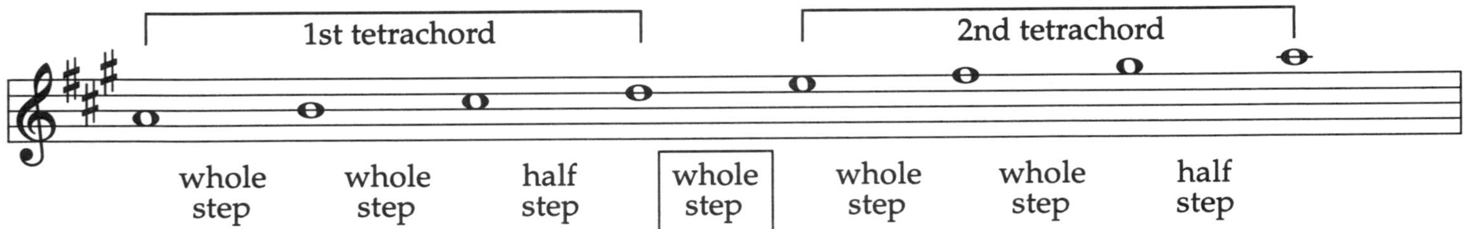

Primary Chords in the Key of A Major

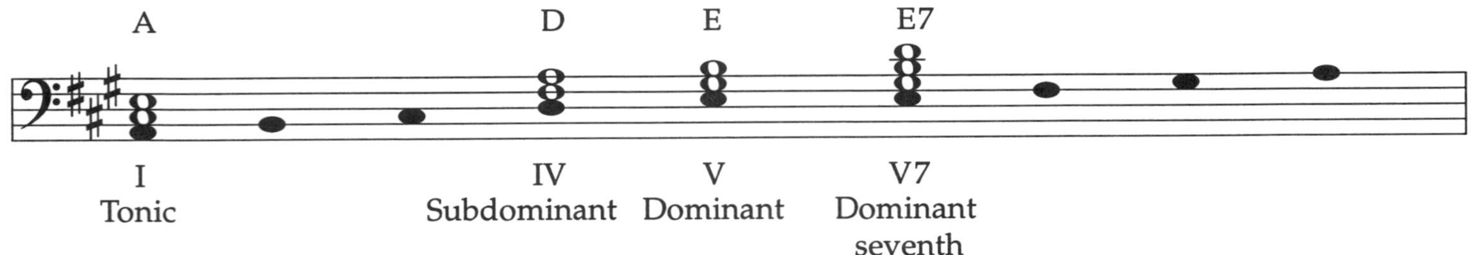

A MAJOR SCALE AND CHORDS

Play hands separately first. Memorize the fingering.

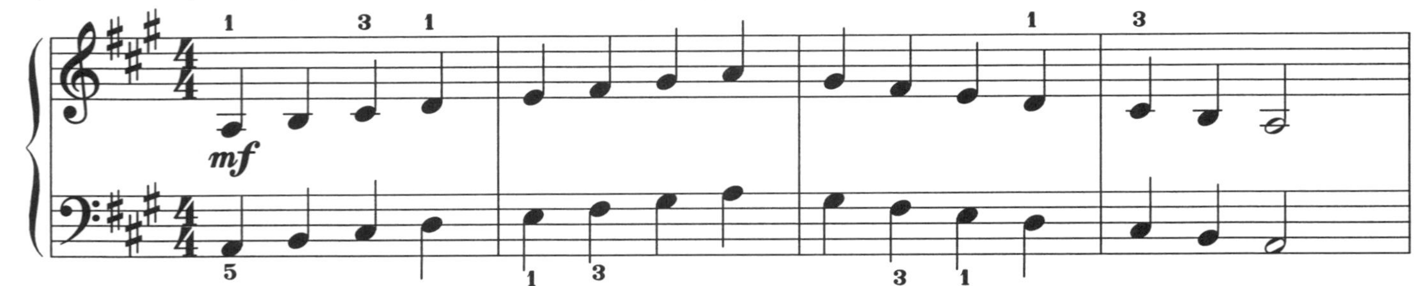

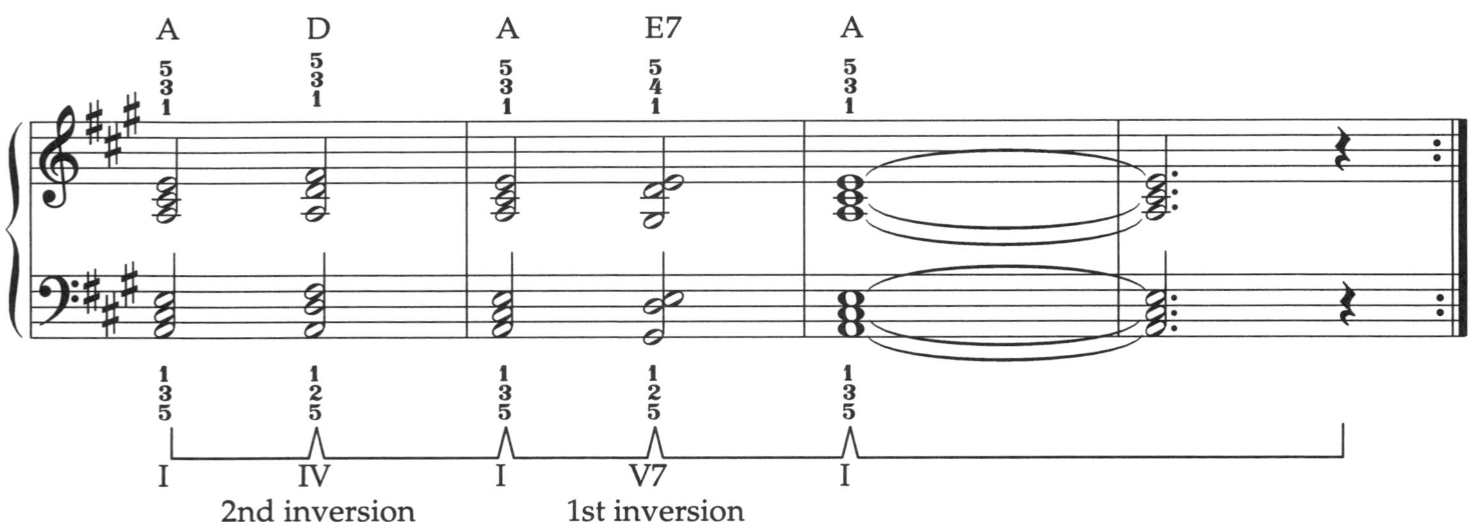

BARCAROLLE

from the opera *Les Contes D'Hoffmann*

Jacques Offenbach

Sixteenth Notes

Four sixteenth notes are equal to one quarter note in duration. = = 1 beat

Two sixteenth notes are equal to one eighth note in duration. = = 1/2 of a beat

Two or more sixteenth notes are connected by a double beam.

To count sixteenth notes, it is helpful to divide each beat into four parts.

Clap and count the following rhythms. Use one of these methods or any other one your teacher suggests for counting sixteenths notes.

Count:
1. 1 e & a 2 e & a | 1 e & a 2 e & a
2. Four six - teenth notes two eighths | Four six - teenth notes two eighths
3. Mis - sis - sip - pi Riv - er | Mis - sis - sip - pi Riv - er

WARM UP

After playing *Warm Up* in the key of C Major, transpose to F Major and D Major.

THEME FROM SURPRISE SYMPHONY

Franz Joseph Haydn

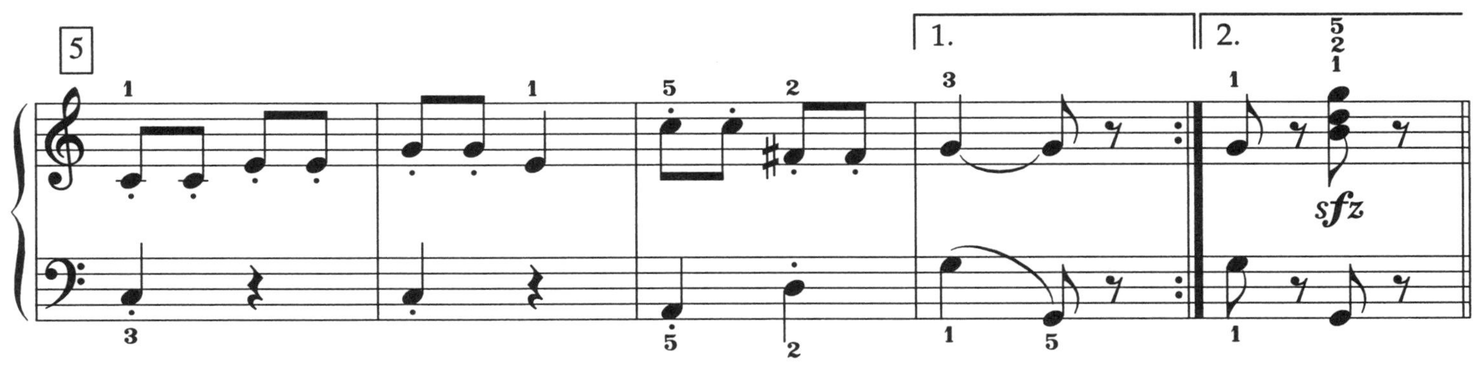

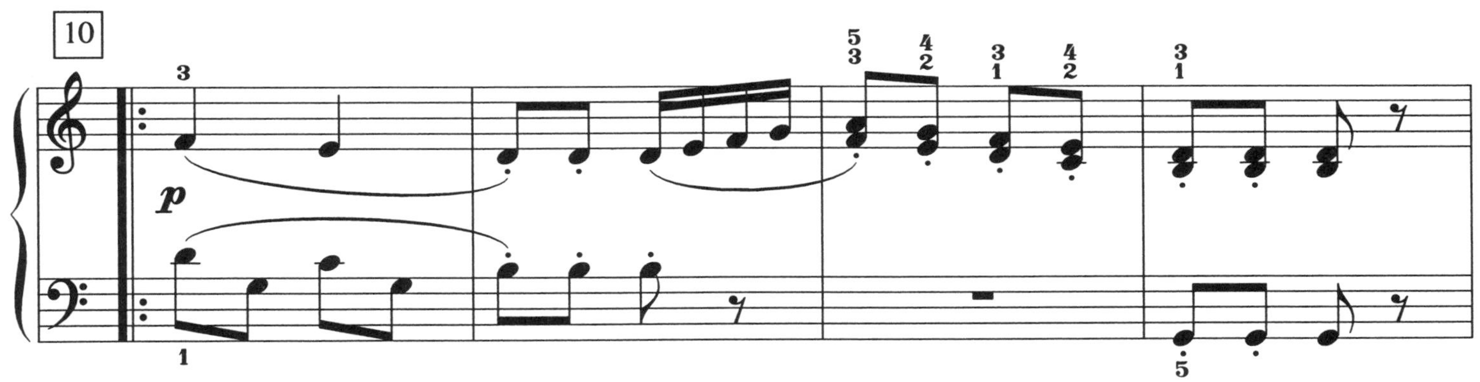

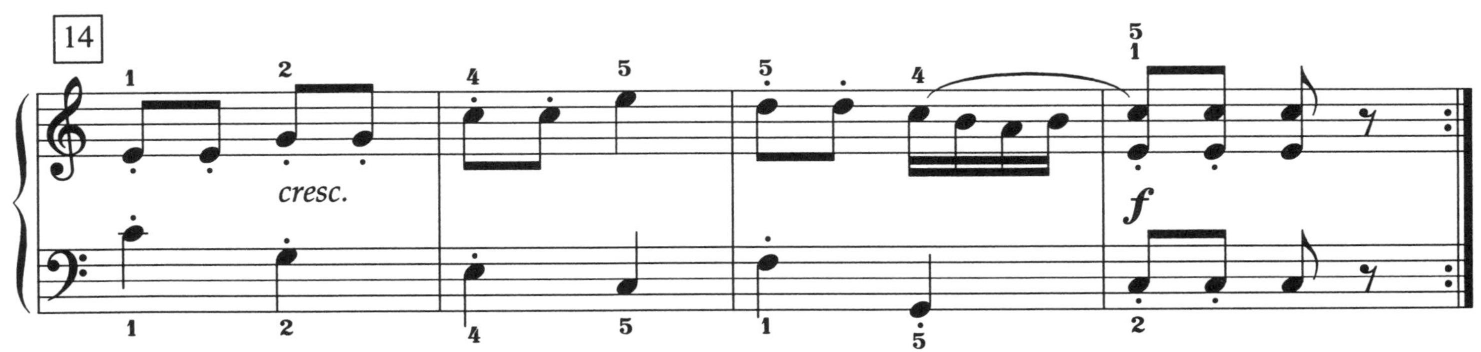

ENTRANCE OF THE EMPEROR

Broadly

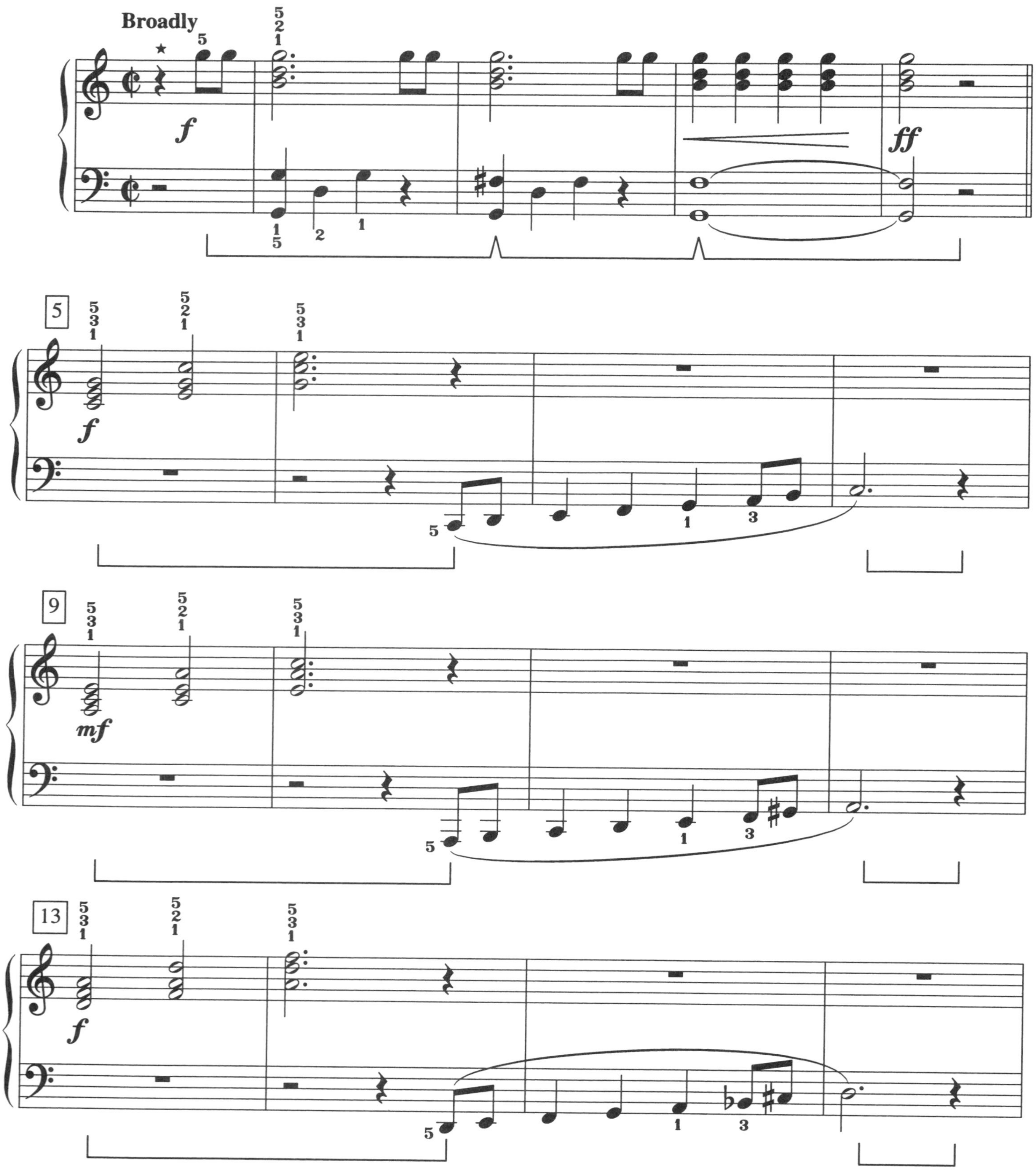

★ The rest appears for those playing with the accompaniment CDs.

17
mf
mp
21
mf
25
cresc.
29
f
33
ff

Grace Notes

A small note 𝅘𝅥𝅮 before a main note is called a **grace note**. It is a note which is considered additional to the melody and is inserted as an ornament. A grace note is played immediately before the main note and does not add value to or take value away from the main note. There may be more than one grace note before a main note ♬.

Technic

ROLLING HOOPS

A SCALE ETUDE

Challenge Piece

CANON IN D

Johann Pachelbel

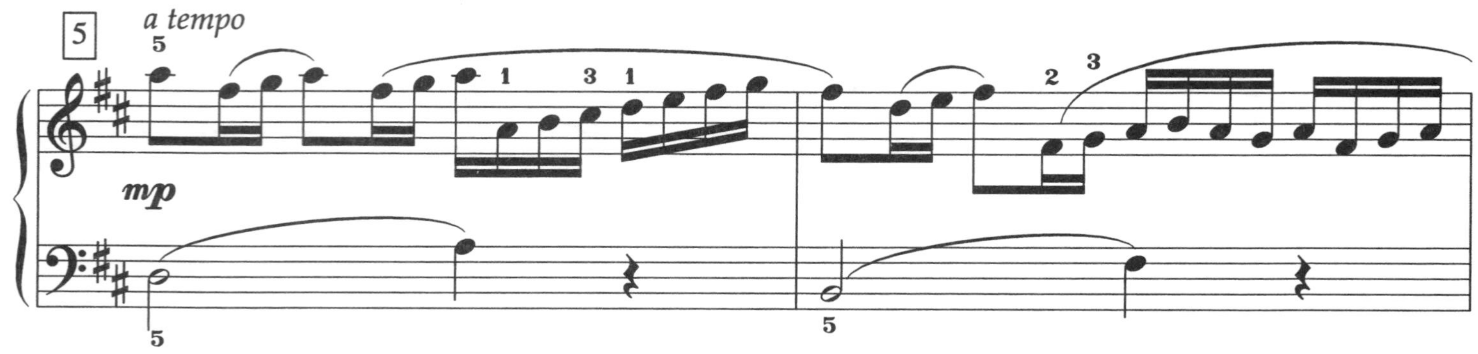

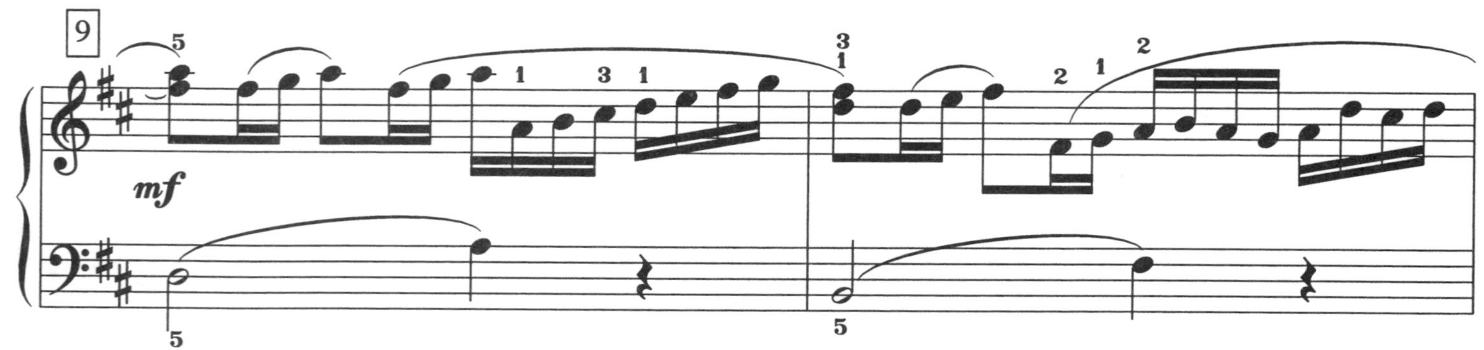

11
13
f–mf
16
mp–p
19
pp

Review

A. Write the A Major scale ascending and descending. Circle the half steps.
B. Write the primary chords in root position.

C. Write the chord symbols (A, E7, or D) in the boxes provided, then play the chords.

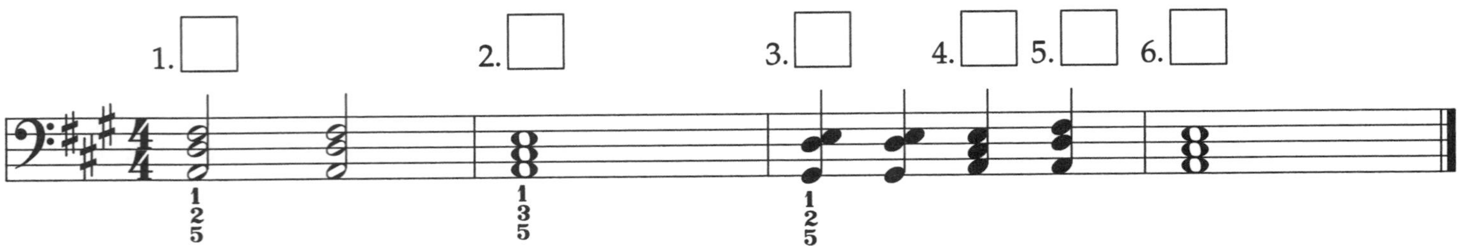

D. Match each note or group of notes with the rest of equal value. You may use letters more than once.

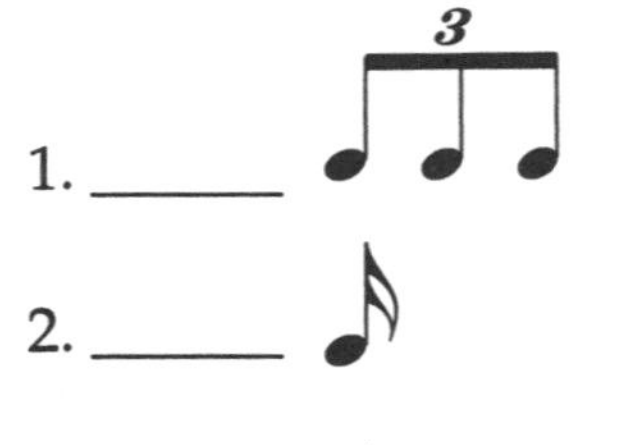

1. ______

2. ______

3. ______

4. ______

5. ______

6. ______

7. ______

8. ______

a.

b.

c.

d.

e.

f.

E. Add barlines to complete each measure.

F. Circle the root of each 1st inversion triad below.
G. Name each chord in the blank provided.
H. Play the chords on the keyboard.

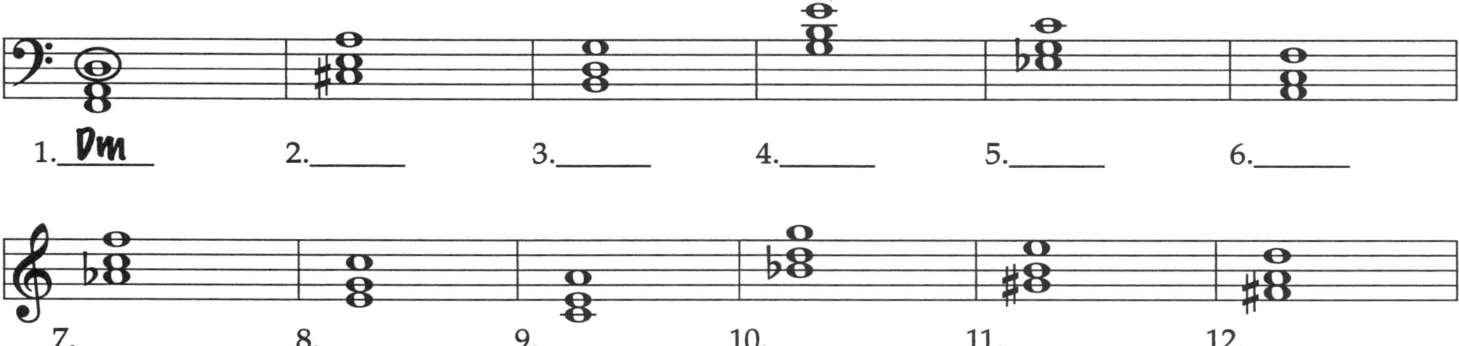

For each key signature there is a Major and a minor key.

I. Write the Major and minor names of the keys indicated by these key signatures.

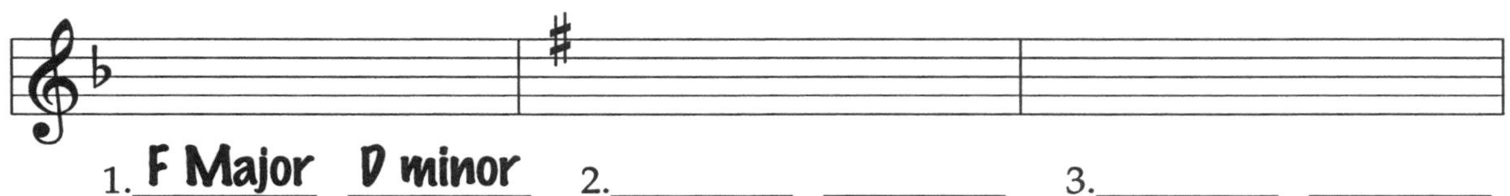

J. The relative minor scale begins on the ______ tone of the Major scale.

K. Write the names of these ledger line and space notes.

L. What do these signs mean?

1. **C** ____________________ 2. **₵** ____________________

Chapter 7
Reading in E Major

NEW CONCEPTS

- E Major Scale and Chords
- Tenuto

REVIEW CONCEPTS

- Identifying 2nd Inversion Triads

BIG SKY BOOGIE

DISC TWO 20 ♩= 60

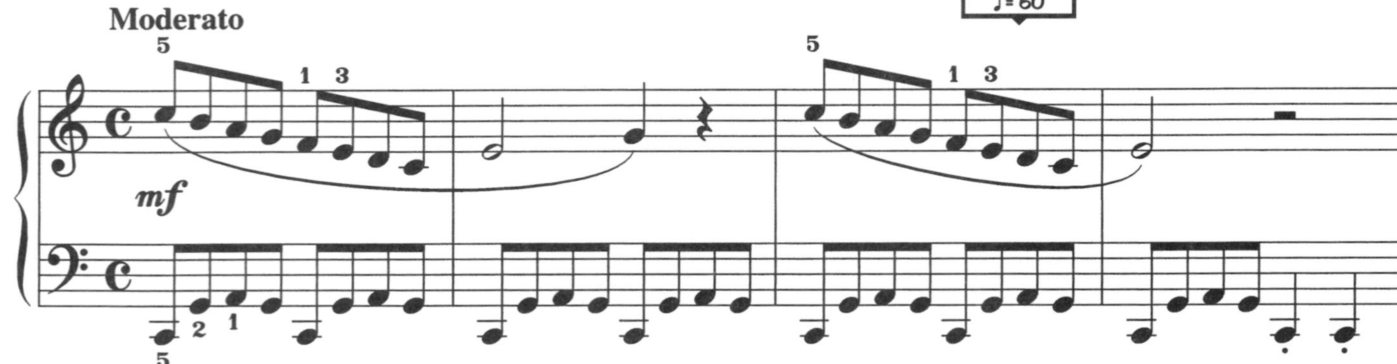

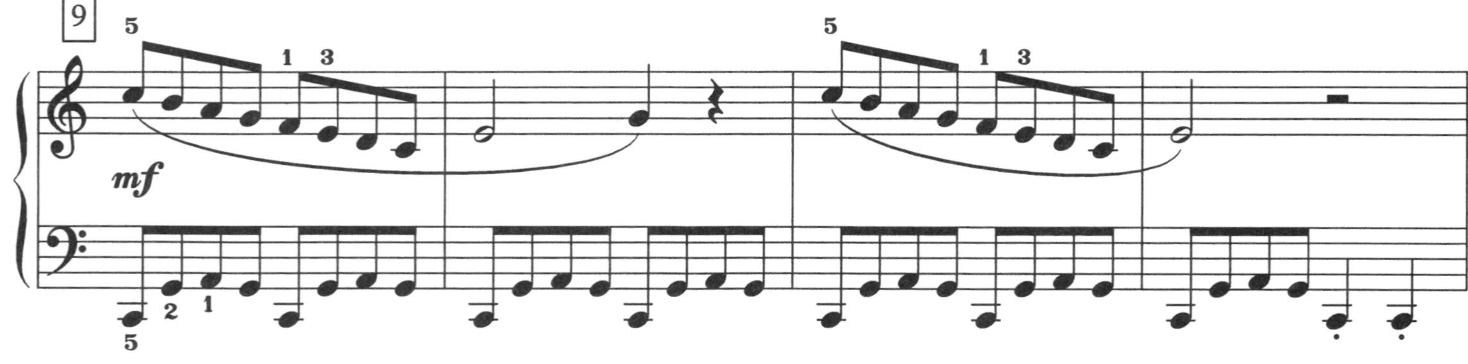

BRAZILIAN BOOGIE

Moderato

E Major Scale

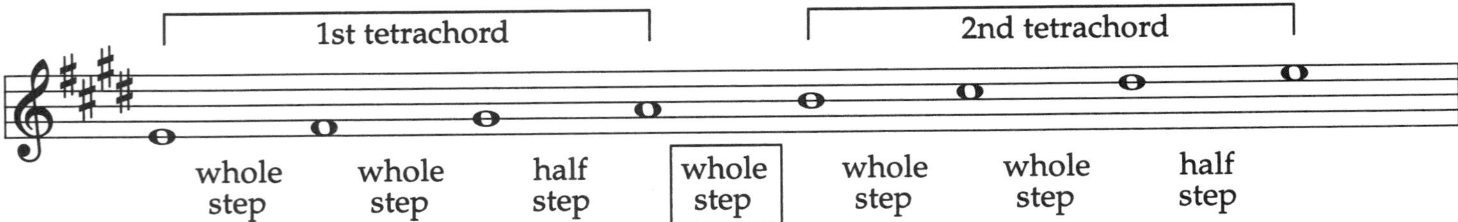

Primary Chords in the Key of E Major

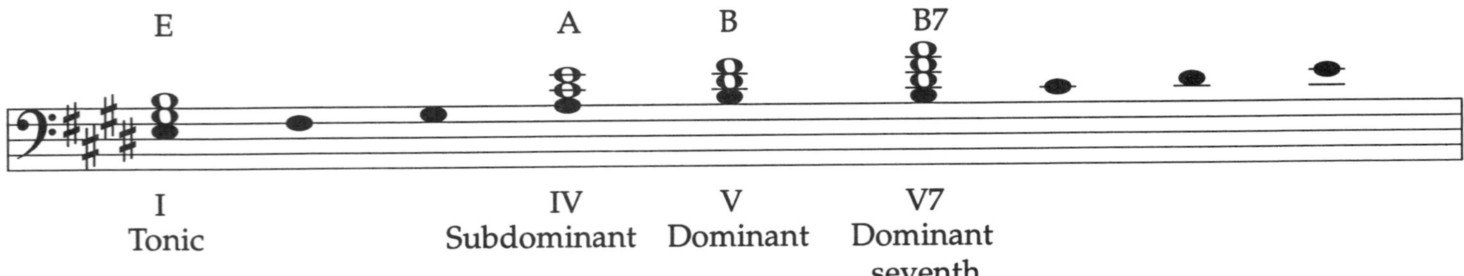

E MAJOR SCALE AND CHORDS

Play hands separately first. Memorize the fingering.

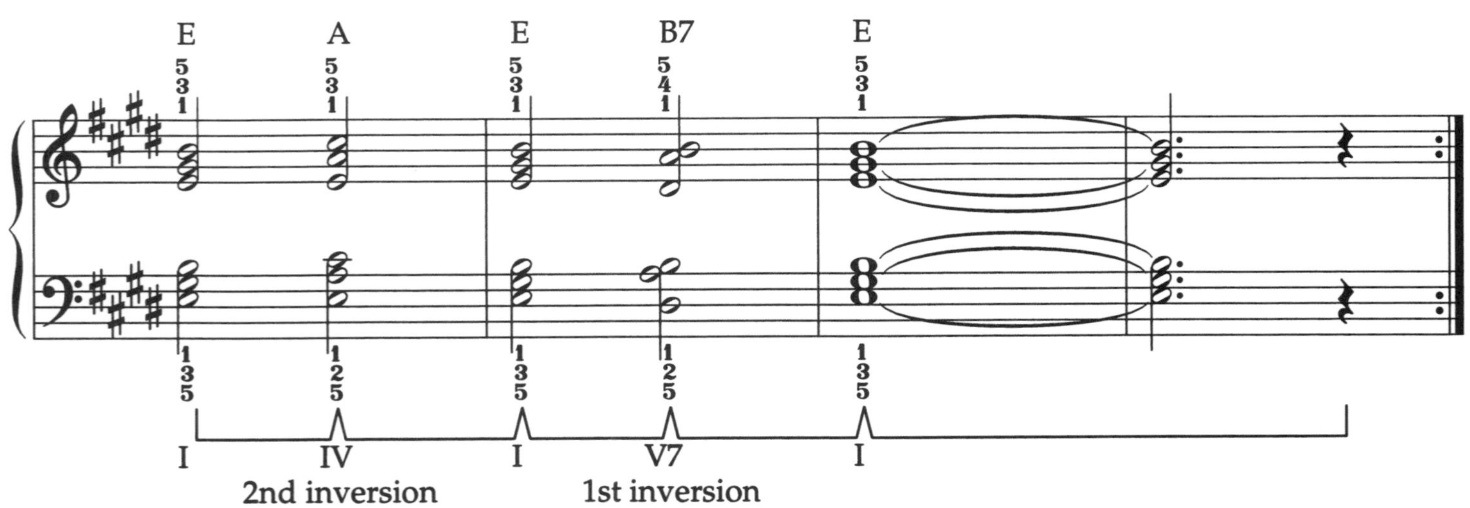

$\frac{6}{8}$ = 6 beats in a measure
= ♪ receives 1 beat

In $\frac{6}{8}$ time:

♬ = ♪ = 1 beat

Clap and count this rhythm:

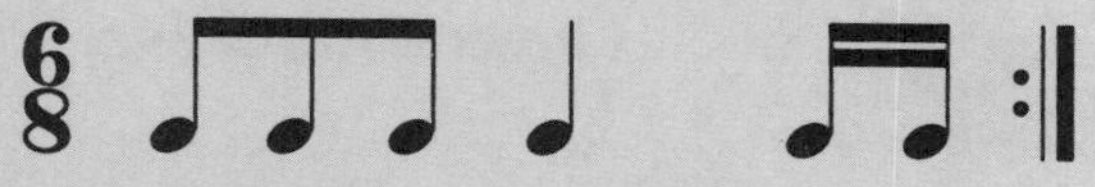

Count: 1 & 2 & 3 & 4 & 5 & 6 &

THE IRISH WASHERWOMAN

Con spirito

Traditional Irish Dance

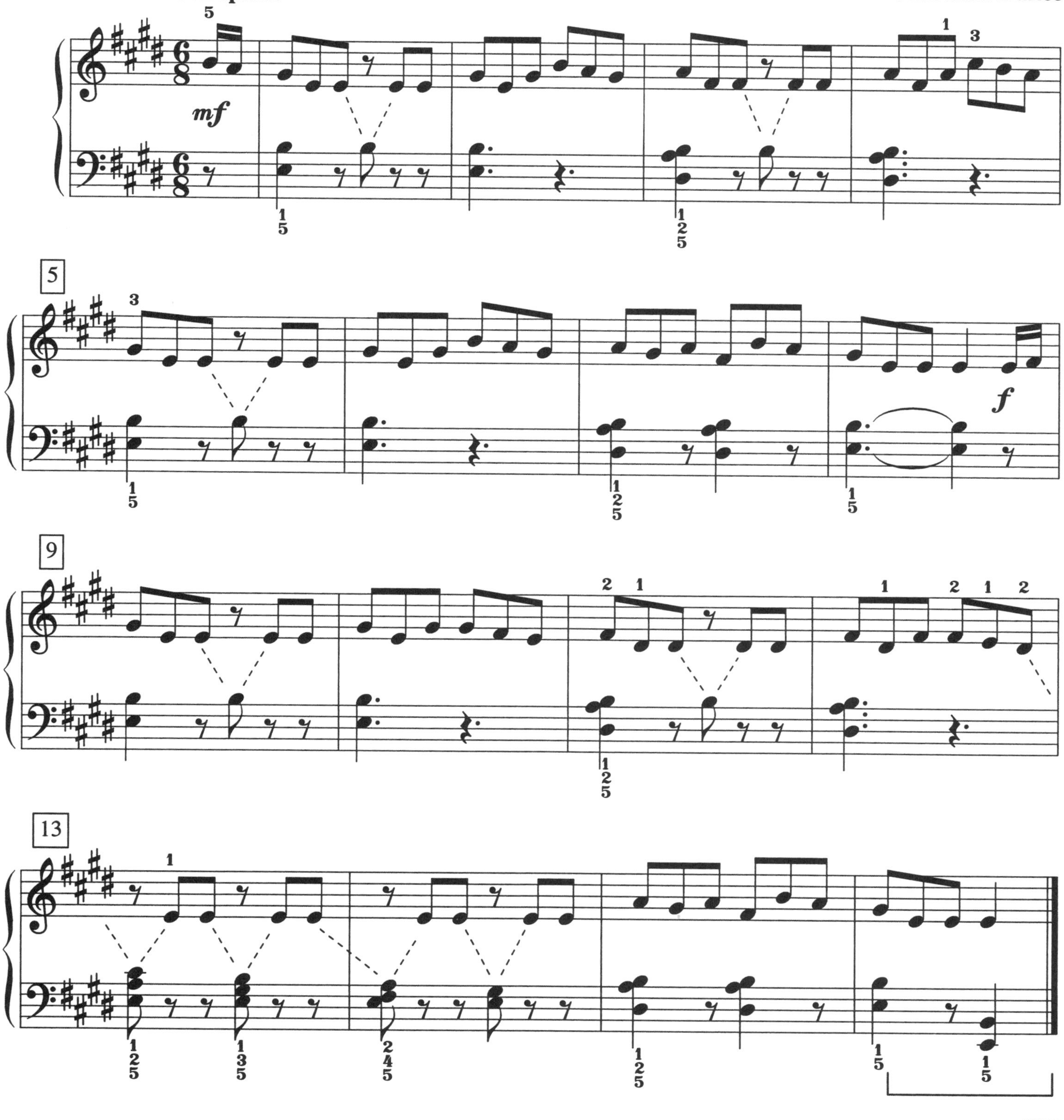

Identifying 2nd Inversion Triads

In **2nd inversion triads** the root is in the middle of the triad.

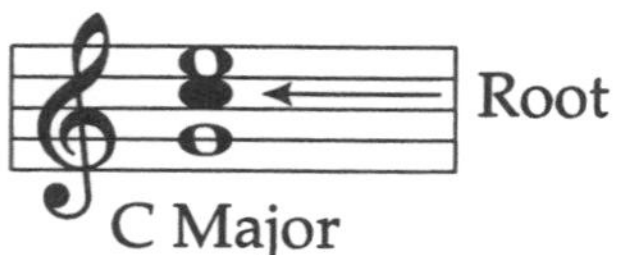

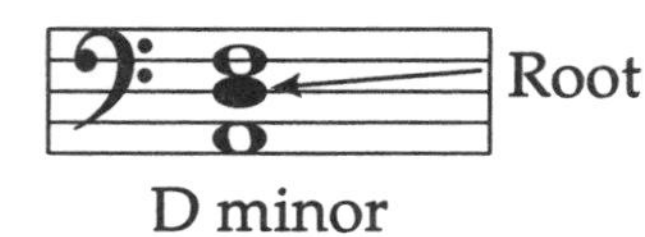

Review

Write the names of these 2nd inversion triads, then play them on the keyboard.

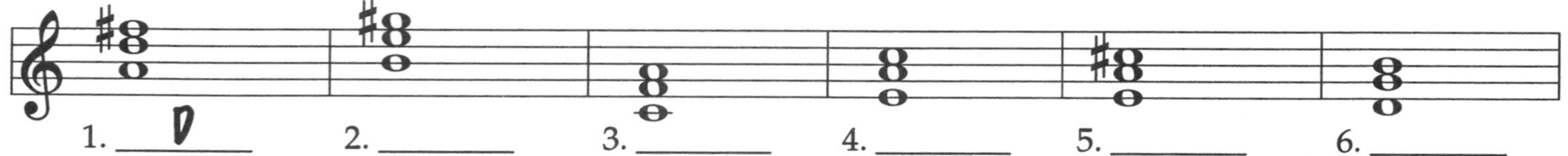

1. D_______ 2. _______ 3. _______ 4. _______ 5. _______ 6. _______

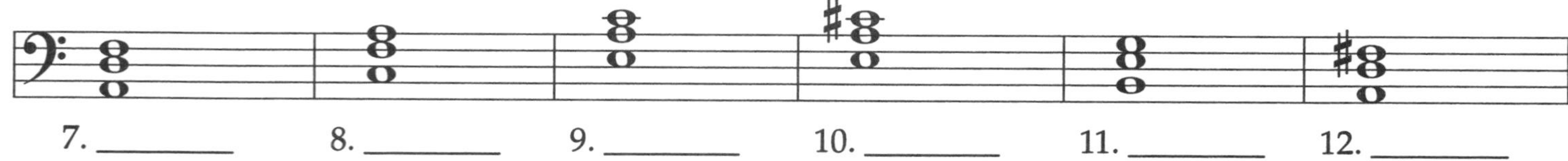

7. _______ 8. _______ 9. _______ 10. _______ 11. _______ 12. _______

2nd Inversion Triads

Play these 2nd inversion triads. Practice hands separately first.
Play as written, then transpose to G Major and F Major.

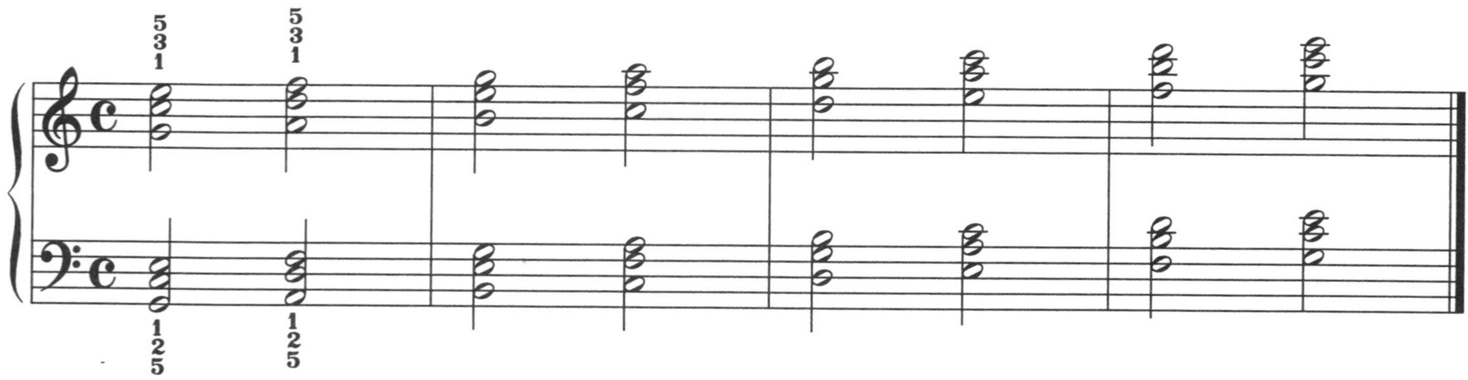

Note: When playing in G Major, remember the F♯'s.
When playing in F Major, remember the B♭'s.

Technic

2ND INVERSION ETUDE

SWAN WALTZ

Moderato con moto

2nd time R.H. plays one octave higher

To Coda ⊕

17
cresc.
21
mf
l.h.
pp
rit.
D.C. al Coda
25
Coda
loco
mf
r.h.
mp
29
l.h.
8va
pp

Technic

ETUDE IN F

from *Selected Pianoforte Studies, Vol. 1*

Carl Czerny

★Vivace

mf

5

9

13

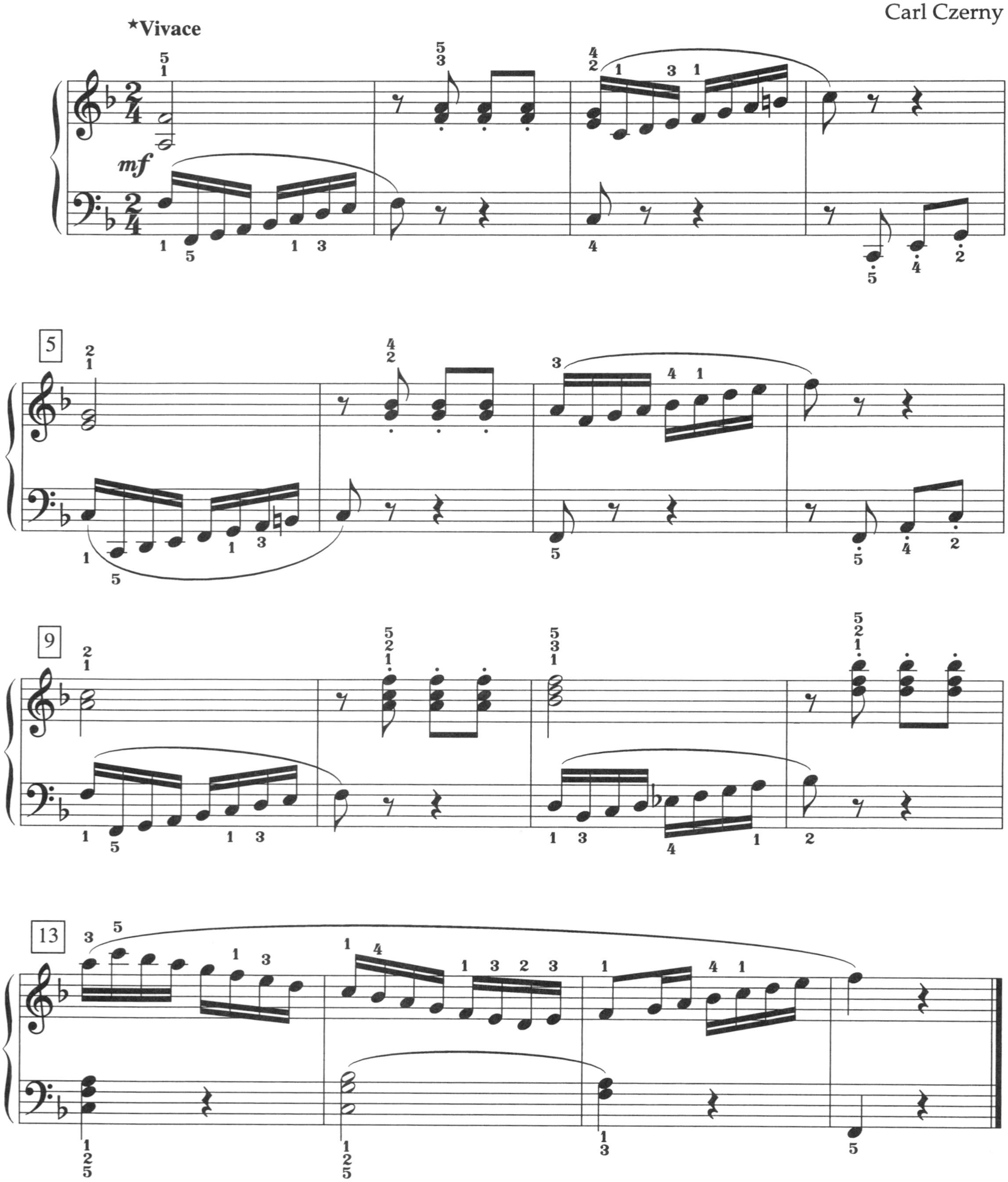

★ The term **Vivace** means lively.

Technic

E CHORD ETUDE

E SCALE ETUDE

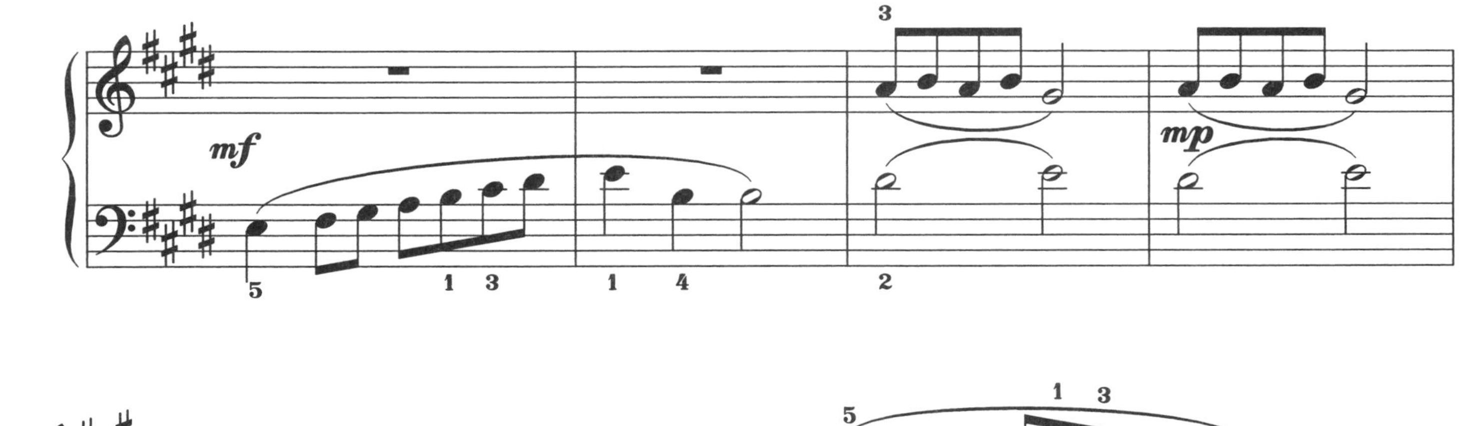

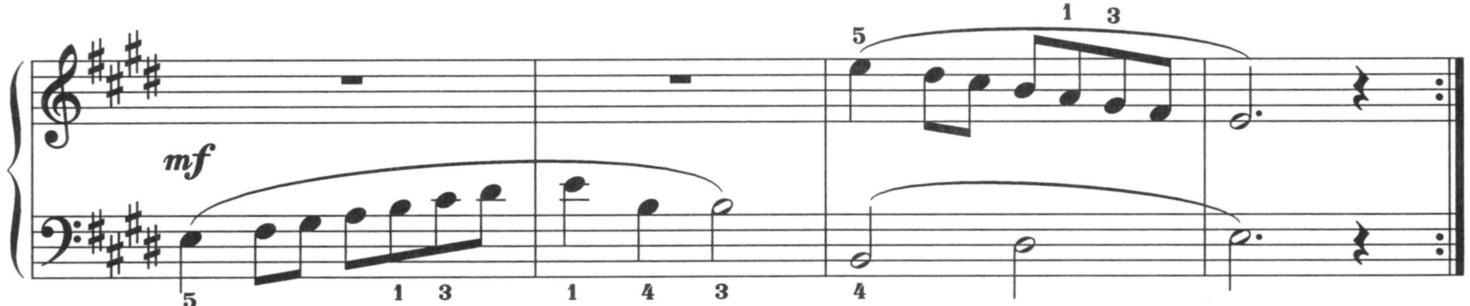

Challenge Piece

Around the late 1500s, the French became fascinated with the alluring and exotic qualities of Chinese and Turkish taste. This trend caught on and continued in Austria into the 1700s, as is evidenced in *Rondo Alla Turca*, the third movement from Wolfgang Amadeus Mozart's *Sonata in A Major, K. 331*. This, Mozart's most unique and famous sonata, was composed in the summer of 1778 during a trip to Paris. The first movement is a theme with six variations. The second movement, a minuet, contains a romantic trio more illustrative of the character of nineteenth century works. The third movement, also known as *Turkish March*, is the most popular of the three movements. It is written in sonata-rondo form, which means that the first theme returns after each new theme is introduced. Below is an arrangement of a section from this movement.

A small note before a main note is called a **grace note**. It is a note which is considered additional to the melody and is inserted as an ornament. A grace note is played immediately before the main note and does not add value to or take value away from the main note. There may be more than one grace note before a main note .

Tenuto

A small line over or under a note is a tenuto mark. It means to stress the note and hold it for its full value.

RONDO ALLA TURCA

Wolfgang Amadeus Mozart

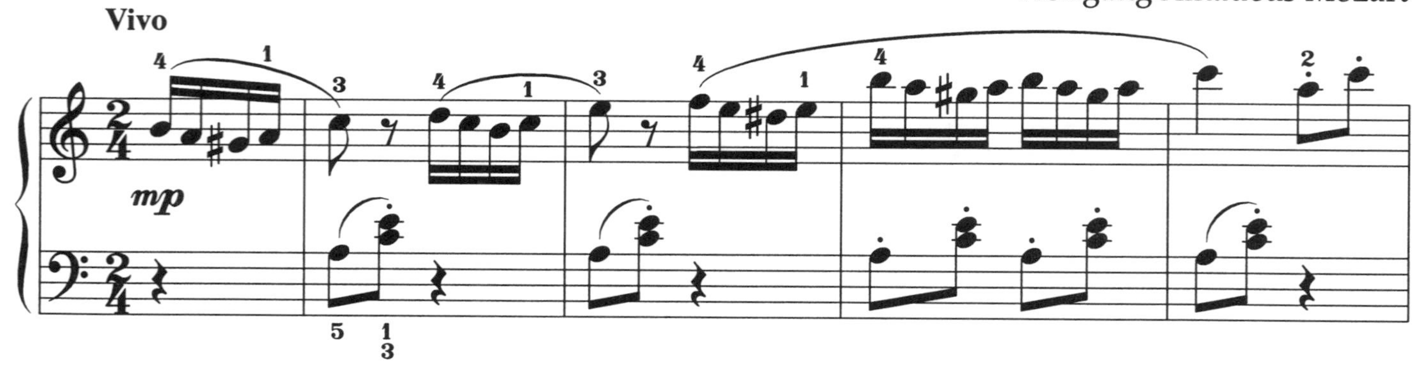

9
p
13
mp
17
cresc.
mf
21

Review

A. Circle the root of each 2nd inversion triad below.
B. Name each chord in the blank provided.
C. Play the chords on the keyboard.

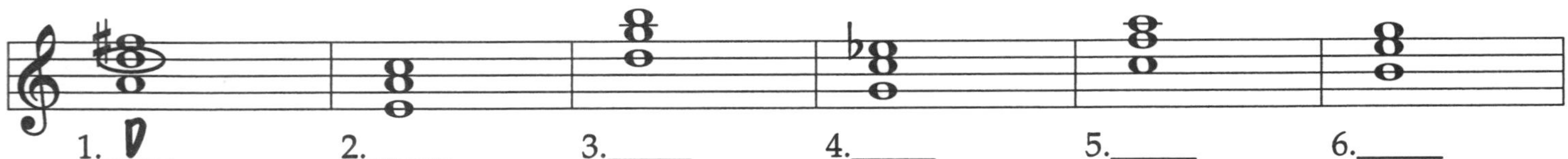

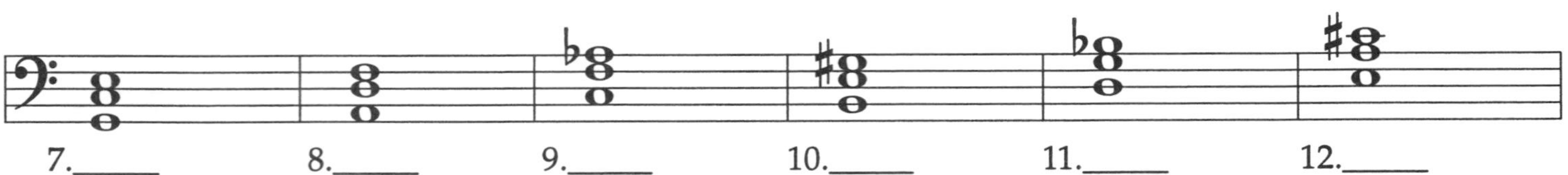

D. Complete the following sentences.

1. *ff* means fortissimo or very loud.
2. *f* means __________ or __________.
3. *mp* means __________ or __________.
4. *p* means __________ or __________.
5. *pp* means __________ or __________.

E. Define the following tempo markings.

1. Allegro __________ 2. Andante __________
3. Allegretto __________ 4. Moderato __________

F. Write the correct time signature for each rhythm below.

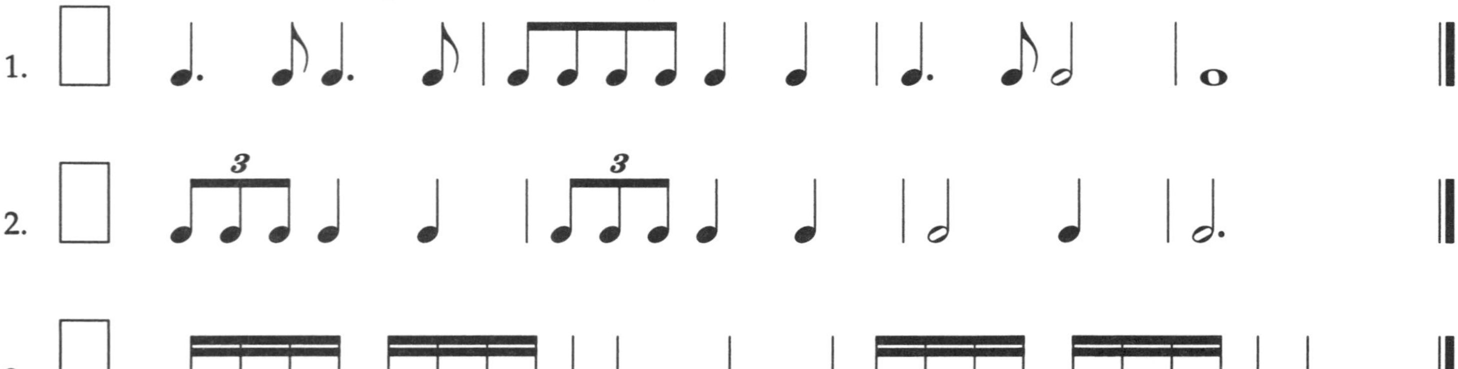

G. Draw accidentals to form the following scales and primary chords.

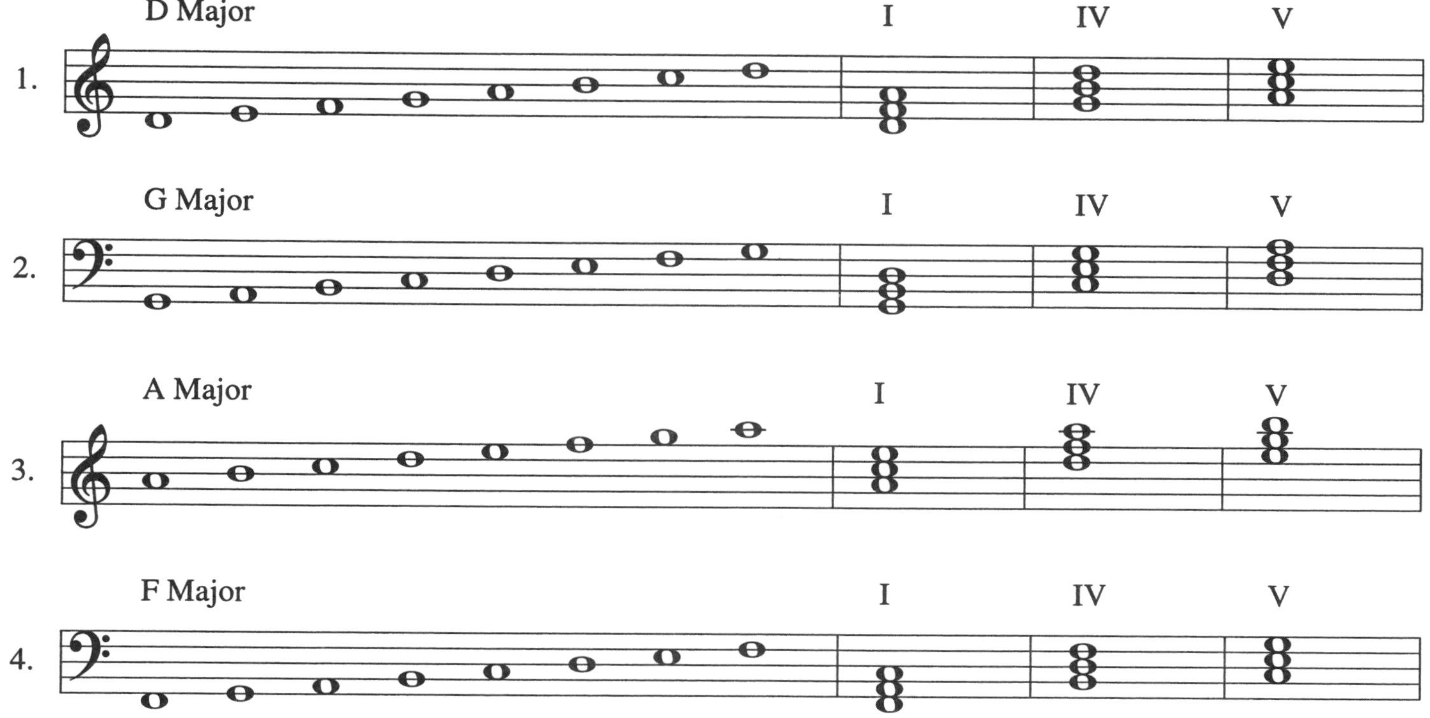

H. Write the E Major scale ascending and descending. Circle the half steps.
I. Write the primary chords in root position.

J. Write the chord symbols (E, B7, or A) in the boxes provided, then play the chords.

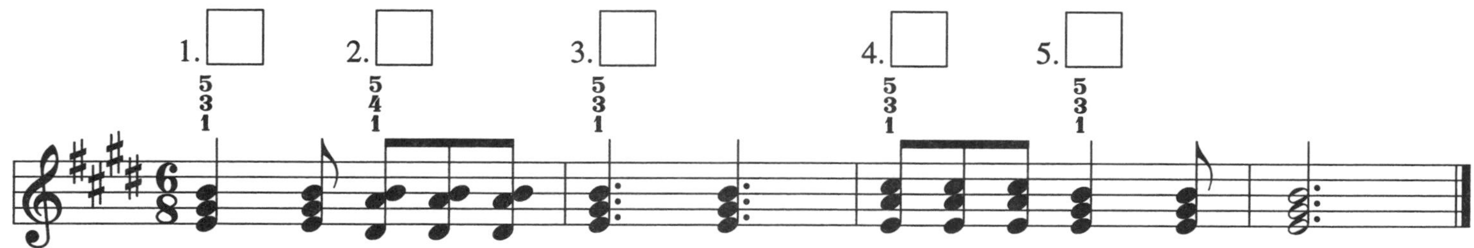

K. Harmonize
Add your own choice of L.H. chords (E, B7, or A) to the following R.H. melody line.
Write chord symbols in the boxes provided.

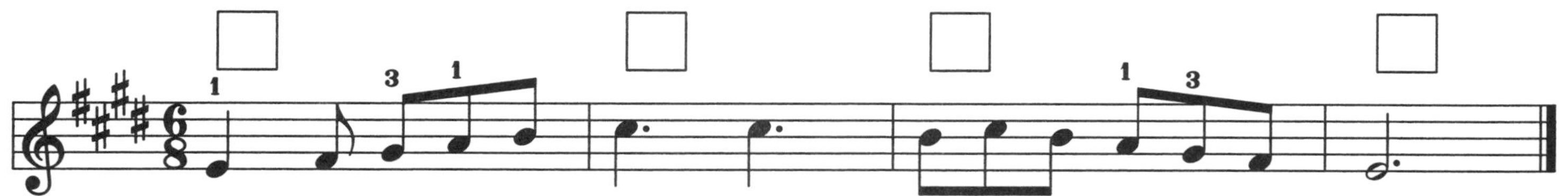

Chapter 8
New Scales and Triads

NEW CONCEPTS

- Parallel Major and Minor Scales
- Augmented Triads
- Diminished Triads
- Dotted Eighth Note
- Single Sixteenth Note
- Sixteenth Rest
- New Rhythm

Parallel Major and Minor Scales

Parallel Major and minor scales begin on the same tone.
The two scales have **different** key signatures.

D Major

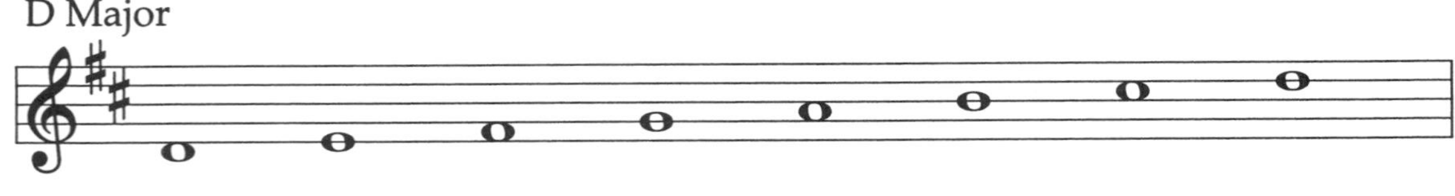

D minor (harmonic)

Practice the following parallel Major and minor scales.
Note: These Major and minor scales have the **same** fingering.

C MAJOR SCALE

C HARMONIC MINOR SCALE

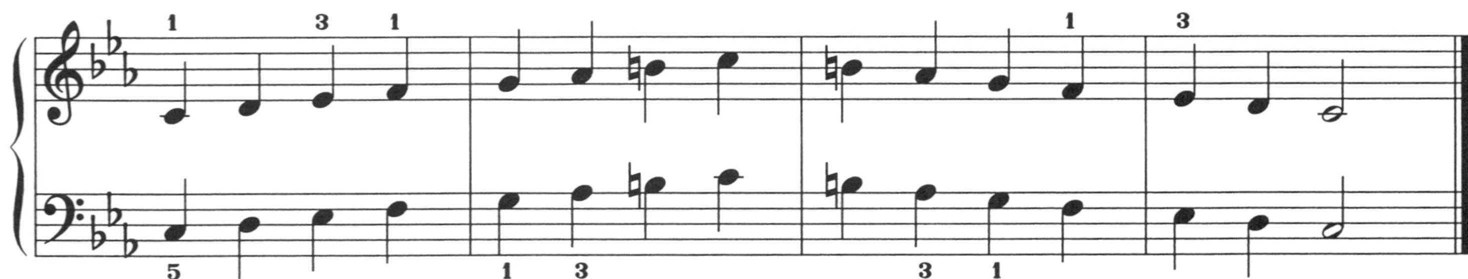

THE MIDNIGHT EXPRESS

Augmented Triads

An **Augmented triad** is made up of a:
Major 3rd (four half steps) and a
Major 3rd

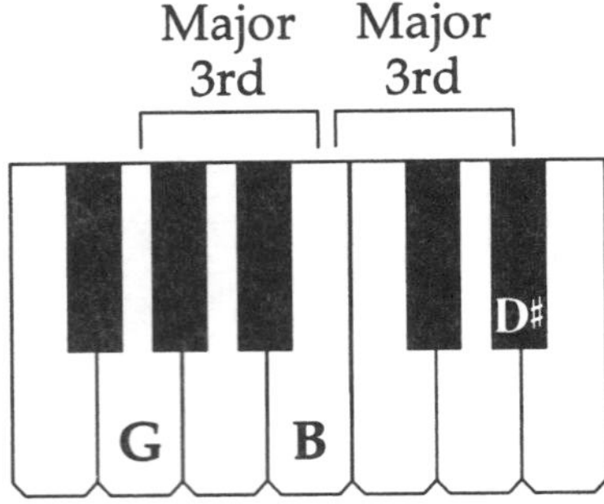

The symbol for an Augmented chord is + (Example: G+). From every Major triad, an Augmented triad may be formed by raising the **5th** (top note) one half step.

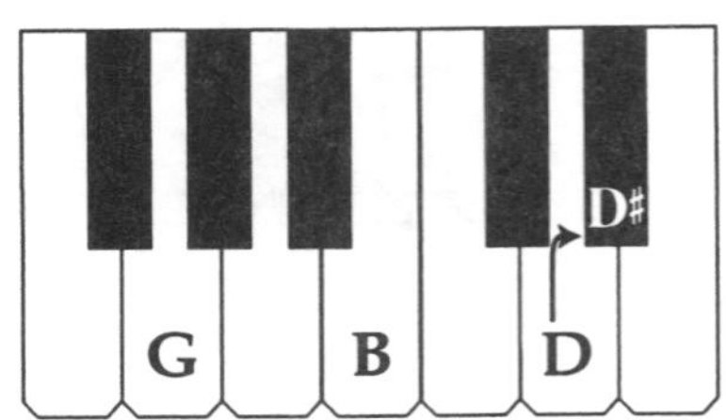

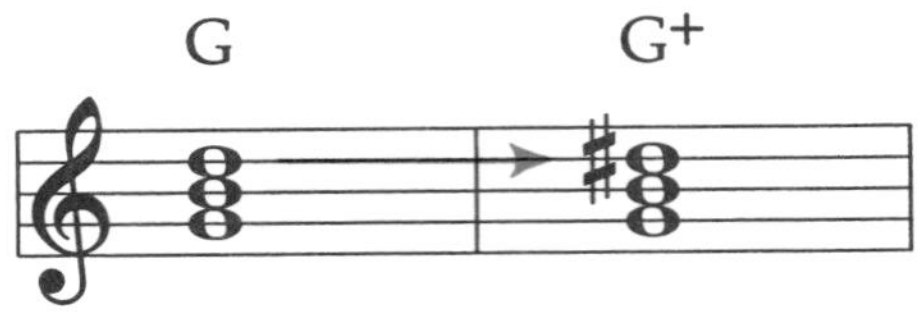

A. Name the Major and Augmented triads below.

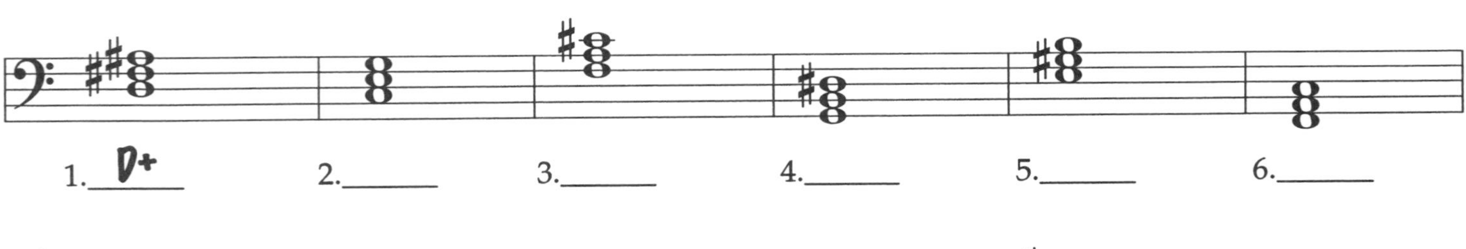

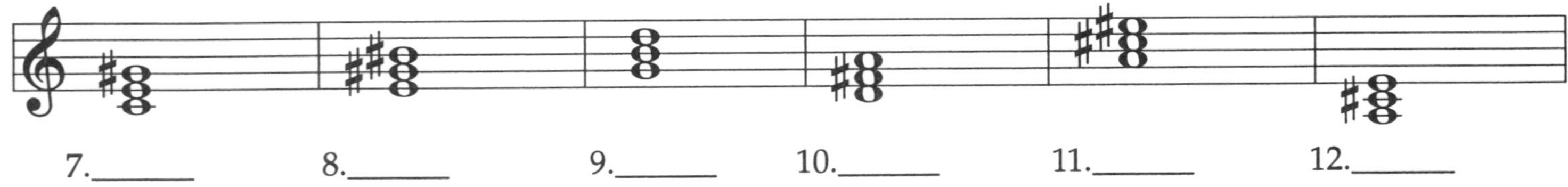

B. Name the Major triads below.
C. Draw and name the corresponding Augmented triads.
D. Play the triads on the keyboard.

MAJOR AND AUGMENTED CHORD WARM UP

Use the correct fingering. Circle the Augmented chords.

A VISIT TO THE ROYAL COURT

James Bastien

Johann Friedrich Franz Burgmüller (1806-1874), German composer, was the son of Johann August Franz Burgmüller, who founded, organized, and directed the Lower Rhine Music Festival in 1818, an important musical festival in Germany to this day. Johann Friedrich grew up surrounded by music; both he and his brother Norbert became prominent composers and pianists. Johann Friedrich settled in Paris after 1832 where he composed fashionable songs, stage works including a ballet, *La peri*, and descriptive teaching pieces for piano. His most famous piano teaching volume is his *25 Progressive Pieces*, op. 100. *Arabesque* is from that collection.

ARABESQUE

DISC TWO 34 ♩= 72

Johann Friedrich Burgmüller

*Allegro scherzando

leggiero

* The term **Allegro scherzando** means fast and playful.

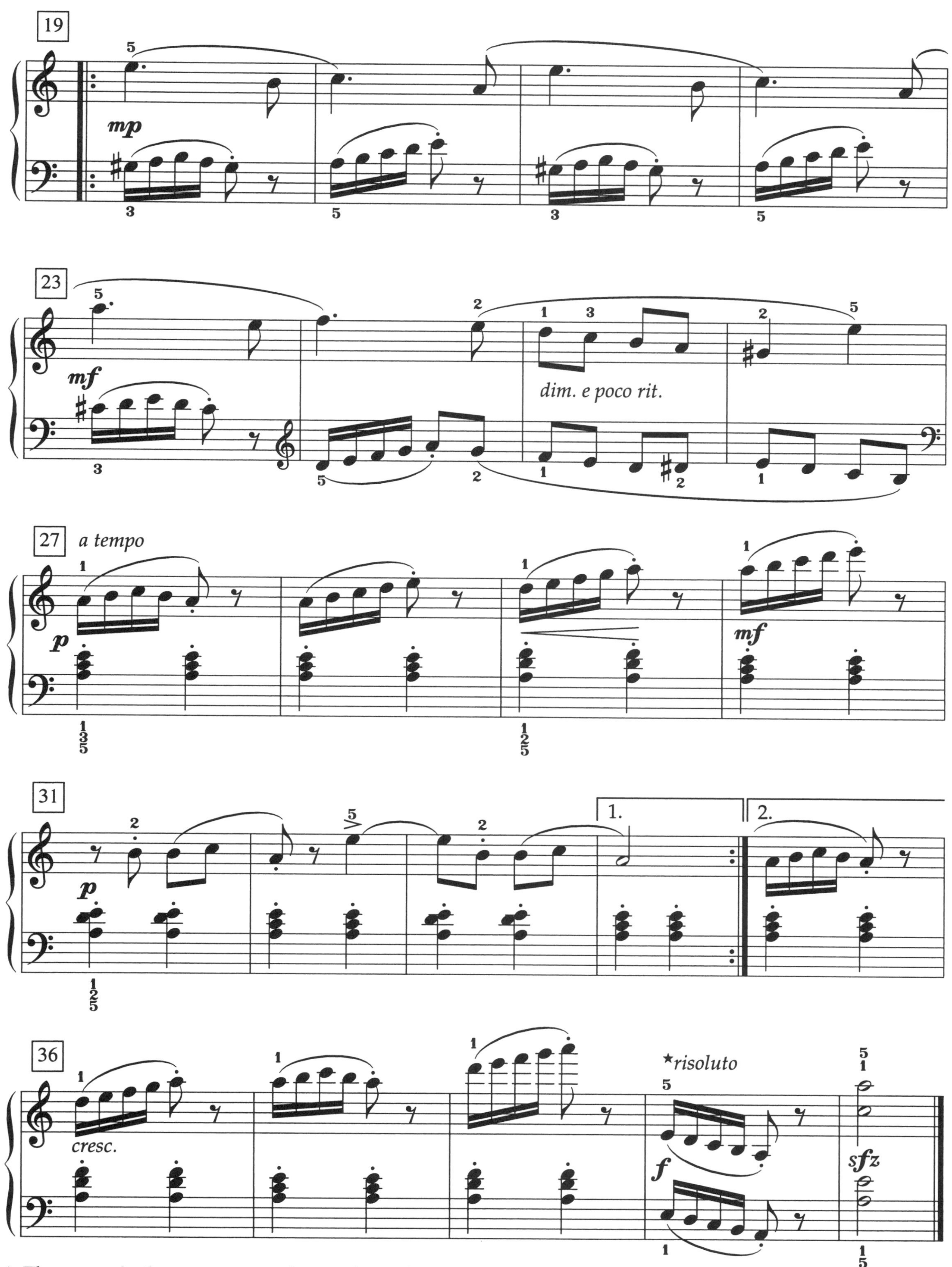

★ The term **risoluto** means to play with resolve.

Diminished Triads

A **diminished triad** is made up of a:
minor 3rd (three half steps) and a
minor 3rd

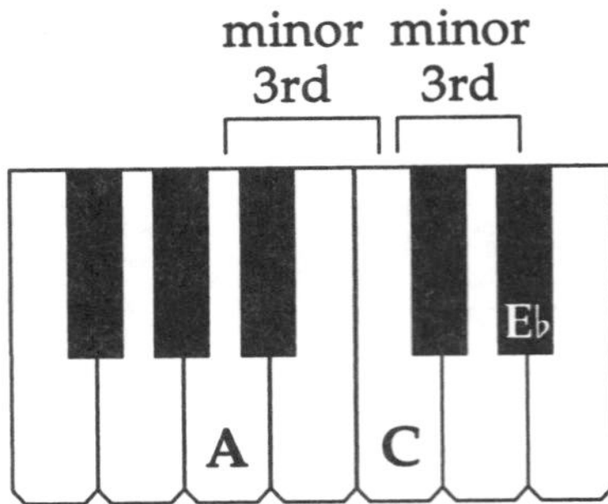

The symbol for a diminished chord is ° (Example: A°). From every minor triad, a diminished triad may be formed by lowering the **5th** (top note) one half step.

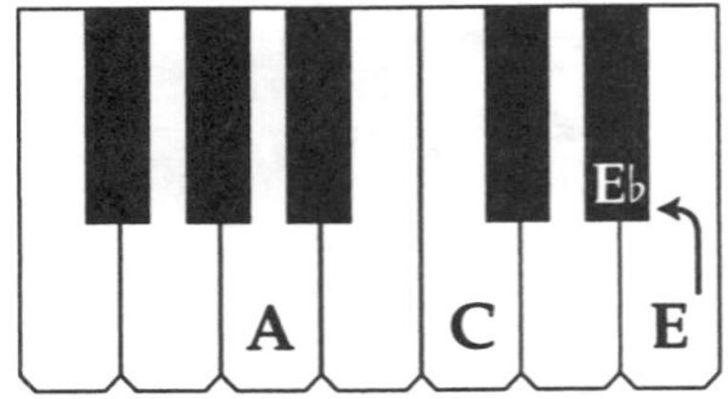

A. Name the minor and diminished triads below.

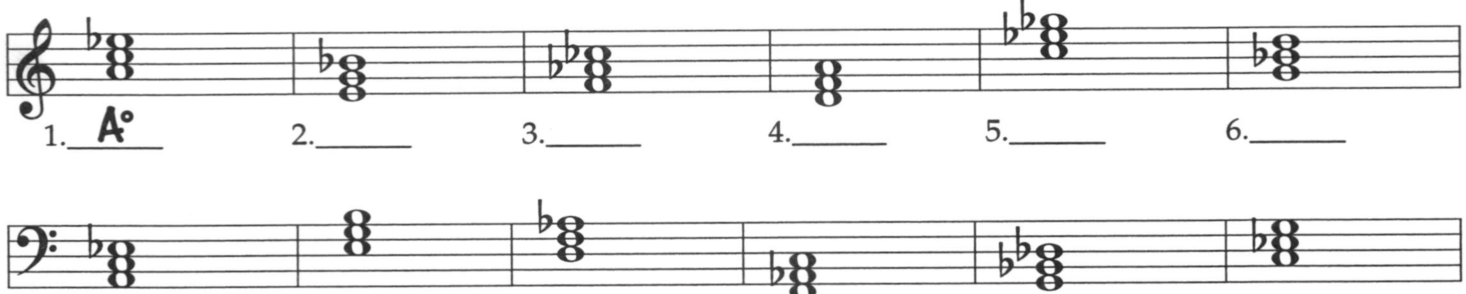

B. Name the minor triads below.
C. Draw and name the corresponding diminished triads.
D. Play the triads on the keyboard.

IN THE SHADE OF THE OLD APPLE TREE

 ★ The term **Allegro grazioso** means fast and graceful.

12
16
p
mp
cresc.
mf
20
p
cresc.
poco rit.
24
a tempo
mf
mp
28
p

JESU, JOY OF MAN'S DESIRING

from *Cantata No. 147*

Johann Sebastian Bach

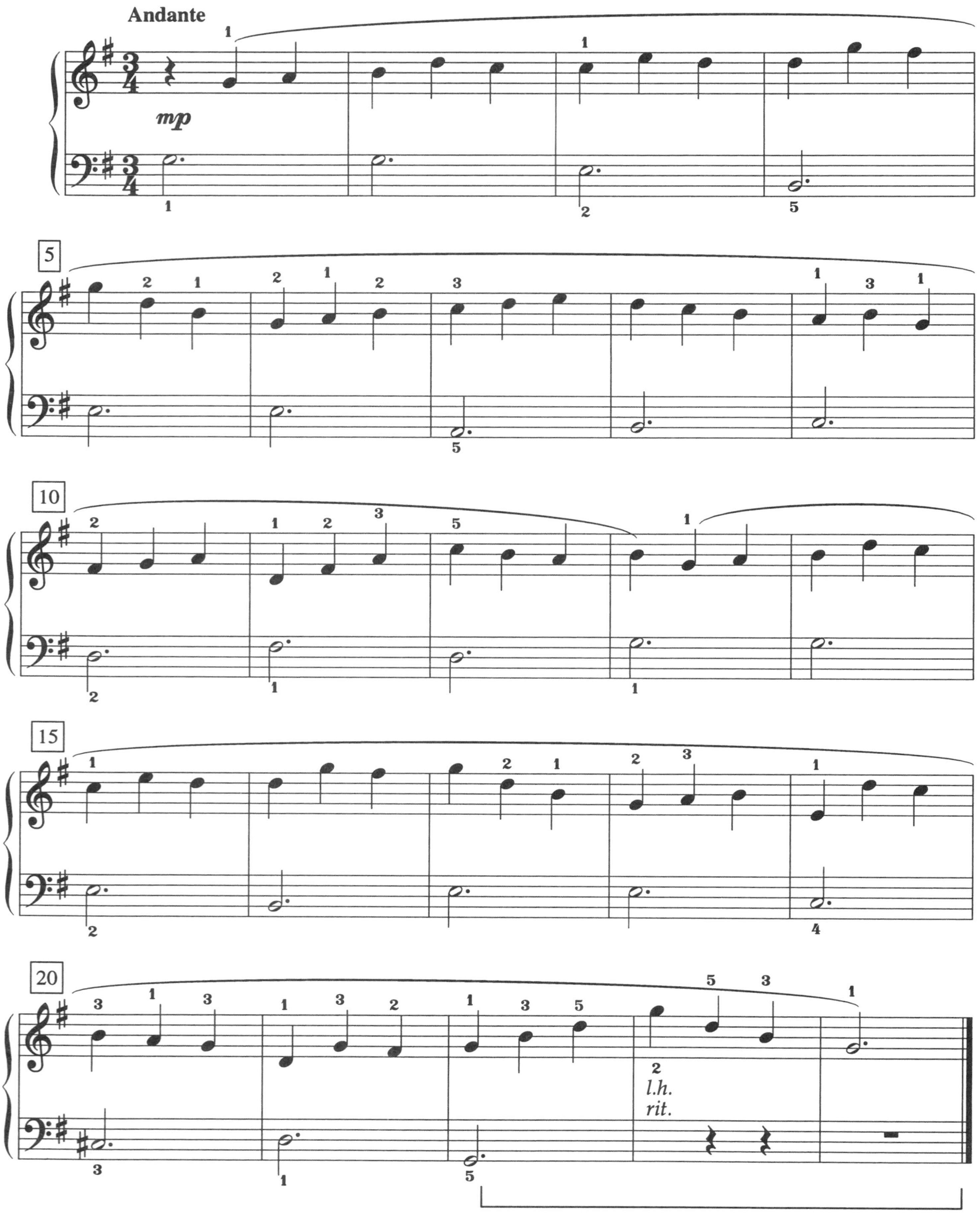

Andante

mp

5

10

15

20

l.h.

rit.

PRELUDE IN C MAJOR

from *Twelve Short Preludes*

Johann Sebastian Bach

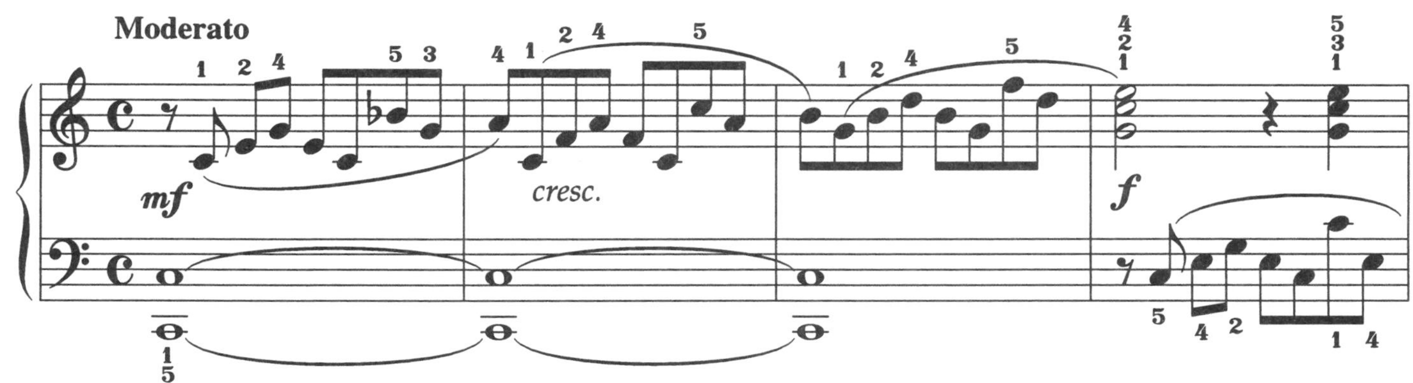

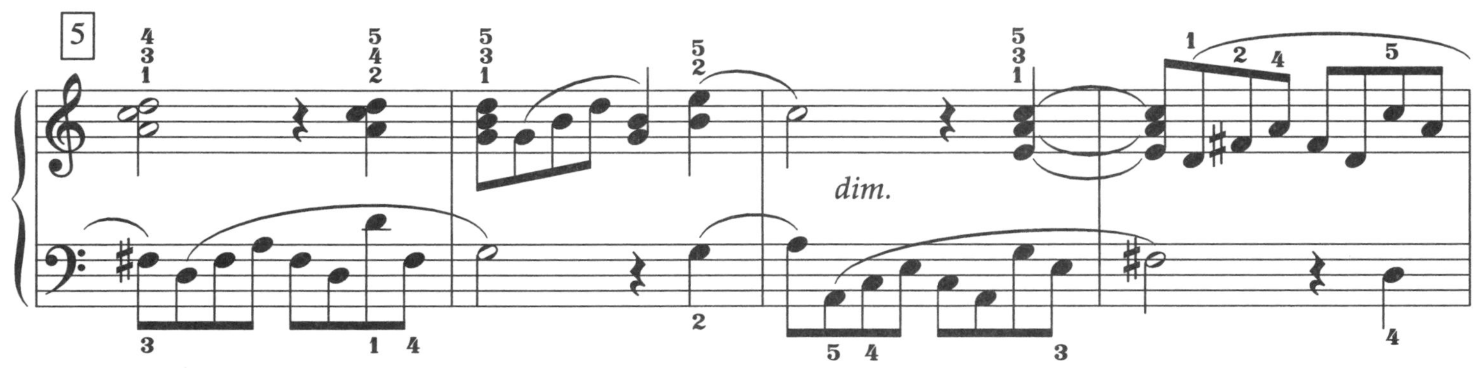

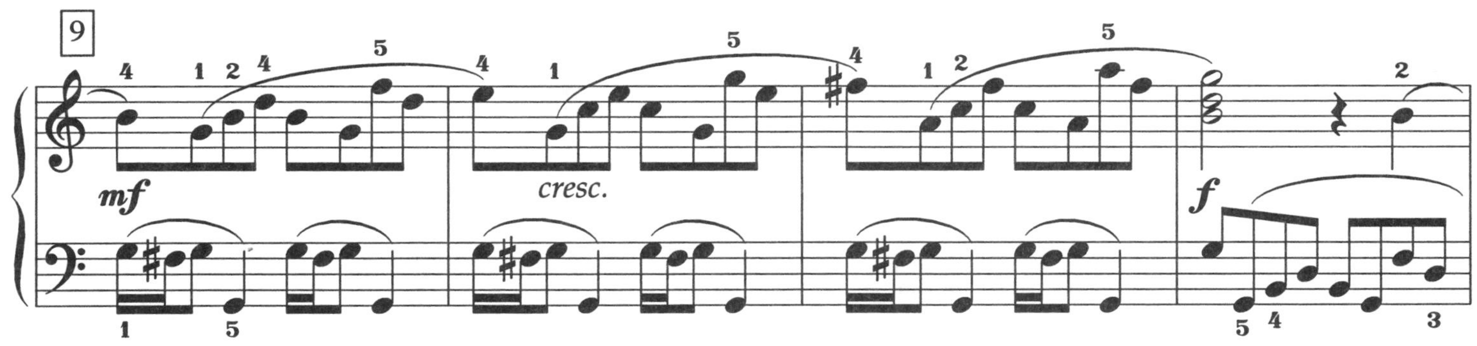

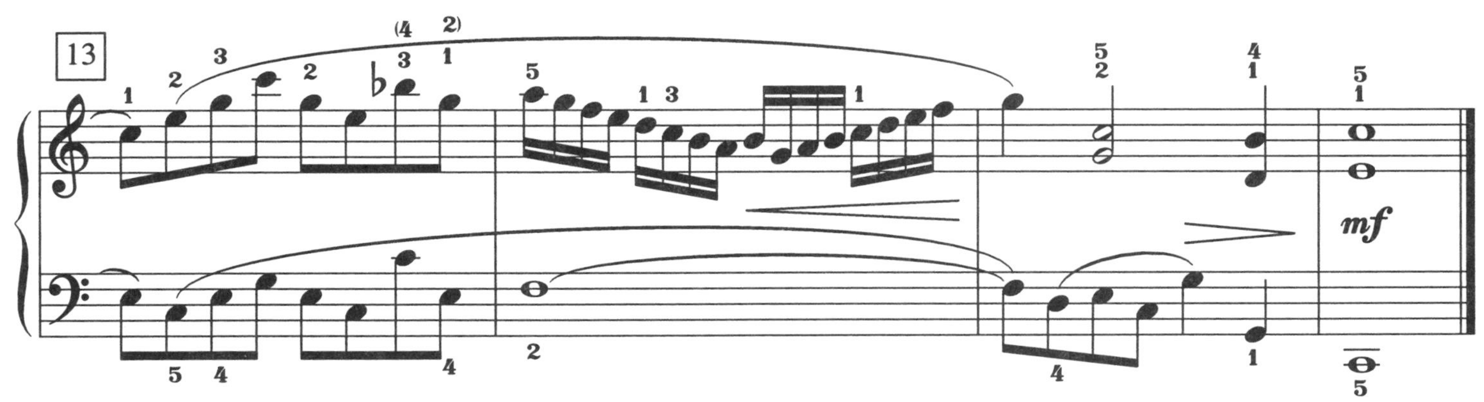

ST. LOUIS BLUES

W. C. Handy

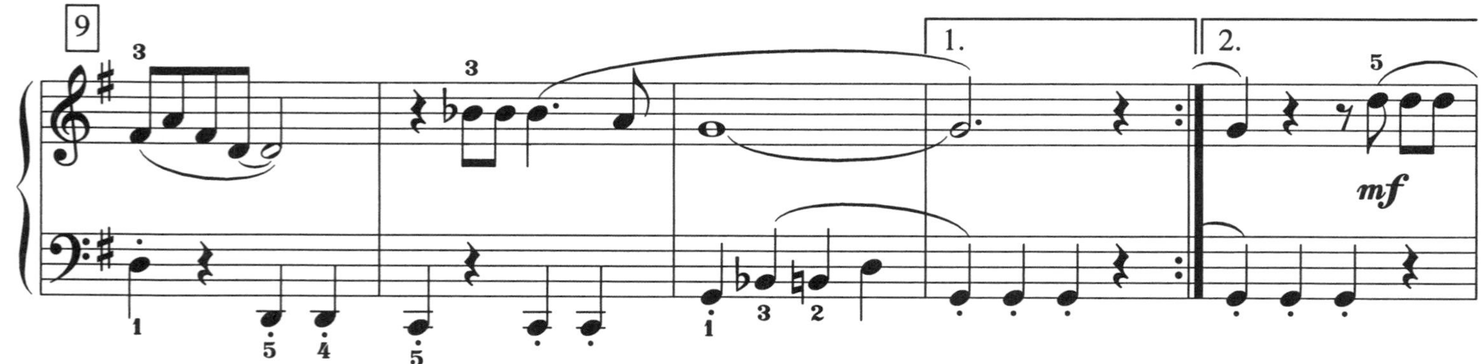

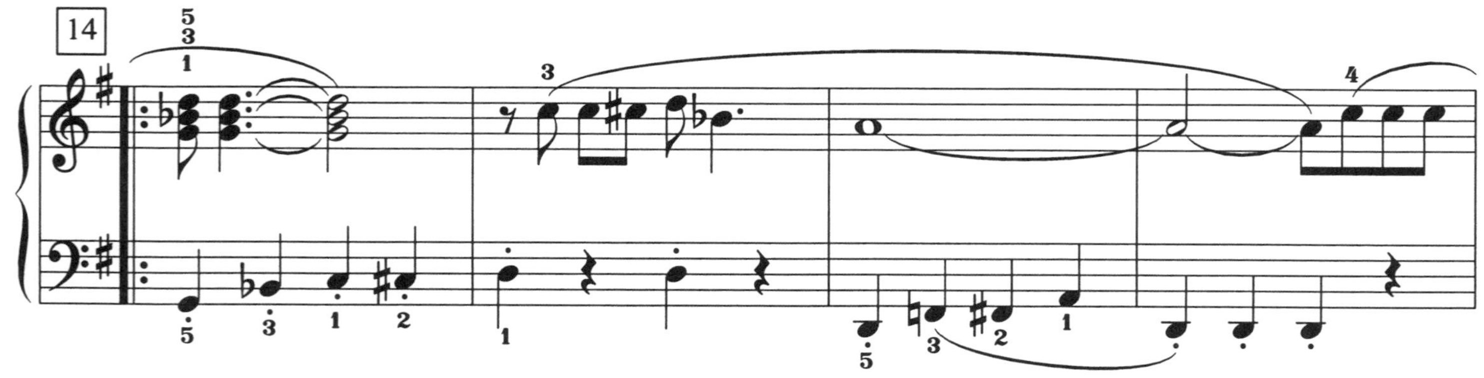

18
1.
22
2.
cresc.
f
26
30
34
1.
2.
dim. e rit.
r.h.
p
8va

ANSWER KEY

Review

From every Major chord, an Augmented chord may be formed by raising the **5th** (top note) one half step.

From every minor chord, a diminished chord may be formed by lowering the **5th** (top note) one half step.

CHORD DRILL

A. Write the correct chord symbols in the boxes.
B. Play the chords on the keyboard.

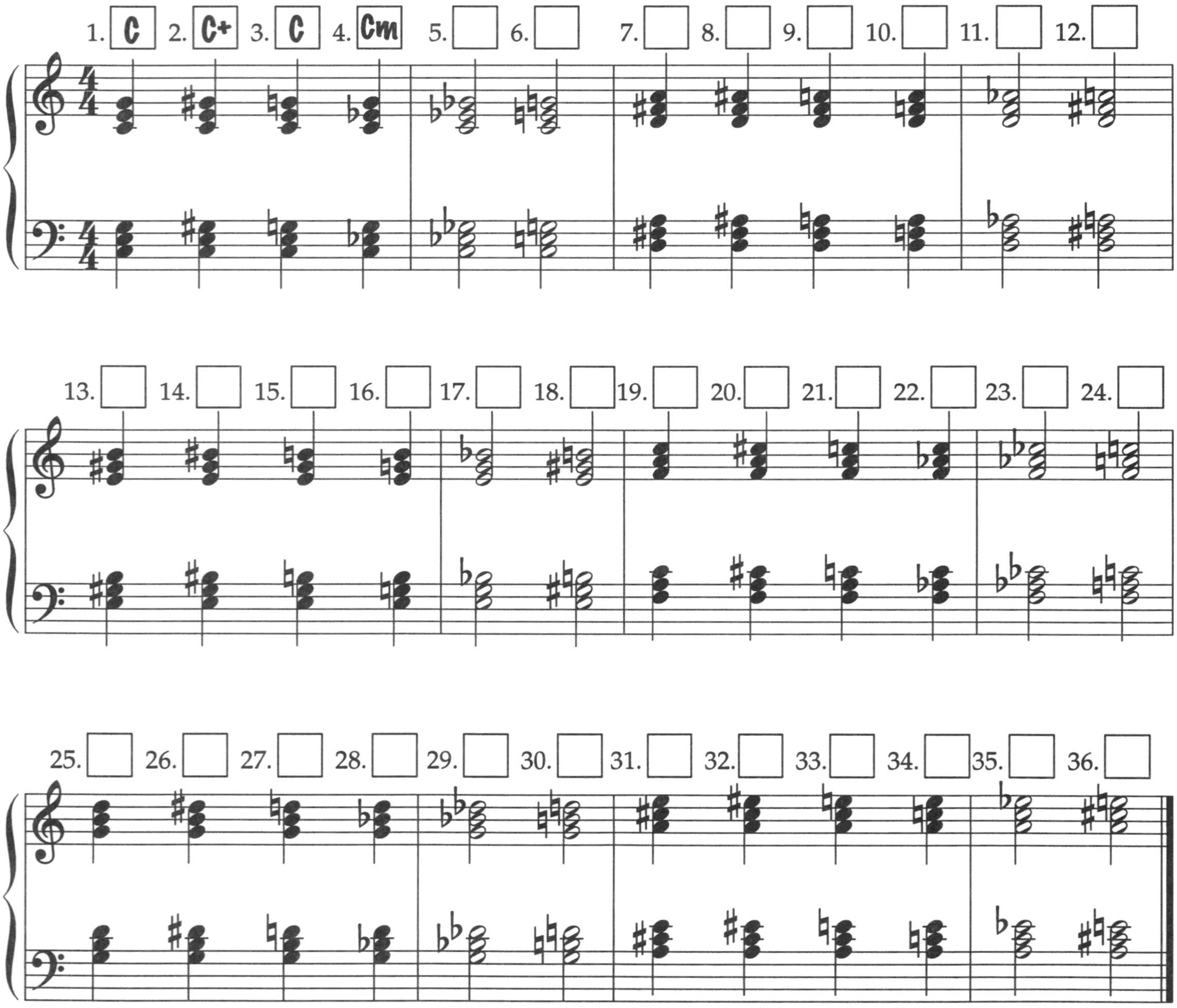

1. C 2. C+ 3. C 4. Cm 5. 6. 7. 8. 9. 10. 11. 12.

13. 14. 15. 16. 17. 18. 19. 20. 21. 22. 23. 24.

25. 26. 27. 28. 29. 30. 31. 32. 33. 34. 35. 36.

Technic

PARALLEL SCALE ETUDE

Challenge Piece

MOONLIGHT SONATA

from *Sonata No. 14*, op. 27

Ludwig van Beethoven

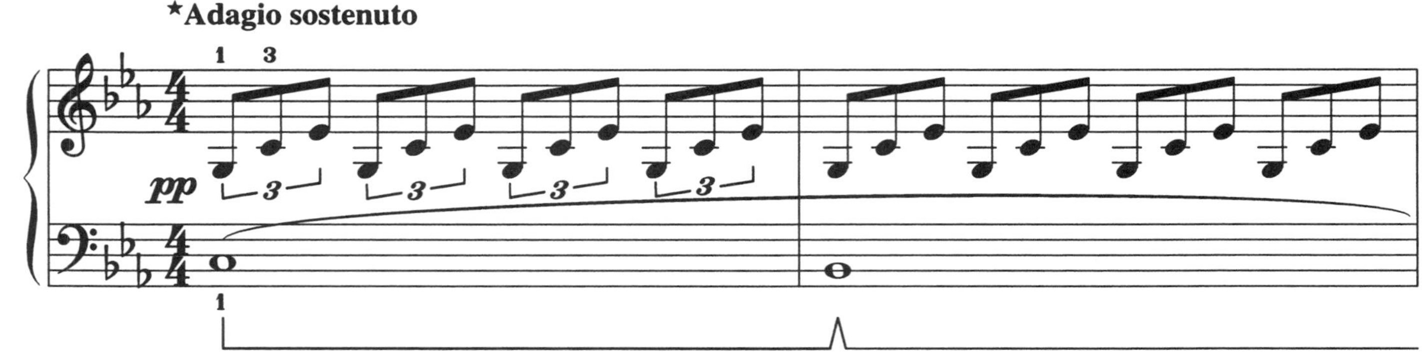

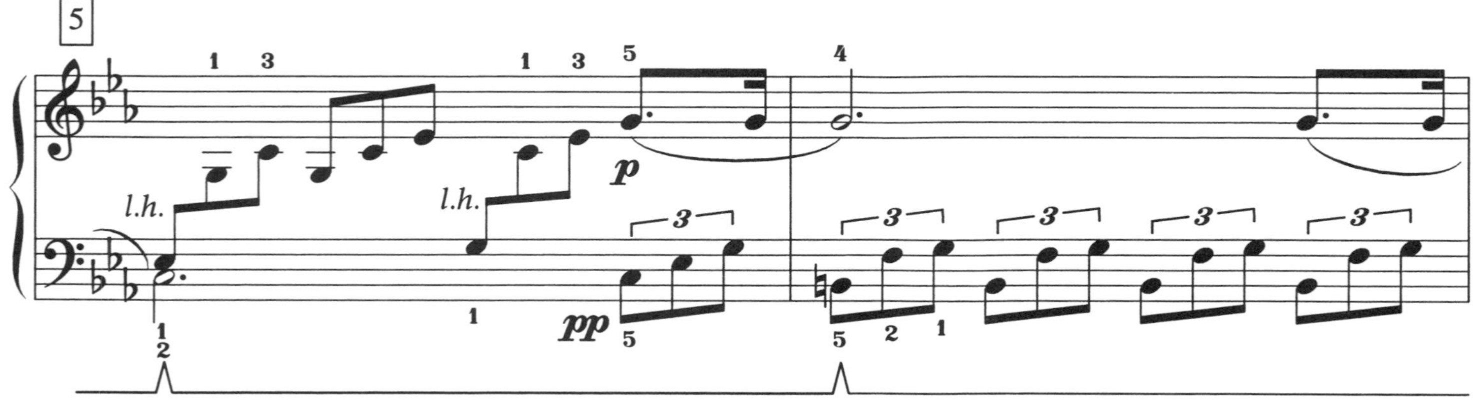

★ The term **Adagio sostenuto** means slow and sustained.

9
mp
11
13
dim.
p
15
17

Review

A. Name the Major and Augmented triads below.

1. E+ 2.____ 3.____ 4.____ 5.____ 6.____

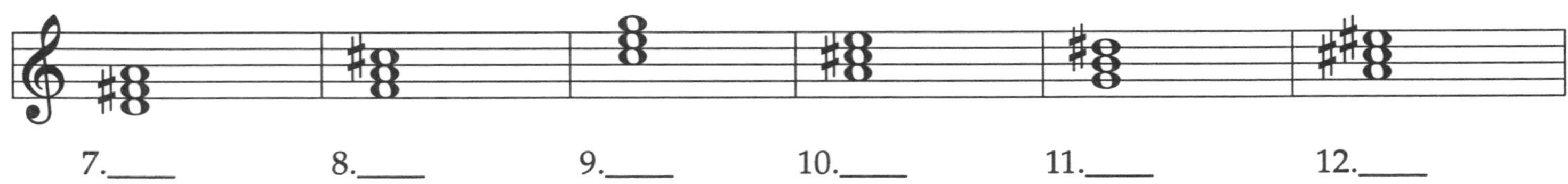

7.____ 8.____ 9.____ 10.____ 11.____ 12.____

B. Name the minor and diminished triads below.

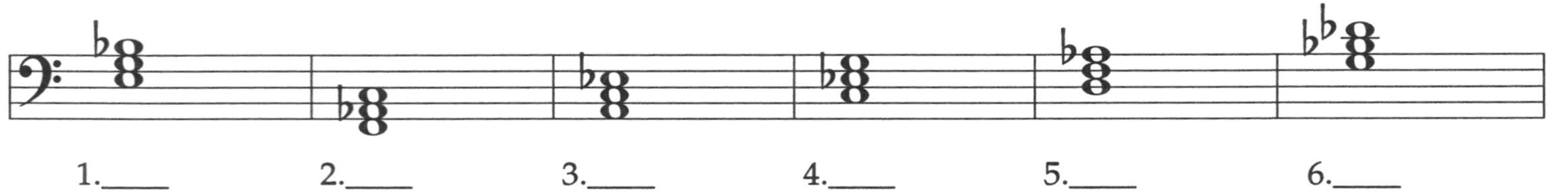

1.____ 2.____ 3.____ 4.____ 5.____ 6.____

7.____ 8.____ 9.____ 10.____ 11.____ 12.____

C. Name the following bass styles.

1. broken chord 2.____________ 3.____________ 4.____________

D. Name the keys indicated by these key signatures.

1.________ 2.________ 3.________ 4.________ 5.________ 6.________

E. The relative minor scale begins on the _____ tone of the Major scale.

F. 1. C Major is relative to __A__ minor.
2. G Major is relative to ____ minor.
3. F Major is relative to ____ minor.

G. Draw accidentals to form the following scales and primary chords.

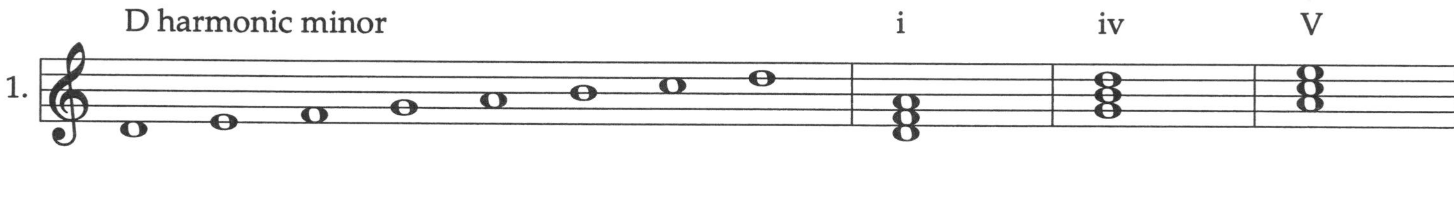

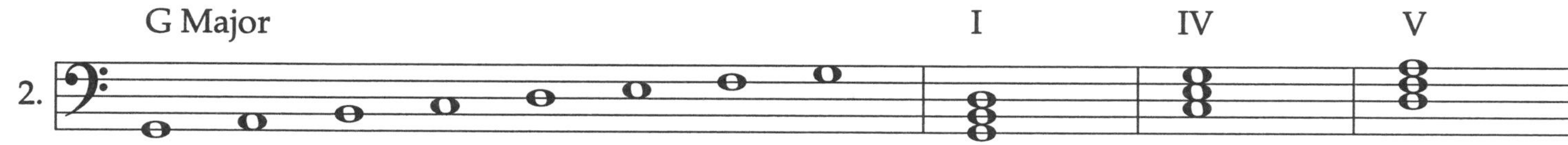

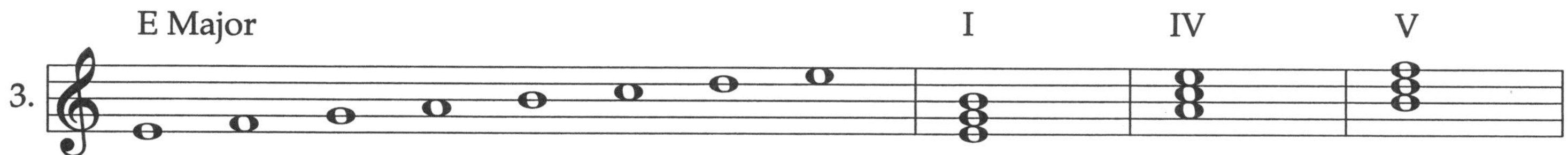

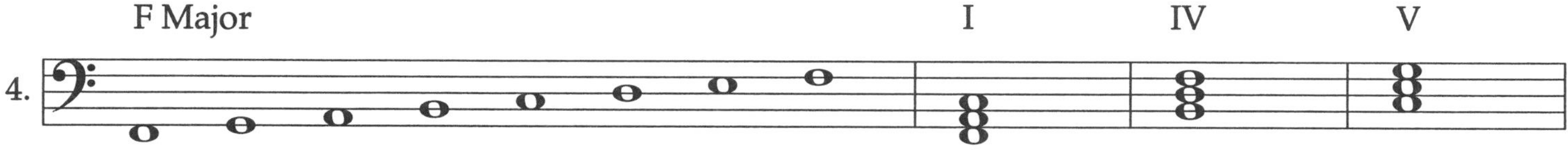

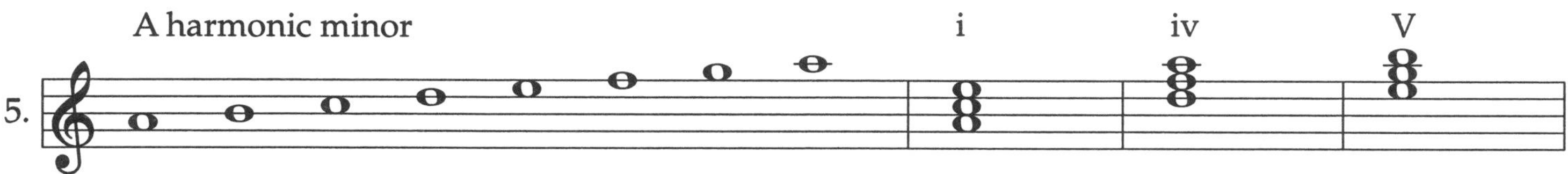

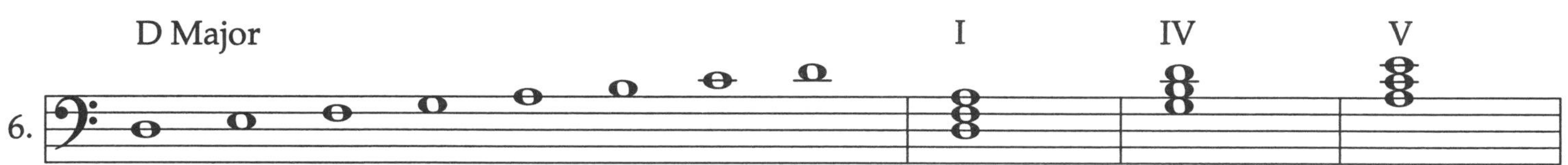

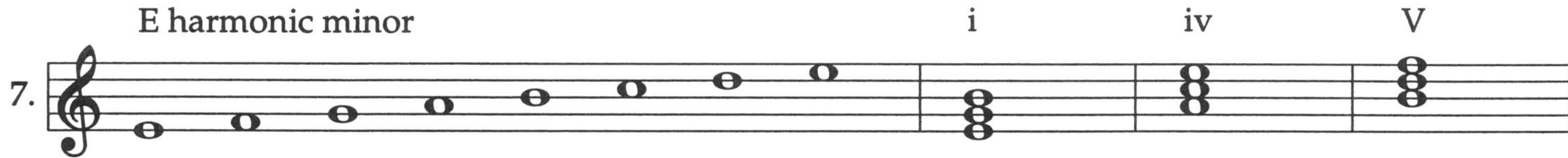

Music Dictionary

Term	Sign or Abbreviation	Meaning
A Tempo		return to the original tempo
Accent *(p. 31)*	>	a symbol placed over or under a note, indicating to stress or accent the note
Accidental *(p. 4)*		a sharp (♯), flat (♭), or natural (♮) sign that does not appear in the key signature and applies for the duration of the measure
Adagio Sostenuto *(p. 138)*		slow and sustained
Allegretto		moderately fast
Allegro		fast
Allegro Grazioso *(p. 130)*		fast and graceful
Allegro Non Troppo *(p. 48)*		fast, but not too fast
Allegro Scherzando *(p. 126)*		fast and playful
Animato *(p. 61)*		with animation
Andante		slowly (walking tempo)
Augmented Triad *(p. 124)*		a triad made up of a Major 3rd (four half steps) and a Major 3rd
Block Chord *(p. 10)*		notes in a chord played simultaneously
Broken Chord *(p. 10)*		notes in a chord played one at a time
Chord Progression		two or more chords played consecutively
Chord Symbol		a letter name placed over a note to indicate a chord that could be played with that note
Clef		
Treble Clef	𝄞	the staff sign used for middle and high tones
Bass Clef	𝄢	the staff sign used for middle and low tones
Coda	𝄌	a section at the end of a composition added as a conclusion
Common Time *(p. 15)*	𝄴	another way to indicate the 4/4 time signature
Con		with
Con Moto		with motion
Con Spirito *(p. 66)*		with spirit
Cut Time *(p. 16)*	𝄵	another way to indicate the 2/2 time signature
Crescendo	*cresc.,* 𝆒	gradually play louder
Da Capo al Coda *(p. 39)*	*D.C. al Coda,* 𝄌	return to the beginning and play until the directions or the *Coda* sign (𝄌) indicate to skip to the *Coda*, which ends the piece
Da Capo al Fine *(p. 9)*	*D.C. al Fine*	return to the beginning and play to the *Fine*
Dal Segno al Fine	*D.S. al Fine,* 𝄋	return to the sign (𝄋) and play to the *Fine*
Dal Segno al Coda	*D.S. al Coda,* 𝄋, 𝄌	return to the sign (𝄋) and play until the directions or the *Coda* sign (𝄌) indicate to skip to the *Coda*, which ends the piece
Damper Pedal	└─^─┘	the pedal on the right that is used to sustain tones
Decrescendo	*decresc.,* 𝆓	gradually play softer
Degrees		the Roman numerals that name the tones within each key
Diminished Triad *(p. 128)*		a triad made up of a minor 3rd (three half steps) and a minor 3rd
Diminuendo	*dim.*	gradually play softer
Dominant Seventh Chord *(p. 8)*		a seventh chord built on degree V of the scale
Dominant Note		degree V within any key
Dynamics	***pp, p, mp, mf, f, ff***	signs in music that indicate how loudly or softly to play
Fermata	𝄐	a sign indicating a pause in music, when the note or notes under the fermata sign are held longer than their original time value
Fine		the end
Flat Sign	♭	a sign indicating to play the nearest key to the left
Forte	***f***	loud
Fortissimo	***ff***	very loud
Grace Note *(p. 102)*	𝆔, ♬	a small note which is played immediately before the main note and does not add value to or take value away from the main note; there may be more than one grace note before a main note
Grand Staff		an arrangement of two staffs connected by a brace, the upper staff usually with a treble clef and the lower staff usually with a bass clef
Half Step		the distance from one key to the very next key with no key in between
Harmonic Minor Scale *(p. 28, 46)*		a scale which uses the same tones as the relative Major scale with one exception: the 7th tone in the harmonic minor scale is raised one half step
Interval		the distance between two notes
Inversion *(p. 18, 60)*		a different arrangement of notes in a chord
Key Signature *(p. 8)*		the sharp(s) or flat(s) located at the beginning of each staff
Legato		smooth and connected tones, usually indicated by a slur
Leggiero *(p. 42)*		lightly
Loco		an instruction placed after an *8va* or *15ma* sign is completed, indicating to return to the octave written
Major Scale *(p. 8, 40, 82, 96, 110)*		eight tones formed in a pattern of whole and half steps: whole, whole, half, whole, whole, whole, half

Term	Symbol	Definition
Major Triad *(p. 24)*		a triad made up of a Major 3rd (four half steps) and a minor 3rd (three half steps)
Mezzo Piano	***mp***	medium soft
Mezzo Forte	***mf***	medium loud
Minor Triad *(p. 24)*		a triad made up of a minor 3rd (three half steps) and a Major 3rd (four half steps)
Moderato		moderately
Molto		much
Natural Sign	♮	a sign before a note which cancels a sharp or flat
Note Values		indicate the duration of each tone
Dotted Eighth Note *(p. 130)*	♪.	
Sixteenth Note(s) *(p. 98, 130)*		
Triplet *(p. 64)*		
Order of Sharps *(p. 80, 85)*		the order of sharps as they always appear in the key signature: F, C, G, D, A, E, B
Octave Sign	*8va*	a sign indicating to play one octave higher or one octave lower
Octave Sign	*15ma*	a sign indicating to play two octaves higher or two octaves lower
Parallel Major and Minor Scales *(p. 122)*		Major and minor scales which begin on the same tone but have different key signatures, for example: D Major and D minor
Phrase		a musical thought indicated by a slur
Piano	***p***	soft
Pianissimo	***pp***	very soft
Poco		little
Primary Chords *(p. 8, 28)*		the three most important chords in any key: I, IV, V in Major; i, iv, V in minor
Relative Minor Scale *(p. 28, 46)*		eight tones formed in a pattern of whole and half steps using the 6th tone of the Major scale for its starting note
Repeat Sign		a sign indicating to repeat (play again) from the beginning of a piece
Repeat Signs		signs indicating to repeat (play again) the music between the pairs of dots and barlines
Rest Signs		indicate measured silence in music
Dotted Half Rest *(p. 66)*		
Dotted Quarter Rest *(p. 38)*		
Sixteenth Rest *(p. 130)*		
Rhythm		combination of short and long tones
Risoluto *(p. 127)*		with resolve
Ritardando	*rit.*	gradually slow down
Ritmico *(p. 16)*		to play in strict rhythm with a steady beat
Root *(p. 18)*		the note from which a chord originates
Root Position *(p. 18)*		a chord in its most basic form: root on the bottom, other notes stacked in intervals of thirds
Rubato *(p. 26)*		time is "borrowed," or some tones are held longer than their actual values, while others are curtailed, in order to allow more freedom and spontaneity
Seventh Chord *(p. 10)*		a four-note chord consisting of a root, 3rd, 5th, and 7th
Sforzando *(p. 34)*	***sfz***	to play with a sudden accent
Sharp Sign	♯	a sign before a note indicating to play the nearest key to the right
Simile		the same as
Slur		a curved line over or under two or more different notes that are to be played legato (smooth, connected)
Staccato		a dot placed over or under a note indicating to play in a short or detached manner
Staff		a group of five horizontal lines on which notes are placed
Subdominant Chord		a chord built on degree IV in any key
Subdominant Note		degree IV in any key
Swing *(p. 50)*		a style of playing jazz in which eighth notes are played "long-short"
Syncopation *(p. 30)*		to stress or accent weak beats
Tempo		rate of speed
Tenuto *(p. 118)*		a symbol which means to stress the note and hold it for its full value
Tetrachord		four tones formed in a pattern of whole and half steps: whole, whole, half
Tie		a curved line that connects notes on the same line or space, which indicates to play the first note only and hold it for the value of both notes
Time Signature	2/4, 3/4, 4/4, 2/2, 6/8, 6/4	the two numbers written at the beginning of each piece: the top number indicates the number of beats per measure; the bottom number indicates which note value receives one beat.
Tone		sound of a definite pitch
Tonic Chord		a chord built on degree I in any key
Tonic Note or Key Note		degree I in any key
Transpose *(p. 60)*		to play in a different key than written
Triad *(p. 18)*		a three-note chord
Upbeat		note(s) that come before the first full measure
Vivace *(p. 116)*		lively
Vivo *(p. 41)*		lively
Whole Step		the distance from one key to the next key, with one key in between

CHORD DICTIONARY

TRIADS

Note: When the symbol 𝄫 is used, it indicates to move down a half step from a flatted note. This is called a **double flat**. When the symbol 𝄪 is used, it indicates to move up a half step from a sharp note. This is called a **double sharp**.

SEVENTH CHORDS

	Major Seventh	Dominant Seventh	Minor Seventh	Half-Diminished Seventh	Diminished Seventh
 C	CMa7	C7	Cm7	Cø7	C°7
D♭	D♭Ma7	D♭7	D♭m7	D♭ø7	D♭°7
D	DMa7	D7	Dm7	Dø7	D°7
E♭	E♭Ma7	E♭7	E♭m7	E♭ø7	E♭°7
E	EMa7	E7	Em7	Eø7	E°7
F	FMa7	F7	Fm7	Fø7	F°7
G♭	G♭Ma7	G♭7	G♭m7	G♭ø7	G♭°7
G	GMa7	G7	Gm7	Gø7	G°7
A♭	A♭Ma7	A♭7	A♭m7	A♭ø7	A♭°7
A	AMa7	A7	Am7	Aø7	A°7
B♭	B♭Ma7	B♭7	B♭m7	B♭ø7	B♭°7
B	BMa7	B7	Bm7	Bø7	B°7

MAJOR SCALES AND PRIMARY CHORDS

SHARP KEYS

FLAT KEYS

F Major
F Bb F C7 F
I IV I V7 I
Bb Major
Bb Eb Bb F7 Bb
Eb Major
Eb Ab Eb Bb7 Eb
Ab Major
Ab Db Ab Eb7 Ab
Db Major
Db Gb Db Ab7 Db
Gb Major
Gb Cb Gb Db7 Gb

HARMONIC MINOR SCALES AND PRIMARY CHORDS

FLAT KEYS

D minor (relative to F Major)
Dm Gm Dm A7 Dm
i iv i V7 i
G minor (relative to B♭ Major)
Gm Cm Gm D7 Gm
C minor (relative to E♭ Major)
Cm Fm Cm G7 Cm
F minor (relative to A♭ Major)
Fm B♭m Fm C7 Fm
B♭ minor (relative to D♭ Major)
B♭m E♭m B♭m F7 B♭m
E♭ minor (relative to G♭ Major)
E♭m A♭m E♭m B♭7 E♭m

THE CIRCLE OF FIFTHS

The **Circle of Fifths** shows the relationship between relative Major and minor keys and the number of accidentals in their key signatures. The Circle is based on the fact that beginning with any tone and moving up by intervals of fifths (C, G, D...) will eventually lead back to the starting tone.

Start with C Major/A minor and follow the circle clockwise, moving up by 5ths. Notice that one sharp is added to the key signature each time you get to a new key.

Start with C Major/A minor and follow the circle counter clockwise, moving down by 5ths. Notice that one flat is added to the key signature each time you get to a new key.

Three keys overlap in the circle: B Major/C♭ Major, F♯ Major/G♭ Major, C♯ Major/D♭ Major. These keys are called enharmonic equivalents because their tones sound the same on the piano, but are named and written differently.

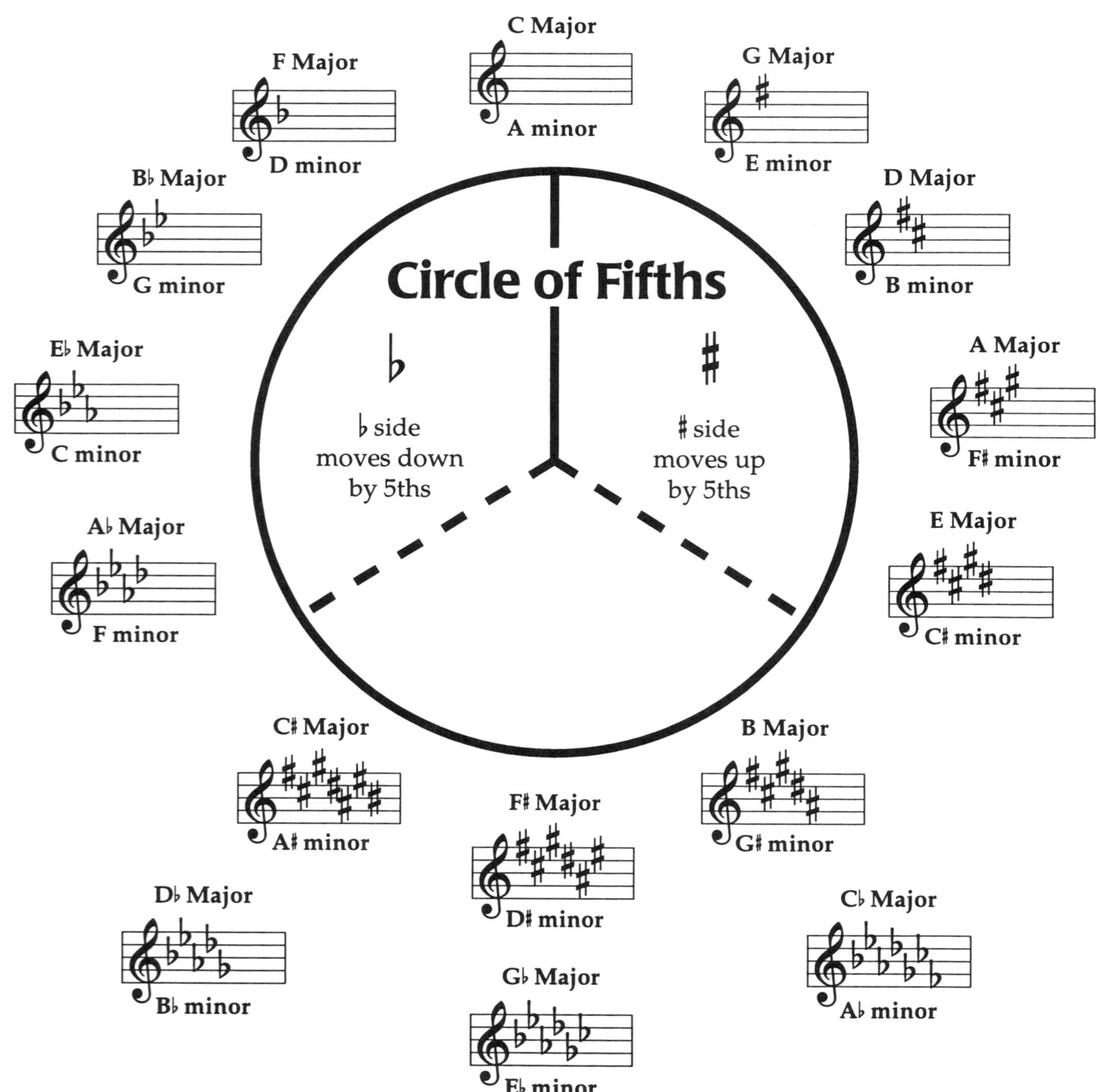

Answer Key for Review Pages

Chapter 1

Page 18

A. and B.

1. 5th, F, C
2. 8th, D, D
3. 2nd, F, G
4. 7th, B, C
5. 4th, E, A
6. 6th, B, G
7. 4th, E, A
8. 5th, G, D
9. 4th, B, F
10. 3rd, A, C
11. 2nd, F, E
12. 3rd, D, F
13. 6th, G, E
14. 8th, C, C
15. 7th, G, A

D.

1. Whole
2. Half
3. Whole
4. Half
5. Whole
6. Half

Page 19

E. and F.

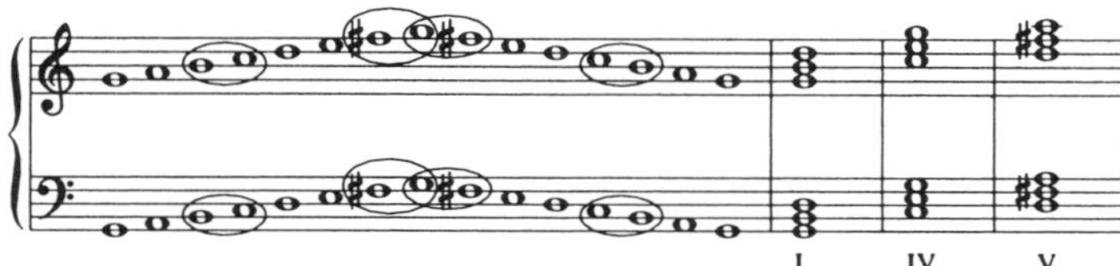

G.

1. G
2. G
3. C
4. C
5. D
6. D

H.

1. G
2. G
3. C
4. C
5. G
6. D7
7. G

Chapter 2

Page 24

A.

1. Cm
2. F
3. Gm
4. C
5. G
6. Fm
7. C
8. Am
9. G
10. Fm
11. Cm
12. Gm

Page 36

A.

1. h
2. f
3. e
4. c or k
5. l
6. i
7. b
8. c or k
9. g
10. a
11. j
12. d

Page 37

B. and C.

D.

1. 
2. E
3. E
4. A
5. A
6. B
7. B
8. minor
9. Major

E.

1. Em
2. B7
3. Em
4. B7
5. Em
6. Am
7. B7
8. Em

G.

1. Gm
2. Cm
3. Am
4. Em
5. G
6. C

Chapter 3

Page 56

A.

1. 6
2. 1
3. 3
4. 1
5. 6
6. 2
7. 2
8. 3

E.

1. c
2. f
3. h
4. i
5. g
6. b
7. d
8. j
9. e
10. a

Page 57

F. and G.

H.

1. 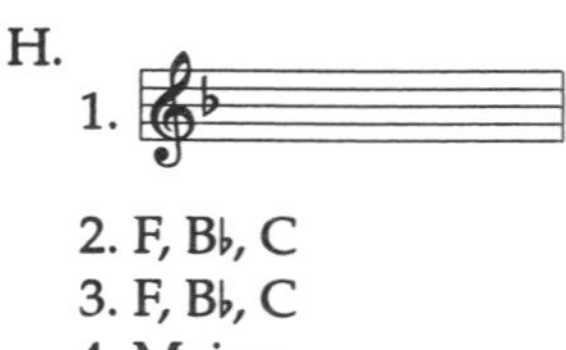

2. F, B♭, C
3. F, B♭, C
4. Major

I. and J.

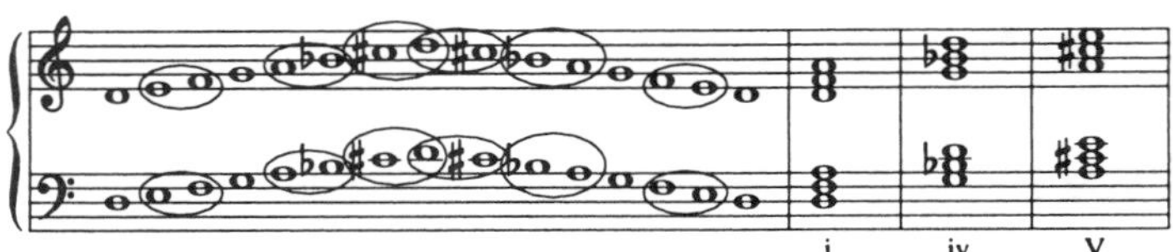

K.

1. 

2. D, G, A
3. D, G, A
4. minor
5. Major

Chapter 4

Page 63

A. and B.

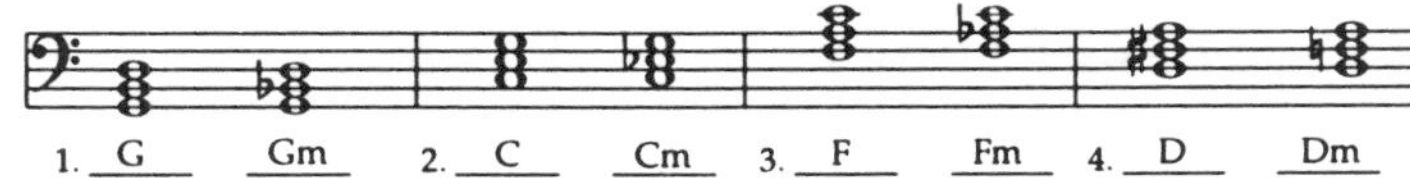

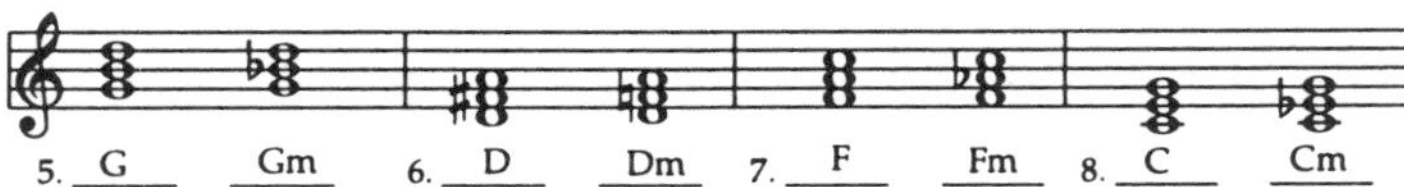

D.

1. Fm
2. Gm
3. Dm
4. F
5. Em
6. Cm

Page 76

A.

1. F Major

2. D minor

3. C Major

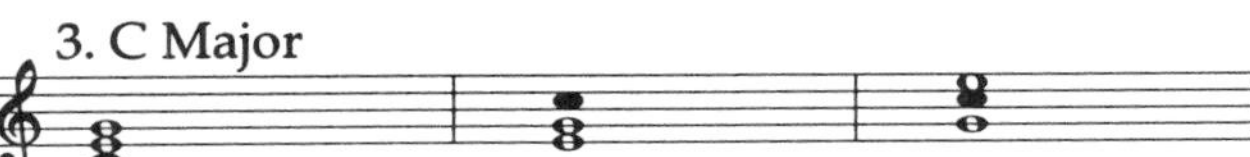

4. A minor

5. G Major

6. E minor

Page 77

B.

1. C, F, G
2.

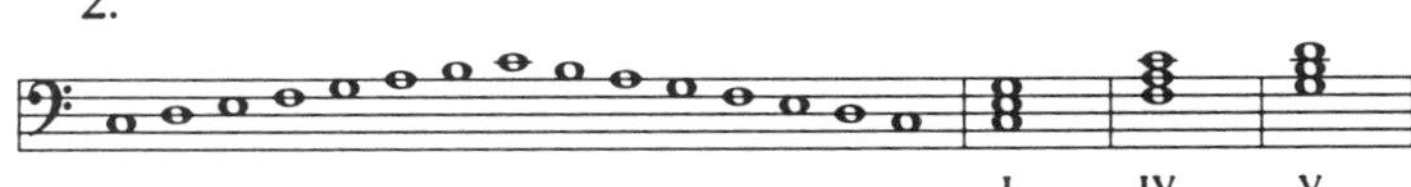

C.

1.

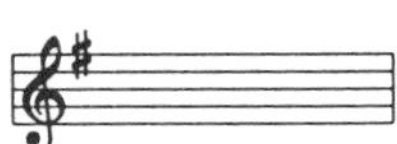

2. G, C, D
3.

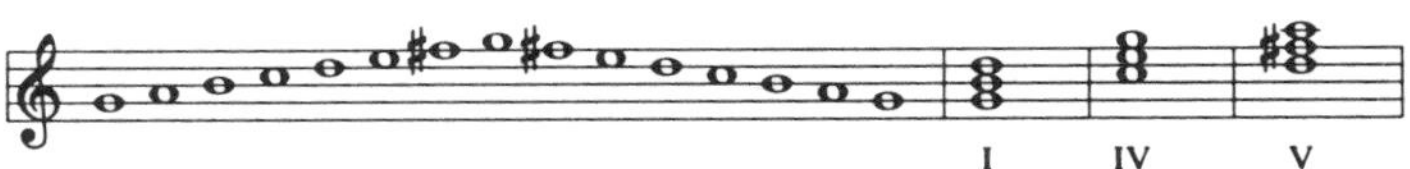

D.

1.

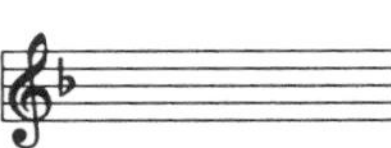

2. F, B♭, C
3.

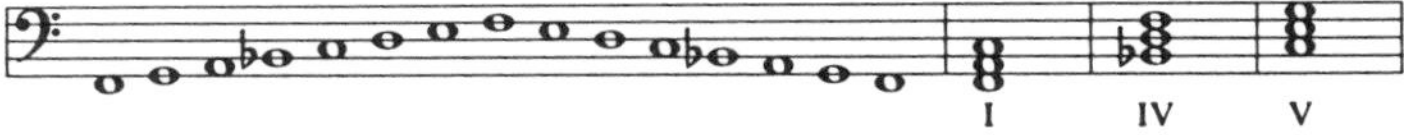

Chapter 5

Page 80
1. G Major
2. A Major
3. D Major
4. E Major

Page 85
A.

B.
1. D Major
2. E Major
3. C Major
4. G Major
5. A Major
6. F♯ Major
7. B Major
8. G Major
9. C♯ Major
10. E Major

Page 86
1. D
2. Em
3. F
4. Am
5. Dm
6. G
7. Dm
8. F
9. Am
10. G
11. Em
12. E

Page 92
A.

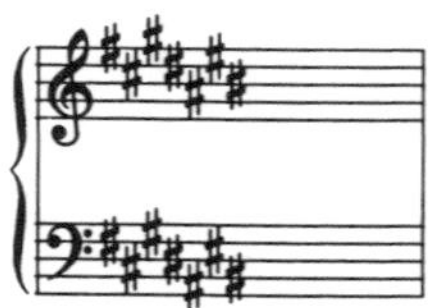

B.
1. A Major
2. E Major
3. G Major
4. C Major
5. B Major
6. F♯ Major
7. D Major
8. C♯ Major
9. A Major
10. E Major

C. and D

F.

Page 93
G. and H.

I.
1. A7
2. D
3. G
4. D
5. D
6. G
7. D
8. A7
9. D

K.
1. c
2. e
3. b
4. d
5. f
6. g
7. a

Chapter 6

Page 106

A. and B.

C.

1. D
2. A
3. E7
4. A
5. D
6. A

D.

1. b
2. f
3. a
4. b
5. e
6. b
7. d
8. c

E.

Page 107

F. and G.

I.

1. F Major, D minor
2. G Major, E minor
3. C Major, A minor

J. 6th

K.

1. G	13. D
2. B	14. B
3. A	15. C
4. C	16. E
5. D	17. E
6. A	18. F
7. C	19. D
8. B	20. C
9. A	21. B
10. G	22. C
11. D	23. D
12. C	24. C

L.

1. Common Time or $\frac{4}{4}$ time signature
2. Cut Time or $\frac{2}{2}$ time signature

Chapter 7

Page 112

1. D
2. E
3. F
4. Am
5. A
6. G
7. Dm
8. F
9. Am
10. A
11. Em
12. D

Page 120

A. and B.

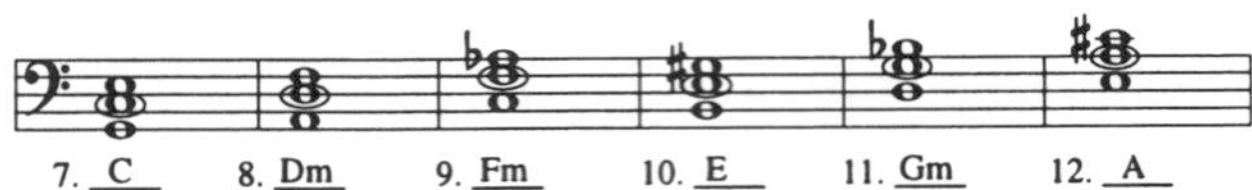

D.

1. fortissimo, very loud
2. forte, loud
3. mezzo piano, moderately soft
4. piano, soft
5. pianissimo, very soft

E.

1. fast
2. slowly (walking tempo)
3. moderately fast
4. moderate

F.

1. $\frac{4}{4}$
2. $\frac{3}{4}$
3. $\frac{2}{4}$

Page 121

G.

1. D Major

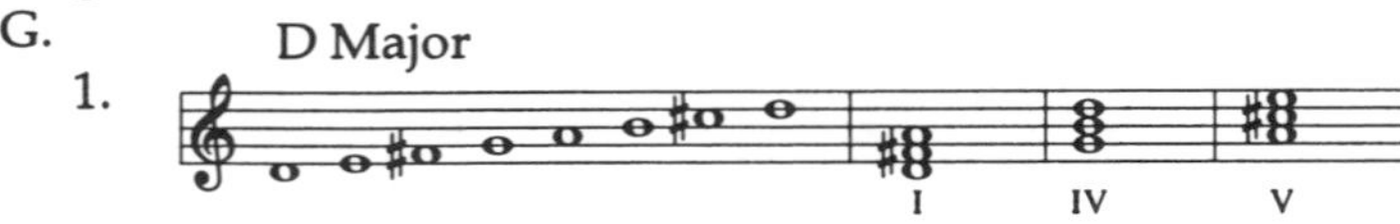

2. G Major

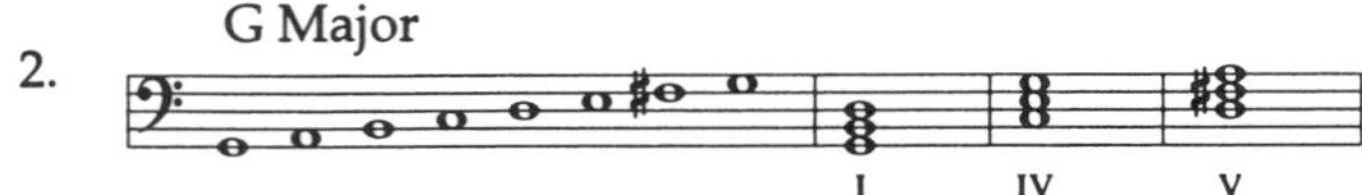

3. A Major

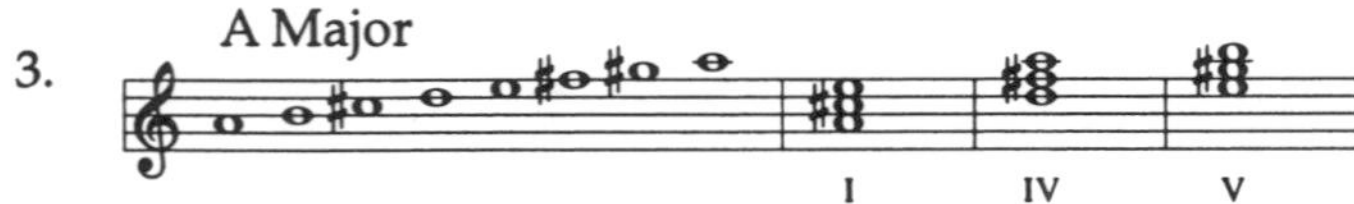

4. F Major

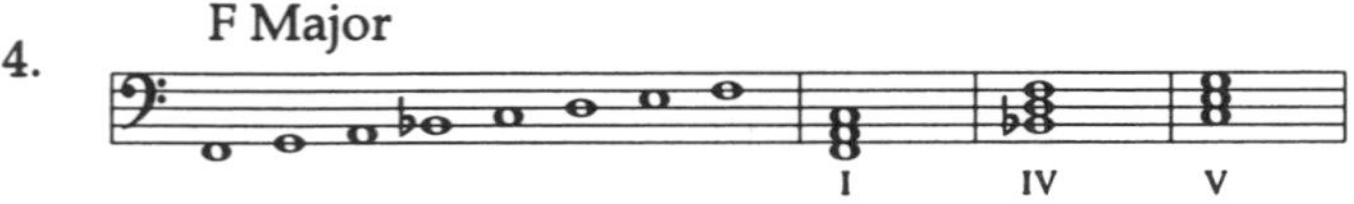

H. and I.

J.

1. E
2. B7
3. E
4. A
5. E

Chapter 8

Page 124
A.
1. D+
2. C
3. F+
4. G+
5. E
6. F
7. C+
8. E+
9. G
10. D
11. A+
12. A

B. and C.

Page 128
A.
1. A°
2. E°
3. F°
4. Dm
5. C°
6. Gm
7. A°
8. Em
9. D°
10. Fm
11. G°
12. Cm

B. and C.

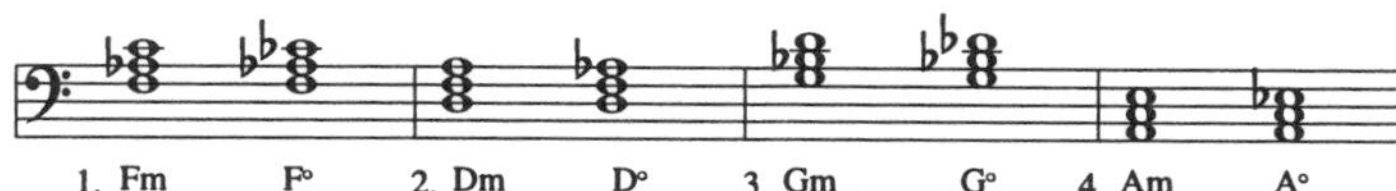

Page 136
A.

1. C	13. E	25. G
2. C+	14. E+	26. G+
3. C	15. E	27. G
4. Cm	16. Em	28. Gm
5. C°	17. E°	29. G°
6. C	18. E	30. G
7. D	19. F	31. A
8. D+	20. F+	32. A+
9. D	21. F	33. A
10. Dm	22. Fm	34. Am
11. D°	23. F°	35. A°
12. D	24. F	36. A

Page 140
A.
1. E+
2. G
3. D+
4. F
5. E
6. C+
7. D
8. F+
9. C
10. A
11. G+
12. A+

B.
1. E°
2. Fm
3. A°
4. Cm
5. D°
6. G°
7. Dm
8. Em
9. F°
10. C°
11. Gm
12. Am

C.
1. broken chord
2. waltz bass
3. boogie bass
4. broken chord

D.
1. A Major
2. B Major
3. E Major
4. C Major
5. G Major
6. D Major

Page 141

E. 6th

F.

1. A
2. E
3. D

G.

1. D harmonic minor

2. G Major

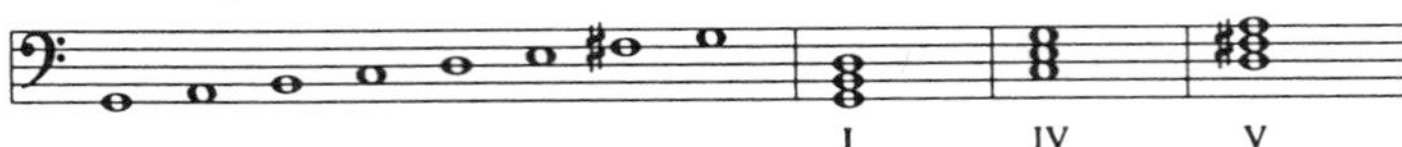

3. E Major

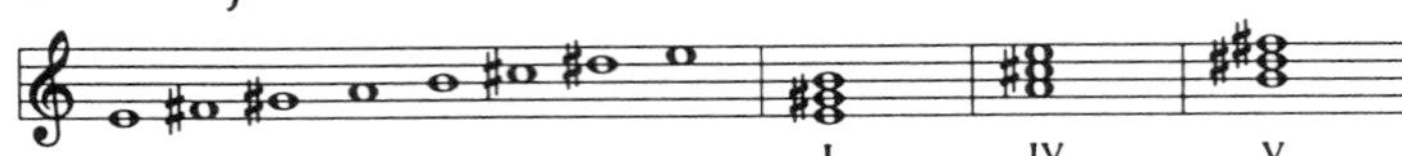

4. F Major

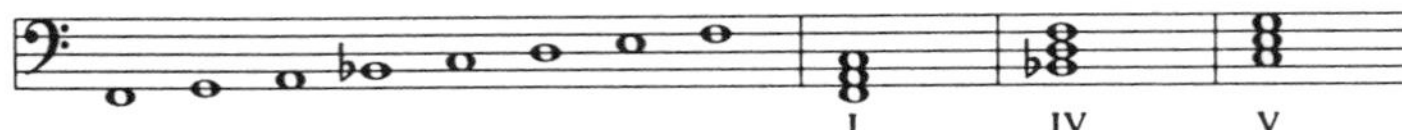

5. A harmonic minor

6. D Major

7. E harmonic minor

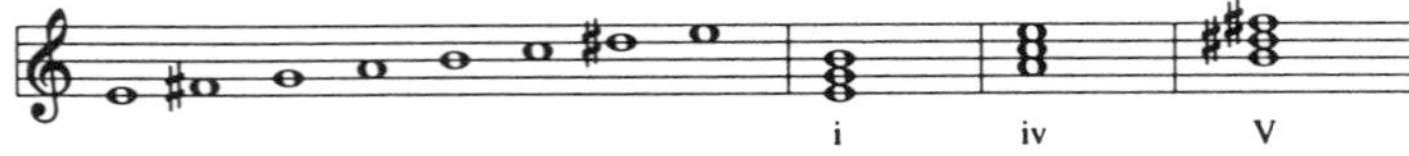